Sensors and Actuators in Smart Cities

Special Issue Editors

Mohammad Hammoudeh
Mounir Arioua

MDPI • Basel • Beijing • Wuhan • Barcelona • Belgrade

Special Issue Editors
Mohammad Hammoudeh
Manchester Metropolitan University
UK

Mounir Arioua
Abdelmalek Essaadi University
Morocco

Editorial Office
MDPI
St. Alban-Anlage 66
Basel, Switzerland

This edition is a reprint of the Special Issue published online in the open access journal *Journal of Sensor and Actuator Networks* (ISSN 2224-2708) from 2013–2014 (available at: http://www.mdpi.com/journal/jsan/special_issues/smart_cities).

For citation purposes, cite each article independently as indicated on the article page online and as indicated below:

Lastname, F.M.; Lastname, F.M. Article title. *Journal Name* **Year**, *Article number*, page range.

First Editon 2018

ISBN 978-3-03842-873-2 (Pbk)
ISBN 978-3-03842-874-9 (PDF)

Table of Contents

About the Special Issue Editors

Mohammad Hammoudeh, PhD, is currently the Head of the MMU IoT Laboratory and a Senior Lecturer in computer networks and security with the School of Computing, Math and Digital Technology, Manchester Metropolitan University. He has been a researcher and publisher in the field of big sensory data mining and visualization. Dr. Hammoudeh is a highly proficient, experienced, and professionally certified cybersecurity professional, specializing in threat analysis, and information and network security management. His research interests include highly decentralized algorithms, communication, cross-layered solutions to the Internet of Things, and wireless sensor networks.

Mounir Arioua, PhD, is currently an associate professor at the National School of Applied Sciences of Tetuan, University of Abdelmalek Essaadi. He received his PhD degree in Telecommunications and Computer Science and joined the National School of Applied Sciences of Marrakech as a research assistant. He is a member of various international scientific organizations and organizing and scientific committees of many international workshops and conferences and a referee of several international journals. He has authored or co-authored more than 50 papers in recognized journals and international conferences. His research interests include communication reliability, data compression in wireless sensor networks and embedded system-based wireless communication, and the Internet of Things.

Journal of
*Sensor and
Actuator Networks*

Editorial

Sensors and Actuators in Smart Cities

Mohammad Hammoudeh [1,*,†] **and Mounir Arioua** [2,†]

1   School of Computing, Mathematics & Digital Technology, Manchester Metropolitan University, Manchester M15 6BH, UK
2   National School of Applied Sciences, Abdelmalek Essaadi University, Tétouan 93000, Morocco; m.arioua@uae.ma
*   Correspondence: M.Hammoudeh@mmu.ac.uk; Tel.: +44-(0)161-247-2845
†   These authors contributed equally to this work.

Received: 9 February 2018; Accepted: 14 February 2018; Published: 16 February 2018

---

1. Scope and Aim

With the city, from its earliest emergence in the Near East between 4500 and 3100 BCE, came a wide range of new discoveries and inventions, from synthetic materials to wheeled vehicles. Through its dense population, irrigation, social continuity and physical security, emerged civil engineering, monumental construction, sculpture, mathematics, arts and law. Today, there is an enormous set of ideas and notions with respect to our ways of living, e.g., the ramp and the lever, which are still fundamental to cities' environmental, social, and economic structures. Modern-day smart cities compete for the introduction of smart technologies and applications to improve key areas of urban communities, such as system automation, sustainability, and quality of life. Technology research experts paint thrilling images of futuristic cities. What's glossed over, however, is the sensor and actuator technologies that enable these smart cities; in particular, the reliable, heterogeneous, wireless networks specifically designed to provision communication across a countless number of sensors embedded in almost everything.

The world is on the verge of a new epoch of innovation and change with the emergence of Wireless Sensor Networks (WSN). The convergence of smaller, more powerful processors, smart mobile devices, low-cost sensing, big data analytics, cloud hosting and new levels of connectivity allowed by the Internet is fuelling the latest wave of Machine-to-Machine (M2M) technology. The merits of this marriage of machines and the digital world are multiple and significant. It holds the potential to dramatically alter the way in which most global industries, such as buildings, rail transportation, power grids and healthcare operate on daily basis. WSNs expand to include our vehicles and homes, as well as newly developed wearable and implanted sensors, which brings fundamental transformations to many aspects of daily life.

WSN innovations promise to integrate and optimise smart buildings, autonomous vehicles, power grids, etc., to enable a successful transition towards smart, user-driven and demand-focused city infrastructures and services [1,2]. There is a wide range of current smart cities applications, which make our lives easier and more efficient, e.g., a smart phone application that let users find free parking spaces in the centre of town. However, cities are notoriously inefficient. As populations grow, everything from garbage collection and public transport becomes more expensive and complex. Away from increasing spending, there is also a demand from citizens for smarter services driven by sensor- and actuator-based infrastructure.

In this Special Issue, we accepted submissions that focus on implementing intelligent sensing infrastructure to solve the smart cities conundrum. This Special Issue attracted contributions from academic researchers in computer science, communication engineering and physics, as well as information technology industry consultants and practitioners, in various aspects of sensors and actuators for smart cities. In the next section, we present a brief review of the papers published, highlighting their objectives and contributions.

2. A Review of Contributions in this Special Issue

Zhang et al. [3] address the challenge of large scale data analytics for smart cities. Typically, multi-modal sensor data collected from cyber physical environments, such as smart cities, must be processed before it can be can be used by data discovery, integration and mash-up protocols. With heterogeneous, noisy and incomplete data, clustering algorithms are used to organise the data in a dataset into clusters. The authors propose a new peak searching algorithm that uses Bayesian optimisation to find probability peaks in a dataset to increase the speed and accuracy of data clustering algorithms. This proposed clustering algorithm was thoroughly evaluated in simulation and results show that it significantly decreases the required number of clustering iterations (by 1.99 to 6.3 times), and produce clustering which, for a synthetic dataset, is 1.69 to 1.71 times more accurate than it is for traditional expectation-maximization (EM). Moreover, the algorithm correctly identified the outliers in a real dataset, decreasing iterations by approximately 1.88 times, while being 1.29 times more accurate than EM at a maximum.

Ateya et al. [4] contribution addresses the development of intelligent core network for Tactile Internet and future smart systems. Tactile Internet is an extremely low latency communication network with high availability, reliability and security. Tactile Internet is predicted to bring a new dimension to human-to-human and human-to-machine interaction in a multitude of different smart city aspects such transport, power grid, education, healthcare and culture. This paper presents a Tactile Internet system structure, which employs software defined networking in the core of the cellular network and mobile edge computing at multi-levels. The contribution focuses on the structure of the core network. The proposed system is simulated under reliable environmental conditions and results shows that it achieved a round trip latency of orders of $1ms$ by the reducing the number of intermediate nodes that are involved in the communication process.

Jiang et al. [5] address the problem of establishing a good measure of the agreement between the activities detected from sensor-generated data and those recorded in self-reported data. The contribution reports on a trial conducted in three single-occupancy households from which data is collected from a set of sensors and from time use diaries completed by the occupants. The authors demonstrate the application of Hidden Markov Models with features extracted from mean-shift clustering and change points analysis. Then, a correlation-based feature selection is applied to reduce the computational cost. Finally, a method based on Levenshtein distance for measuring the agreement between the sensor-detected activities and that reported by the participants is demonstrated. The authors conclude their paper by an exciting discussion on lessons learnt on how the features derived from sensor data can be used in activity recognition and how they relate to activities recorded in time use diaries.

Taking the work in the previous contribution [5] one step further, Castro et al. [6] present a system based on the Internet of Things (IoT) to Human Activity Recognition (HAR) that monitors vital body signs remotely. The authors employ machine learning algorithms to determine activities that occur within four pre-defined categories (lie, sit, walk and jog). Evaluation using advanced real-world hardware platform shows that the proposed system is able to give feedback during and after the activity is performed, using a remote monitoring component with remote visualization and programmable alarms. This system was successfully implemented with a 95.83% success ratio.

The contribution of Riouali et al. [7] addresses another vital area of sensing and actuation in smart cities. The authors present a road traffic management system based on wireless sensor networks. This paper introduces the functional and deployment architecture of this system with particular focus on the data analytics component, which uses a new extension of batches Petri nets for modelling road traffic flow. The evaluation of the proposed system was performed using a real world implementation of visualization and data analysis components.

Voutos et al. [8] present a social environmental sensor network integrated within a web GIS platform. Controls, user interface and extensions of the proposed system are presented. The key novel aspect of this contribution is the fact that the gathered data from the proposed system carries spatial information, which is fundamental for the successful correlation between pollutants and their place of origin. The latter is implemented by an interactive Web GIS platform operating oversight in situ and on a timeline basis.

Catania et al. [9] contribute a user-generated services composition in smart multi-user environments. In this contribution, the focus is on security issues raised by services generated by users, User-Generated Services (UGSs). UGSs are characterized by a set of features that distinguish them from conventional services. To cope with UGS security problems, the authors introduce three different policy management models, analysing benefits and drawbacks of each approach. Finally, a cloud-based solution that enables the composition of multiple UGSs and policy models, allowing users' devices to share features and services in IoT based scenarios is proposed.

Obinikpo et al.'s [10] contribution demonstrates how big sensed data meets deep learning for smarter health care in smart cities. Healthcare lends itself as a natural fit for IoT technology and smart city concepts. The authors advocate that integrating sensory data (hard sensing) with external data sources (soft sensing, e.g., crowd-sensing) could reveal new data patterns and information. This research addresses this challenge through hidden perception layers in the conventional artificial neural networks, namely by deep learning. The paper starts by reviewing deep learning techniques that can be applied to sensed data to improve prediction and decision making in smart health services. Then, a comparison and taxonomy of these methodologies based on types of sensors and sensed data is presented. Finally, a thorough discussions on the open issues and research challenges in each category is given.

Arbia et al.'s [11] contribution targets smart city critical infrastructure, particularly, an IoT enabled end-to-end emergency and disaster relief system. This paper presents a new enhancement for an emergency and disaster relief system called Critical and Rescue Operations using Wearable Wireless sensors networks (CROW 2). CROW 2 addresses the reliability challenges in setting up a wireless autonomous communication system to offload data from the disaster area (rescuers, trapped victims, civilians, media, etc.) back to a command centre. The proposed system connects deployed rescuers to extended networks and the Internet. The system integrates heterogeneous wireless devices and different communicating technologies to enable end-to-end network connectivity, which is monitored by a cloud-based IoT platform. The overall performance of CROW 2 is evaluated using end-to-end link quality estimation, throughput and end-to-end delay. Finally, the system architecture is validated through deployment and motion detection and links unavailability prevention are highlighted.

3. Conclusions and Remarks

Sensors and actuators are the building blocks for the forth industrial revolution. They have already transformed the way humans perceive their environment. Sensor-enabled smart cities are paving the way for a more sustainable future, from urban planning to social conscience. The papers published in this special issue put humans at the centre of smart cities. From traffic management to assisted living, human centred design of smart city services is a detrimental factor to the success of smart cities. It is evident that we are still at the start of the smart cities revolution and the full economical, environmental and social benefits are yet to be achieved.

Conflicts of Interest: The authors declare no conflict of interest.

References

1. Coates, A.; Hammoudeh, M.; Holmes, K.G. Internet of Things for Buildings Monitoring: Experiences and Challenges. In Proceedings of the International Conference on Future Networks and Distributed Systems, ICFNDS '17, Cambridge, UK, 19–20 July 2017; ACM: New York, NY, USA, 2017.

2. Jogunola, O.; Ikpehai, A.; Anoh, K.; Adebisi, B.; Hammoudeh, M.; Son, S.Y.; Harris, G. State-of-the-art and prospects for peer-to-peer transaction-based energy system. *Energies* **2017**, *10*, 2106.

3. Zhang, T.; Zhao, Q.; Shin, K.; Nakamoto, Y. Bayesian-Optimization-Based Peak Searching Algorithm for Clustering in Wireless Sensor Networks. *J. Sens. Actuator Netw.* **2018**, *7*, 2.

4. Ateya, A.A.; Muthanna, A.; Gudkova, I.; Abuarqoub, A.; Vybornova, A.; Koucheryavy, A. Development of Intelligent Core Network for Tactile Internet and Future Smart Systems. *J. Sens. Actuator Netw.* **2018**, *7*, 1.

5. Jiang, J.; Pozza, R.; Gunnarsdóttir, K.; Gilbert, N.; Moessner, K. Using Sensors to Study Home Activities. *J. Sens. Actuator Netw.* **2017**, *6*, 32.

6. Castro, D.; Coral, W.; Rodriguez, C.; Cabra, J.; Colorado, J. Wearable-Based Human Activity Recognition Using and IoT Approach. *J. Sens. Actuator Netw.* **2017**, *6*, 28.

7. Riouali, Y.; Benhlima, L.; Bah, S. Extended Batches Petri Nets Based System for Road Traffic Management in WSNs. *J. Sens. Actuator Netw.* **2017**, *6*, 30.

8. Voutos, Y.; Mylonas, P.; Spyrou, E.; Charou, E. A Social Environmental Sensor Network Integrated within a Web GIS Platform. *J. Sens. Actuator Netw.* **2017**, *6*, 27.

9. Catania, V.; La Torre, G.; Monteleone, S.; Panno, D.; Patti, D. User-Generated Services Composition in Smart Multi-User Environments. *J. Sens. Actuator Netw.* **2017**, *6*, 20.

10. Obinikpo, A.A.; Kantarci, B. Big Sensed Data Meets Deep Learning for Smarter Health Care in Smart Cities. *J. Sens. Actuator Netw.* **2017**, *6*, 26.

11. Ben Arbia, D.; Alam, M.M.; Kadri, A.; Ben Hamida, E.; Attia, R. Enhanced IoT-Based End-To-End Emergency and Disaster Relief System. *J. Sens. Actuator Netw.* **2017**, *6*, 19.

Journal of
*Sensor and
Actuator Networks*

Article

Bayesian-Optimization-Based Peak Searching Algorithm for Clustering in Wireless Sensor Networks

Tianyu Zhang *, Qian Zhao, Kilho Shin and Yukikazu Nakamoto

Graduate School of Applied Informatics, University of Hyogo, Computational Science Center Building 5-7F
7-1-28 Minatojima-minamimachi, Chuo-ku Kobe, Hyogo 6570047, Japan; zhaoqian_sunny@yahoo.co.jp (Q.Z.);
kilhoshin314@gmail.com (K.S.); nakamoto@ai.u-hyogo.ac.jp (Y.N.)
* Correspondence: tenngre@yahoo.co.jp

Received: 31 October 2017; Accepted: 29 December 2017; Published: 2 January 2018

Abstract: We propose a new peak searching algorithm (PSA) that uses Bayesian optimization to find probability peaks in a dataset, thereby increasing the speed and accuracy of clustering algorithms. Wireless sensor networks (WSNs) are becoming increasingly common in a wide variety of applications that analyze and use collected sensing data. Typically, the collected data cannot be directly used in modern data analysis problems that adopt machine learning techniques because such data lacks additional information (such as data labels) specifying its purpose of users. Clustering algorithms that divide the data in a dataset into clusters are often used when additional information is not provided. However, traditional clustering algorithms such as expectation–maximization (EM) and *k-means* algorithms require massive numbers of iterations to form clusters. Processing speeds are therefore slow, and clustering results become less accurate because of the way such algorithms form clusters. The PSA addresses these problems, and we adapt it for use with the EM and *k-means* algorithms, creating the modified *PSEM* and *PSk-means* algorithms. Our simulation results show that our proposed *PSEM* and *PSk-means* algorithms significantly decrease the required number of clustering iterations (by 1.99 to 6.3 times), and produce clustering that, for a synthetic dataset, is 1.69 to 1.71 times more accurate than it is for traditional EM and enhanced *k-means* (*k-means*++) algorithms. Moreover, in a simulation of WSN applications aimed at detecting outliers, *PSEM* correctly identified the outliers in a real dataset, decreasing iterations by approximately 1.88 times, and *PSEM* was 1.29 times more accurate than EM at a maximum.

Keywords: peak searching; clustering; Gaussian mixture model; Bayesian optimization; Gaussian process; outlier detection

---

1. Introduction

Over the past decade, wireless sensor networks (WSNs) have been widely applied in applications that involve analyzing collected data to improve quality of life or secure property. For example, sensor nodes are present in homes, vehicle systems, natural environments, and even satellites and outer space. These sensors collect data for many different purposes, such as health monitoring, industrial safety and control, environmental monitoring, and disaster prediction [1–4]. In such WSN applications, sensing data can be manually or automatically analyzed for specific purposes. However, in the age of big data, an increasing amount of sensing data is required for precise analysis in the WSN applications. Consequently, it is difficult or, in some cases, even impossible to manually analyze all of the collected data.

There are several conventional ways to automatically manage the collected data. The most typical and the easiest method is to set threshold values that correspond to sensing events. Events are triggered once the data exceed these thresholds. However, the thresholds in large-scale WSNs vary, and change due to environment changes. Moreover, precise analysis results cannot be obtained through the use of thresholds alone.

A complementary approach uses supervised machine learning. In this approach, a model is trained that can categorize sensing data into the different states required by an application. However, because sensing data labels are required in the training phase, extra work is required to manage the data. This process is particularly difficult when the dataset is large. Moreover, if the sensing environment changes, certain labels must also change. It is difficult to maintain a functional model under conditions where labels change frequently; this affects the analysis results.

Unsupervised machine learning methods are feasible and well-studied, and are not associated with the data labeling problems described above. Clustering is an important and common method in such approaches. In clustering, the overall features of the dataset are extracted. Then, the data are divided into clusters according to their features. As a result, data labeling is not required, and the data-labeling difficulties that occur in supervised approaches can be avoided. However, in state-of-the-art clustering methods such as the *expectation-maximization (EM)* [5] and *k-means* [6] algorithms, a massive number of iterations must be performed in order to form clusters, and a significant amount of computation time is required. Furthermore, because these algorithms use random starting data points as initial center points to form clusters, and because the number of clusters is not precisely determined, the clustering results become less accurate. To address these problems, in this paper, we propose a peak searching algorithm (*PSA*) for improving clustering algorithm capabilities.

Our approach should be applicable to different dataset distributions. Therefore, the collected sensing dataset is considered to be generated by a Gaussian mixture model composed of several different Gaussian distributions. If the number of Gaussian distributions and appropriate initial center points are known, clustering algorithms can appropriately divide the dataset into different clusters because each Gaussian distribution corresponds to a cluster. The proposed *PSA* employs a Bayesian optimization (BO) strategy that uses a Gaussian process [7]. Bayesian optimization is typically used for hyper-parameter optimizations; to the best of our knowledge, our approach is the first to use BO to improve clustering. Moreover, other Bayesian theorem based algorithms, such as [8–11], are also appropriate optimization strategies for training online and offline machine learning algorithms.

Given a collected dataset, the *PSA* searches for the data points with the highest probability values (i.e., peaks in the dataset). A Gaussian distribution peak is a point that corresponds to the mean. By searching the peaks, we can obtain appropriate initial center points of Gaussian distributions, hence, the corresponding clusters. This method overcomes the difficulties associated with the hard determination of starting data points in traditional cluster algorithms, thereby reducing the number of iterations. By using the *PSA*, cluster algorithms can form clusters using peak points instead of random starting points, which improves the clustering accuracy.

We used simulations to investigate the potential of the proposed *PSA* for improving algorithm performance. To measure performance improvements, we applied the *PSA* to the *EM* and *k-means* algorithms. We refer to these modified algorithms as *PSEM* and *PSk-means*, respectively. The simulation results showed that, for *PSEM* and *PSk-means*, the required numbers of clustering iterations were significantly reduced by 1.99 to 6.3 times. Additionally, for synthetic datasets, clustering accuracy was improved by 1.69 to 1.71 times relative to the traditional *EM* and enhanced version of *k-means*, i.e., *k-means++* [12].

The proposed method can accurately group data into clusters. Therefore, any outliers in a dataset can be clustered together, making them possible to identify. Because outliers obviously reduce the capabilities of the WSN applications, we also conducted a simulation using a real WSN dataset from the Intel Berkeley Research lab (Berkeley, CA , USA). This allowed us to compare the outlier-detection capabilities of *PSEM* and *EM*. Our simulation results showed that *PSEM* correctly identified outliers, decreased iterations by approximately 1.88 times, and improved accuracy by 1.29 times at a maximum.

The remainder of this paper is organized as follows. Section 2 outlines related works, while Section 3 introduces BO. Section 4 describes the proposed *PSA* and Section 5 presents the simulation results. Section 6 presents a discussion of this work. Section 7 summarizes key findings, presents conclusions, and describes potential future work.

2. Related Works

This section describes the techniques used in the clustering algorithms, which are used to automatically divide a collected dataset into different clusters. There are two main types of clustering approaches. The first is based on parametric techniques. To cluster a dataset, the parameters of the statistical model for a dataset must be calculated. The *EM* algorithm is a parametric technique. The second type of clustering approach uses non-parametric techniques, in which the calculated parameters of a statistical model are not required for clustering a dataset. *k-means* and *k-means++* are non-parametric techniques.

We describe the two clustering approaches in the following subsections. Moreover, because outlier detection is critical in the WSN applications, we describe some relevant outlier detection approaches.

2.1. Parametric Techniques

Parametric techniques assume that a dataset is generated from several parametric models, such as Gaussian mixture models. The clustering process is conducted by calculating the parameters of each Gaussian model, and assuming that data points in the same cluster can be represented by the same Gaussian model. Usually, a Gaussian model is chosen as the default model because it conforms to the central limit theorem [13,14] parametric techniques used. From the collected dataset, they calculated detailed a priori estimates of statistical parameters for the assumed statistical model (for example, the mean, median, and variance). This allowed them to fit statistical models.

EM [5] is a famous and widely used algorithm for clustering datasets using parametric techniques. The *EM* algorithm first calculates responsibilities with respect to given parameters (means and variances). This is referred to as the E-step. Then, the *EM* algorithm uses the responsibilities to update the given parameters. This is referred to as the M-step. These two steps are iteratively executed until the parameters approach the true parameters of the dataset. When those parameters are determined, the Gaussian models in the Gaussian mixture model are fixed. Therefore, clustering can be accomplished using the Gaussian models.

There are many benefits associated with parametric techniques: (i) such techniques assign a probability criterion to every data point to determine whether or not it belongs to a cluster; and (ii) such techniques do not require additional information (for example, labels on data points that indicate their statuses). On the other hand, parametric techniques cannot be deployed in a distributed way because a significant number of data points are required to estimate the mean and variance. Thus, methods that use parametric techniques are deployed in a centralized way.

2.2. Non-Parametric Techniques

Some algorithms use non-parametric techniques, which cluster datasets without using statistical models. Non-parametric techniques make certain assumptions, such as density smoothness. Typical methods use histograms, as in [15–17]. Histogram-based approaches are appropriate for datasets in low-dimensional spaces because the calculations in histogram-based techniques have an exponential relationship with the dimensions of a dataset. Therefore, this type of approach has low scalability to problems with larger numbers of data points and higher-dimensional spaces.

One typical non-parametric cluster algorithm is *k-means* [6]. In *k-means*, when candidate cluster centers are first provided to the algorithm, the number of centers is equal to the number of clusters. Then, *k-means* is used to calculate the sum of the distances from the center of each cluster to every data point. These two steps are iteratively executed, and *k-means* updates the given cluster centers by minimizing the calculated sum. When cluster centers are determined, clusters are formed.

However, *k-means* cannot guarantee that the candidate centers will be close to the true cluster centers. The iterations and clustering accuracy of the algorithm are not satisfying.

To overcome the disadvantages of *k-means*, Arthur and Vassilvitskii [12] proposed *k-means++*, which is based on the *k-means* algorithm. *k-means++* and *k-means* are different because *k-means++* uses the number of *k* values to execute a calculation that identifies the appropriate data points to use as the initial centers. In contrast, in the *k-means* algorithm, the initial centers are randomly selected, which increases the number of clustering iterations. Therefore, *k-means++* requires fewer iterations than *k-means*.

In conclusion, there are disadvantages associated with the use of both parametric and non-parametric techniques in the WSNs. Parametric techniques can only estimate a model when sufficient data is available, and they are therefore difficult to use in a distributed way. While non-parametric techniques can be executed in a distributed way in the WSNs, they cannot provide a probability criterion for detection. Moreover, both techniques require a massive number of iterations to form clusters and use random starting data points. These require significant computing power and have low accuracy.

2.3. Outlier Detection in WSN Applications

Outliers are very common in collected datasets for two reasons. First, sensor nodes are vulnerable to failure because the WSNs are often deployed in harsh environments [18–21]. Outliers are commonly found in datasets collected by the WSNs installed in harsh environments [22,23]. Second, noise in wireless signals and malicious attacks both create outliers [24,25], which obviously reduce the WSN capabilities.

The clustering methods are also used for outlier detection in the WSN applications. For instance, to robustly estimate the positions of sensor nodes, Reference [26] used the *EM* algorithm to iteratively detect outlier measurements. The *EM* algorithm was used to calculate variables that could indicate whether or not a particular measurement was an outlier. Reference [27] conducted similar work using *EM* algorithms to detect outliers. Additionally, Reference [28] proposed a novel flow-based outlier detection scheme based on the *k-means* clustering algorithm. This method separated a dataset containing unlabeled flow records into normal and anomalous clusters. Similar research by [29] used *k-means* to detect heart disease. However, approaches using *EM* and *k-means* to detect outliers suffer from the previously mentioned problems of clustering iteration and accuracy. The approach that we introduce later in this paper can solve such problems.

3. Bayesian Optimization

Before a dataset can be divided into clusters, the starting data points of clusters in the dataset must be determined. In particular, the number of peak points (a peak point is a data point corresponding to the maximum probability) in a dataset corresponds to the number of clusters. In this study, we use BO to identify peak points. Typically, we do not know the form of the probability density function $p(x)$. Nevertheless, we can obtain the approximate value $f(x)$ of $p(x)$ at data point x, with some noise. For example, we can approximately compute the density of a certain volume. This density is an approximate value of the probability density (see Section 4). However, obtaining the maximum density can be computationally expensive because of the large number of data points. To reduce computation costs, we used BO [30,31], a very powerful strategy that fully utilizes prior experience to obtain the maximum posterior experience at each step. This allows the maximum density to be approached. Thus, fewer data points are required to obtain the maximum density. In the following subsection, we introduce the Gaussian process used in BO.

3.1. Gaussian Process

In BO, a Gaussian process (GP) is used to build a Gaussian model from the provided information. The model is then updated with each new data point. Assume that a set of data points contains *t* elements: $\{x_1, x_2, \cdots, x_t\}$. We use the notation $x_{1:t}$ to represent the set of data points. Each of these points exists in a *D-dimensional* space. An example data point is $x_i = (x_{i1}, \cdots, x_{iD})$.

There is an intuitive analogy between a Gaussian distribution and a GP. A Gaussian distribution is a distribution over a random variable. In contrast, the random variables of a GP are functions. The mean and covariance are both functions. Hence, function $f(x)$ follows a GP and is defined as follows:

$$f(x) \sim \mathcal{GP}(m(x), k(x, x')), \tag{1}$$

where $m(x)$ is the mean function, and $k(x, x')$ is the kernel function of the covariance function.

Suppose that we have a set of data points $x_{1:t}$ and their corresponding approximate probability density $\{f(x_1), f(x_2), \cdots, f(x_t)\}$. We assume that function $f(x_i)$ can map a data point x_i to its probability density $p(x_i)$ with some noise. For concision, we will use $f_{1:t}$ to represent the set of functions for each data point $\{f(x_1), f(x_2), \cdots, f(x_t)\}$. For the collected dataset, $\mathcal{D}_{1:t} = \{(x_1, f_1), (x_2, f_2), \cdots, (x_t, f_t)\}$ is the given information. For convenience, we assume that $\mathcal{D}_{1:t}$ follows the GP model, which is given by an isotropic Gaussian $\mathcal{N}(0, K)$ whose initial mean function is zero and covariance function is calculated using K, as follows: ($k(x_i, x_j)$ consists of the kernel functions)

$$K = \begin{bmatrix} k(x_1, x_1) & \cdots & k(x_1, x_t) \\ \vdots & \ddots & \vdots \\ k(x_t, x_1) & \cdots & k(x_t, x_t) \end{bmatrix}$$

Once, we have calculated K, we build a GP model from the information provided.

A new data point x_{t+1} also follows $f_{t+1} = f(x_{t+1})$. According to the GP properties, $f_{1:t}$ and f_{t+1} are jointly Gaussian:

$$\begin{bmatrix} f_{1:t} \\ f_{t+1} \end{bmatrix} = \mathcal{N}\left(0, \begin{bmatrix} K & k \\ k^T & k(x_{t+1}, x_{t+1}) \end{bmatrix}\right)$$

where

$$k = \begin{bmatrix} k(x_{t+1}, x_1) & k(x_{t+1}, x_2) & \cdots & k(x_{t+1}, x_t) \end{bmatrix}$$

Moreover, we want to predict the approximate probability density f_{t+1} of the new data point x_{t+1}. Using Bayes' theorem and $\mathcal{D}_{1:t}$, we can obtain an expression for the prediction:

$$P(f_{t+1}|\mathcal{D}_{1:t}, x_{t+1}) = \mathcal{N}\left(\mu_t(x_{t+1}), \sigma_t^2(x_{t+1})\right) \tag{2}$$

where

$$\begin{aligned} \mu_t(x_{t+1}) &= k^T K^{-1} f_{1:t}, \\ \sigma_t^2(x_{t+1}) &= k(x_{t+1}, x_{t+1}) - k^T K^{-1} k \end{aligned} \tag{3}$$

We can observe that μ_t and σ_t^2 are independent of f_{t+1} and that we can calculate f_{t+1} using the given information.

3.2. Acquisition Functions for Bayesian Optimization

Above, we briefly describe how to use the given information to fit a GP and update the GP by incorporating a new data point. At this point, we must select an appropriate new data point x_{i+1} to use to update the GP, so that we can obtain the maximum value of $f(x_{i+1})$. To achieve this, we could use BO to realize exploitation and exploration. Here, exploitation means that we should use the data point with the maximum mean in the GP because that point fully uses the given information. However, this point cannot provide additional information about the unknown space. Exploration means that a point with a larger variance in the GP can provide additional information about the unknown area. The acquisition functions used to find an appropriate data point are designed on the basis of exploitation and exploration. There are three popular acquisition functions: probability of improvement, expectation of improvement, and upper confidence bound criterion.

The probability of improvement (PI) function is designed to maximize the probability of improvement over $f(x^+)$, where $x^+ = \text{argmax}_{x_i \in x_{1:t}} f(x_i)$. The resulting cumulated distribution function is:

$$
\begin{aligned}
PI(x) &= P\left(f(x) \geq f(x^+) + \xi\right) \\
&= \Phi\left(\frac{\mu(x) - f(x^+) - \xi}{\sigma(x)}\right)
\end{aligned}
\tag{4}
$$

where ξ is the exploration strength, which is provided by the user.

The expectation of improvement (EI) is designed to account for not only the probability of improvement, but also the potential magnitude of improvement that could be yielded by a point. The EI is expressed as

$$
EI(x) = \begin{cases} (\mu(x) - f(x^+) - \xi)\,\Phi(Z) + \sigma(x)\phi(Z) & \text{if } \sigma(x) > 0 \\ 0 & \text{if } \sigma(x) = 0 \end{cases}
\tag{5}
$$

$$
Z = \begin{cases} \frac{\mu(x) - f(x^+) - \xi}{\sigma(x)}, & \text{if } \sigma(x) > 0 \\ 0, & \text{if } \sigma(x) = 0 \end{cases}
\tag{6}
$$

The upper confidence bound (UCB) criterion uses the confidence bound, which is the area representing the uncertainty between the mean function and variance function in Equation (3). The UCB is compared with the other two acquisition functions, and is relatively simple and intuitive. In detail, it directly uses the mean and variance functions obtained from the given information. A potential new data point is presented by the sum of (*i*) the mean function, and (*ii*) a constant v times the variance function. That is, given several potential new data points, the data point with the largest UCB will be selected as the next new data point. Moreover, v, which is greater than 0, indicates how many explorations are expected. The UCB formula is

$$
\text{UCB}(x) = \mu(x) + v\sigma(x)
\tag{7}
$$

These three acquisition functions are suited to different datasets, and allow us to obtain an appropriate new data point. The BO algorithm (Algorithm 1) is shown below.

Algorithm 1: BO

---

1 **for** $i = 1, 2, \ldots$ **do**
2   Fit a GP to the given information $\mathcal{D}_{1:t}$;
3   Use acquisition functions to find a data point x that has the maximum value $\mu(x|\mathcal{D}_{1:t})$ over GP;
4   Calculate the value of $f(x)$ at x_i;
5   Augment the dataset $\mathcal{D}_{1:t+1} = \{\mathcal{D}_{1:t}, (x_i, f_i)\}$ and update the GP;
6 **end**

---

4. Peak Searching Algorithm

In this section, we first introduce some preliminary information related to our proposed algorithm. Then, we explain the algorithm.

4.1. Preliminary Investigations

In most cases, the environment can be represented as a collection of statuses that indicate whether or not certain events have occurred. Such events include fires, earthquakes, and invasions. The data points collected by the sensor nodes contain measurements that describe the statuses of these events. One can assume that the collected dataset is generated by a Gaussian mixture model (GMM) because the data points contained in the dataset are collected from the normal environment, or from natural events. Thus, before fitting a GMM, it is necessary to clarify the peaks of the GMM because each peak is a point that has the largest probability corresponding to a Gaussian distribution. Therefore, we need to know the probability of each data point when we search for the dataset peaks. Although the probability density function is unknown, it can be approximated using alternative methods, which are shown as follows.

One type of method assumes that the set of data points exists in a *D-dimensional* space. The probability of data point x can then be approximated as follows: (i) set x as the center of a volume with side h. Figure 1 shows an example of a volume in 3D space, where the length of each side is h; and (ii) the density of the volume with center x, calculated using Equation (8) [31], is approximately equal to the probability at data point x. The density $p(x)$ in this formula depends on the length of side h in the volume and the number T (that is, the number of neighbors of data point x in the volume). N is the total number of data points in the dataset and h^D is the size of the volume. Thus, to search for the peaks, we must calculate the densities of all of the different data points using Equation (8). However, this is computationally expensive:

$$p(x) = \frac{T}{Nh^D}.\tag{8}$$

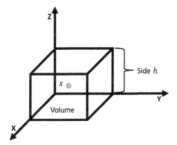

Figure 1. A volume in three-dimensional space.

Another method fixes h and applies a kernel density estimator [31]. In this case, the probability of data point x can be calculated as

$$p(x) = \frac{1}{Nh^D} \sum_{i=1}^{T} K\left(\frac{x - x_i}{h}\right),\tag{9}$$

where $K(\bullet)$ is the kernel function and T is the number of data points in a volume with side h. Then, the largest value of $p(x)$ occurs along the gradient of Equation (9), which is

$$\nabla p(x) = \frac{1}{Nh^D} \sum_{i=1}^{T} K'\left(\frac{x - x_i}{h}\right).\tag{10}$$

By setting Equation (10) equal to zero, we can calculate the point along the gradient that has the largest $p(x)$. With this method, we do not need to search through the unimportant data points, which reduces the time required to identify peaks. However, Equations (9) and (10) are difficult to solve. Moreover, the length of side h affects the peak search results. Firstly, it supposes that all of the volumes have the same size because they have the same h. Secondly, an inappropriate h value will lead to an incorrect result. In particular, h values that are too large cause over-smoothing in high-density areas, while h values that are too small cause significant noise in low-density areas. To overcome these shortcomings, we introduce the PSA, which we describe in the following subsection.

4.2. The Algorithm

We propose a peak searching algorithm (PSA) that does not consider parameter h. We will use simulations to investigate the details of the PSA, which can be used to improve the speed and accuracy of clustering algorithms such as EM and k-*means*.

In Equation (10), $\frac{x-x_i}{h}$ is a vector that starts at point x and ends at neighboring point x_i. Because a kernel function is used to calculate the inner product of the vector, in this case, the inner product is equal to the vector mode. Moreover, it calculates the largest $p(x)$ and the location of data point x where x on the vector at $\frac{1}{Nh^D}$ times the mode of the vector. Therefore, the largest probability for finding the peak lays on this vector. This allows us to concentrate only on the vector, without considering constants $\frac{1}{Nh^D}$ and h. Hence, we propose using V_x to represent the vector in the PSA as

$$V_x = \frac{\sum_{i=1}^T (x - x_i)}{\| \sum_{i=1}^T (x - x_i) \|}. \tag{11}$$

In Equation (11), only V_x is searched. A significant amount of non-important space is not searched. However, many probabilities must be calculated along V_x. Moreover, because there are too many data points on the vector V_x, it becomes impossible to search for the best data point with the largest probability in a limited amount of time. Hence, we apply BO when searching for the largest probability along V_x. BO optimizes the method for searching the maximum probability value mentioned in Algorithm 1. However, as we mentioned in Section 3, the form of probability function $p(x)$ is not known, and it can instead be represented by an approximate probability function, which is $f(x)$ in Algorithm 1 line 4. Therefore, in this paper, we use Equation (8) to calculate the approximate probability function, which we use in the proposed algorithm. Equation (8) is simpler and more practical for finding dataset peaks. The following describes the details of the proposed PSA.

Next, we will explain how the PSA works in accordance with Algorithm 2. The initializing step requires a number of starting data points from which to begin the search for peaksbecause the dataset may contain multiple peaks. Therefore, the PSA randomly selects M starting points, $\{x^{(1)}, x^{(2)}, \cdots, and x^{(M)}\}$. For convenience, we will use starting point $x^{(j)}$ to describe the details of the method. Vector $x^{(j)}$ is calculated using Equation (11) in line 1. The peak searching process shown in Figure 2 contains four steps. In Step 1, the PSA uses Algorithm 1 to search for the peak. That is, data point $x_i^{(j)}$, which has a maximum probability along $V_x^{(j)}$. The probability denoted by $p\left(x_i^{(j)}\right)$ is calculated using Equation (8) as shown in line 4. In Step 2 in line 5, a new vector $V_{x_i}^{(j)}$ is calculated on the basis of $x_i^{(j)}$ and its T neighboring data points. In Step 3, the method searches for the peak $x_{i+1}^{(j)}$ along $V_{x_i}^{(j)}$ in line 6. Notice that data points $x_i^{(j)}$ and $x_{i+1}^{(j)}$ are possible dataset peaks. Step 4 starts from line 7 to 14, and the method repeats these steps until the difference between $p\left(x_i^{(j)}\right)$ and $p\left(x_{i+1}^{(j)}\right)$ gets close enough to zero. At this point, data point $x_{i+1}^{(j)}$ is selected as a dataset peak. The same four steps are used with the other starting data points to identify all peaks in the dataset.

Algorithm 2: PSA

1 Given a starting data point $x^{(j)}$, and calculate the $V_x^{(j)}$;

2 $i = 0$;

3 **while** *True* **do**

4   Search for Max $p\left(x_i^{(j)}\right)$ along $V_x^{(j)}$ by using Algorithm 1 ;

5   Set $x_i^{(j)}$ as a peak and calculate $V_{x_i}^{(j)}$ with $x_i^{(j)}$'s K neighbors;

6   Search for Max $p\left(x_{i+1}^{(j)}\right)$ along $V_{x_i}^{(j)}$ by using Algorithm 1 ;

7   **if** $\left| p\left(x_i^{(j)}\right) - p\left(x_{i+1}^{(j)}\right)\right| < \epsilon$ **then**

8          $x_{i+1}^{(j)}$ is a peak of the dataset ;

9   break ;

10   **else**

11   Set $x_{i+1}^{(j)}$ as a peak and calculate $V_{x_{i+1}}^{(j)}$ with $x_{i+1}^{(j)}$'s T neighbors ;

12         $V_x^{(j)} \leftarrow V_{x_{i+1}}^{(j)}$;

13         $i \leftarrow i+1$;

14   **end**

15 **end**

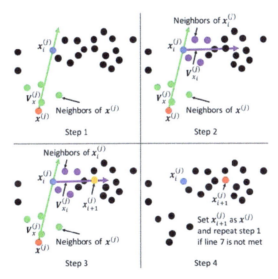

Figure 2. Peak searching.

5. Simulation and Analysis

In this section, we investigate the efficiency of the proposed *PSA*. Because the *PSA* is a method for improving clustering algorithms, we must use it in state-of-the-art clustering algorithms to evaluate the extent to which the *PSA* can improve those algorithms. As mentioned in Section 2, *EM* and *k-means* are common clustering algorithms. Here, variations of those algorithms using the *PSA* are referred to as *PSEM* and *PSk-means*, respectively. In *PSEM* and *PSk-means*, the *PSA* first searches the peaks of the collected dataset. Then, *EM* and *k-means* use the obtained peaks as the initial starting points to start clustering. In the simulations, we assume that the collected datasets follow GMMs, and that the number of peaks found by the *PSA* is equal to the number of Gaussian distributions.

We conducted simulations using synthetic datasets and a real dataset. In simulations with synthetic datasets, we compared the accuracies and iterations of *PSEM* and *PSk-means* with those of the original *EM* (*OEM*), *k-means*, and *k-means++* algorithms. Moreover, because recall and precision are important evaluation indicators, we also used the simulations to compare recalls and precisions. In the simulation using a real dataset, we simulated our methods in order to detect outliers. Because a real dataset could be either isotropic or anisotropic, and because *k-means* has a weak effect on anisotropic datasets, we only compared *PSEM* to *OEM* for the real dataset.

5.1. Simulation on Synthetic Datasets

5.1.1. Synthetic Dataset

We generated two synthetic datasets, whose data points contained two features. Each dataset was generated using a GMM that contained two different Gaussian distributions. The Gaussian distributions in the first dataset were isotopically distributed; their true peaks (means) were $(1, 1)$ and $(2, 2)$ and their variances were 0.6 and 0.5, respectively. The Gaussian distributions in the second synthetic dataset were transformed using the following matrix to create anisotropically distributed datasets:

$$\begin{bmatrix} 0.6 & -0.6 \\ -0.4 & 0.8 \end{bmatrix}.$$

The two synthetic datasets are shown in Figure 3. The two synthetic datasets are appropriate for these types of simulations because they can represent both easy and difficult clustering situations. This allows us to evaluate the effects of our algorithm.

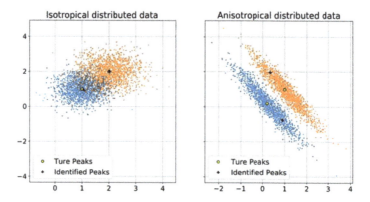

Figure 3. Synthetic dataset.

5.1.2. Simulations and Results

To estimate the extent to which the *PSA* can improve clustering capabilities, we compared *PSEM* with the original *EM* (*OEM*) algorithm. Both *PSEM* and *OEM* use *EM* to fit a GMM, and have a time complexity of $O(N^3)$, where N is the number of data points. Hence, we cannot use time complexity to compare *PSEM* and *EM*. Computational efficiency can also be measured from the number of iterations. The *EM* algorithm contains two steps: the *E*-step and the *M*-step. These two steps are iteratively executed to fit a GMM, and are the core calculations of this algorithm. Hence, we compared the number of iterations in *PSEM* (i.e., how many *E*-steps and *M*-steps were executed) with the number of iterations in *OEM*. Note that the *OEM* algorithm does not use *PSA*, so its calculations start at randomly selected initial starting points.

PSEM and OEM were executed 200 times for the two different datasets. Figure 3 shows 200 peak searching results for *PSA*. The dark crosses indicate the peaks identified by *PSA*. We can see that, in the isotropically distributed dataset, the identified peaks are very close to the true peaks. In the anisotropically distributed dataset, the identified peaks are also close to the true peaks. Figure 4 illustrates the number of iterations (*y*-axis) for each size of dataset (*x*-axis). In the peak searching step, three different acquisition functions are used (*UCB*, *EI*, and *PI*), and their calculation efficiencies are compared. According to the results shown in Figure 4, there were 3.06 to 6.3 times fewer iterations for *PSEM* than *OEM*. In other words, the *PSA* improved the calculation efficiency of *OEM* by 73.9% to 86.3%. Moreover, we can see that there is no obvious difference between the three acquisition functions.

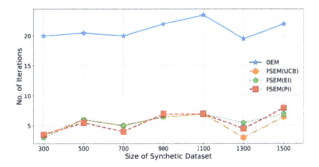

Figure 4. Comparison of iterations: OEM.

Because we wanted to fairly estimate the extent to which the proposed *PSA* improves clustering capabilities, we compared the *PSA* to *k-means++* in another simulation. *k-means++* uses a special method to calculate its initial points, and its clustering method increases the speed of convergence. Note that both *PSk-means* and *k-means++* are based on *k-means*, which has a time complexity $O(N^2 T)$, where N is the number of data points and T is the number of iterations. Similarly, we cannot use time complexity to compare calculation efficiencies. However, we can compare the number of iterations required for *PSk-means* to that required for *k-means++*. Both of these algorithms were executed 200 times with the two different datasets, and the results are shown in Figure 5.

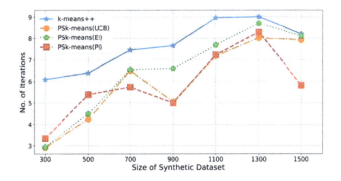

Figure 5. Comparison of iterations: *k-means++*.

The simulation results are shown in Figure 5. The average number of iterations for *PSk-means* is reduced by 1.04 to 1.99 times compared with the number of iterations for *k-means++*. In other words, the PSA improved the calculation efficiency of OEM by 51% to 67%. Additionally, there was no obvious difference between the three acquisition functions.

5.1.3. Performance Estimation of Clustering

Accuracy, precision, and *recall* are three commonly used measurements for estimating machine learning algorithm performance. Therefore, we adopt these measurements to quantify the performances of our proposed algorithm. In simulations, a dataset containing two clusters is generated by GMM. To explain these measurements, we assume that the two clusters are cluster A and cluster B. Data points belonging to cluster A are considered to be positive instances, while those that belong to cluster B are considered to be negative instances. If a data point from cluster A is correctly clustered into cluster A, it is a true positive (TP) result. Otherwise, it is a false positive result (FP). Similarly, if a data point from cluster B is correctly clustered into cluster B, that is a true negative (TN); otherwise, it is a false negative (FN). Overall *accuracy* can be calculated as follows:

$$accuracy = \frac{TP + TN}{TP + FP + TN + FN}. \tag{12}$$

Recall is equal to the ratio of TP to the total number of positive instances. It is based on the total positive instances, and shows how many positive instances can be detected by the algorithm. It is calculated as

$$recall = \frac{TP}{TP + FN}. \tag{13}$$

From a prediction standpoint, *Precision* indicates how many TPs occur in the detected positive instances. It presents the proportion of TP to the total number of data points that are detected as positive, which is equal to TP + FP. *Precision* is calculated as

$$precision = \frac{TP}{TP + FP}. \tag{14}$$

We estimated the *accuracy, precision*, and *recall* of the *PSk-means* and *PSEM* clustering algorithms, and compared the values with those for *k-means, k-means++*, and *OEM*. We repeated this estimation 200 times for each dataset; the average accuracy of each algorithm is shown in Figures 6 and 7. The isotropic datasets shown in Figure 3 are difficult to cluster because the two clusters partially overlap and their centers are very close together. We can see from the simulation results shown in Figure 6 that the estimations of *k-means, k-means++*, and *OEM* are similar. However, *PSk-means* and *PSEM* show a great improvement over their original algorithms. The accuracy of *PSk-means* is 1.69 times higher than that of *k-means++*, while that of *PSEM* is 1.71 times higher than that of *OEM*. The recall of *PSk-means* is 1.66 times higher than that of *k-means++*, and the recall of *PSEM* is 1.83 times higher than that of *OEM*. Moreover, the precision of *PSk-means* is 1.64 times higher than that of *k-means++*'s. The precision of *PSEM* is 1.84 times higher than that of *OEM*.

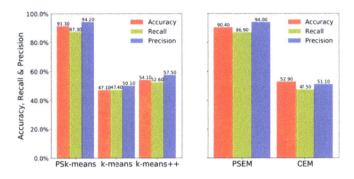

Figure 6. Measurements for isotropic dataset.

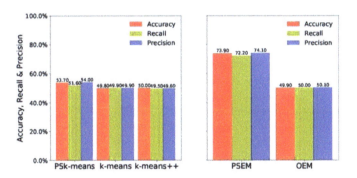

Figure 7. Measurements for anisotropic dataset.

The results for the anisotropic datasets are shown in Figure 7. Because the anisotropic datasets are elliptical, as shown in Figure 3, and the two datasets are very close together, the datasets are very difficult to cluster. As a result, *k-means* and *k-means++* exhibit low estimation performance, and *PSk-means* yields little improvement. However, the accuracy of *PSEM* was 1.48 times higher than that of *OEM*, and its recall and precision were 1.44 and 1.48 times higher, respectively, than they were for *OEM*. Accordingly, we can see that the *PSA* can improve clustering accuracy.

5.2. Simulation on a Real Dataset from Intel Berkeley Research Laboratory

We used a real sensor dataset from the Intel Berkeley Research Laboratory [32] to assess outlier detection performance. In the simulation, we only considered two features for each data point: temperature and humidity. Each sensor node contained 5000 data points, which are shown in Figure 8.

Because the original dataset did not provide any outlier information or labels, we manually cleaned the data by removing values that fell outside a normal data range. All of the remaining data points were considered to be normal. Table 1 lists the normal data ranges.

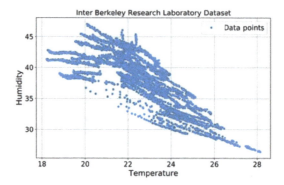

Figure 8. Dataset from Intel Berkeley Research Laboratory.

Table 1. Normal data ranges.

	Range	Average
Temperature (°C)	21.32–28.14	23.14
Humidity (%)	26.39–44.02	37.69

After completing this step, a uniform distribution was used to generate artificial outliers. Temperature outliers were generated within a range of (27–30) °C, and humidity outliers were generated within a range of (42–46)%. Thus, some outliers can fall inside the normal range with the same probability. Outliers were then inserted into the normal dataset. We produced four different cases, in which the outliers accounted for 5%, 15%, 20%, and 25% of the total normal data points.

5.2.1. Setting of WSNs

PSEM and *OEM* were run for a real dataset from the Intel Berkeley Research Laboratory. The deployment of the WSNs is shown in Figure 9. There were 54 sensor nodes, each of which had a *Mica2Dot* sensor for collecting humidity, temperature, light, and voltage values. Temperatures were provided in degrees Celsius. Humidity was provided as temperature-corrected relative humidity, and ranged from 0–100%. Light was expressed in Lux (1 Lux corresponds to moonlight, 400 Lux to a bright office, and 100,000 Lux to full sunlight), and voltage was expressed in volts, ranging from 2–3. The batteries were lithium ion cells, which maintain a fairly constant voltage over their lifetime; note that variations in voltage are highly correlated with temperature. We selected data from 10 sensor nodes (nodes 1 to 10) to test our method, and used only humidity and temperature values.

In this simulation, we assumed that the WSN was hierarchical and consisted of classes. ("Cluster" is used in the WSNs to describe a group of sensor nodes. However, "cluster" can also refer to a group of similar data points in data mining. In this paper, we use "class" instead of cluster to describe a group of sensor nodes). Each class contained one class head (CH) and other member sensor nodes (MSNs). The MSNs sent the data points collected over a certain time period to the CH, which used the proposed method to monitor whether the dataset collected from its members contained outliers. The configuration of the WSNs is shown in Figure 10.

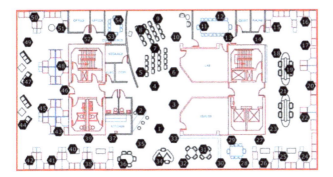

Figure 9. Floor plan of Intel Berkeley Research Laboratory.

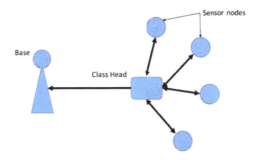

Figure 10. WSN configuration.

5.2.2. Results

Using the real dataset, we tested the proposed *PSEM* and compared it with the *OEM*. The CH executed the *PSEM* or *OEM* to detect outliers, and sent outlier reports to the base station. We generated four different datasets, containing 5%, 15%, 20%, and 25% outliers. (Figures 11 and 12).

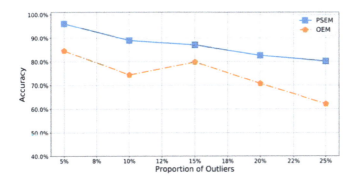

Figure 11. Accuracy of real dataset.

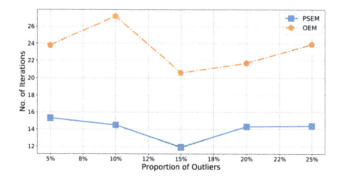

Figure 12. No. of iterations for dataset.

It was relatively easy to detect outliers in the test dataset containing only 5% outliers because the proportion of outliers was so low. Thus, the accuracy of our method approached 100% for 5% outliers. In contrast, the accuracy of the *OEM* was only approximately 85%. In the other datasets, more outliers fell within the normal dataset. In such cases, it was difficult to detect the outliers; the accuracies of both methods decreased as the proportion of outliers increased. However, *PSEM* remained more accurate than *OEM*. In the worst case, with 25% outliers in the test dataset, its accuracy of *PSEM* was approximately 80%, while the accuracy of *OEM* was only approximately 60%. That is, *PSEM* was about 1.09 to 1.29 times more accurate than *OEM*. Moreover, Figure 12 shows the number of iterations was 1.52 to 1.88 times lower for *PSEM*, meaning that *PSEM* improved the calculation efficiency of *OEM* by 60% to 65.2%. Because accuracy and iteration numbers are very important metrics for assessing the clustering algorithm efficiency, this simulation result demonstrated the practical significance of *PESM*, and, therefore, of the *PSA*.

6. Discussion

In this section, we describe other important aspects of the WSNs, such as WSN power consumptions and lifetime. We also discuss the advantages and disadvantages of the proposed method.

Because most sensor nodes in the WSNs are powered by batteries, sensor node power consumptions, WSN lifetime, and energy efficiency are also important problems affecting the quality of a WSN. Mostafaei et al. [33] proposed an algorithm PCLA to schedule sensors into active or sleep states, utilizing learning automata to extend network lifetime. Our previous work attempted to extend battery life by reducing peak power consumption. We scheduled sensor execution times [34], and used optimized wireless communication routes to reduce energy consumption, with the goal of prolonging network lifetimes [35,36]. If the proposed *PSA* can be applied in such approaches to analyze data using clustering methods, then energy consumption can be further reduced. Because the *PSA* can reduce clustering iterations, the required computational power decreases, leading to energy savings.

The proposed algorithm has advantages and disadvantages. In conventional clustering methods such as *EM* and *k-means*, cluster-forming procedures are started at random data points. There are two disadvantages associated with this. First, correct clusters may not be able to form from random starting points. Second, because random staring points may not occur near cluster centers, massive iterations may be needed to update random points to approach the cluster centers. However, because the *PSA* can identify the peak points near cluster centers, it is a better approach for forming clusters than an algorithm starting from a random point. Therefore, clustering algorithms using the *PSA* can form clusters more accurately. Moreover, using peak points as the starting points to form clusters can significantly reduce clustering iterations because peak points are the desired points.

There are some disadvantages associated with the *PSA*. The *PSA* use BO and are, therefore, affected by the problems associated with BO. A particular issue is that a priori design is critical to efficient BO. As mentioned in Section 3, BO uses GPs to build Gaussian models with Gaussian distributions, making the resulting datasets transcendental. If a dataset does not have a Gaussian distribution, the *PSA* may be less efficient. Another weak point of the *PSA* is that it is centralized. It is not suited for highly distributed WSNs where data analyses are conducted at each sensor node.

7. Conclusions

In this paper, we proposed a new *PSA* for improving the performance of clustering algorithms (i.e., for improving accuracy and reducing clustering iterations). BO is used to search for the peaks of a collected dataset in the *PSA*. To investigate the efficiency of the *PSA*, we used the *PSA* to modify *EM* and *k-means* algorithms. The new algorithms were named *PSEM* and *PSk-means*, respectively.

Using simulations, we investigated the performance of *PSEM* and *PSk-means* relative to that of *OEM* and *k-means++*. We conducted simulations using both synthetic datasets and a real dataset. For synthetic datasets, *PSEM* and *PSk-means* reduced iterations by approximately 6.3 and 1.99 times, respectively, at a maximum. Moreover, they improved clustering accuracy by 1.71 times and 1.69 times, respectively, at a maximum. On a real dataset for outliers' detection purpose, *PSEM* reduced iterations about 1.88 times, and improved clustering accuracy by 1.29 times at a maximum. These results show that our proposed algorithm significantly improves performance. We obtained the same conclusions by illustrating the recall and precision improvements for *PSEM* and *PSk-means*.

In the future, we will improve this method so that it can be used with high-dimensional data, such as images collected by a camera. Moreover, we would like to deploy the peak searching algorithm with sensor nodes, in order to allow CHs to obtain peak searching results from their neighbors; this will reduce the calculation time required for the peak search. Thus, clustering can be implemented in the sensor node and communication costs can be reduced.

Acknowledgments: This work was supported by the Japan Society for the Promotion of Science (JSPS KAKENHI Grant Numbers 16H02800, 17K00105, and 17H00762).

Author Contributions: Tianyu Zhang, Qian Zhao, and Kilho Shin conceived and designed the algorithm and experiments. Tianyu Zhang performed the experiments, analyzed the data, and was the primary author of this paper. Yukikazu Nakamoto gave advice on this work and helped revise the paper. Additionally, Qian Zhao and Kilho Shin helped revise the paper.

Conflicts of Interest: The authors declare no conflict of interest.

References

1. Sung, W.T. Multi-sensors data fusion system for wireless sensors networks of factory monitoring via BPN technology. *Expert Syst. Appl.* **2010**, *37*, 2124–2131.
2. Hackmann, G.; Guo, W.; Yan, G.; Sun, Z.; Lu, C.; Dyke, S. Cyber-physical codesign of distributed structural health monitoring with wireless sensor networks. *IEEE Trans. Parallel Distrib. Syst.* **2014**, *25*, 63–72.
3. Oliveira, L.M.; Rodrigues, J.J. Wireless Sensor Networks: A Survey on Environmental Monitoring. *J. Clin. Microbiol.* **2011**, *6*, 143–151.
4. Wu, C.I.; Kung, H.Y.; Chen, C.H.; Kuo, L.C. An intelligent slope disaster prediction and monitoring system based on WSN and ANP. *Expert Syst. Appl.* **2014**, *41*, 4554–4562.
5. Dempster, A.P.; Laird, N.M.; Rubin, D.B. Maximum likelihood from incomplete data via the EM algorithm. *J. R. Stat. Soc. Ser. B* **1977**, *39*, 1–38.
6. Huang, Z. Extensions to the *k-means* algorithm for clustering large data sets with categorical values. *Data Min. Knowl. Discov.* **1998**, *2*, 283–304.
7. Rasmussen, C.E.; Williams, C.K. *Gaussian Processes for Machine Learning*; MIT Press: Cambridge, MA, USA, 2006; Volume 1.
8. Papaioannou, I.; Papadimitriou, C.; Straub, D. Sequential importance sampling for structural reliability analysis. *Struct. Saf.* **2016**, *62*, 66–75.

9. Behmanesh, I.; Moaveni, B.; Lombaert, G.; Papadimitriou, C. Hierarchical Bayesian model updating for structural identification. *Mech. Syst. Signal Proc.* **2015**, *64*, 360–376.
10. Azam, S.E.; Bagherinia, M.; Mariani, S. Stochastic system identification via particle and sigma-point Kalman filtering. *Sci. Iran.* **2012**, *19*, 982–991.
11. Azam, S.E.; Mariani, S. Dual estimation of partially observed nonlinear structural systems: A particle filter approach. *Mech. Res. Commun.* **2012**, *46*, 54–61.
12. Arthur, D.; Vassilvitskii, S. *k-means++*: The advantages of careful seeding. In Proceedings of the Eighteenth Annual ACM-SIAM Symposium on Discrete Algorithms, Society for Industrial and Applied Mathematics, Orleans, LA, USA, 7–9 January 2007; pp. 1027–1035.
13. Wu, W.; Cheng, X.; Ding, M.; Xing, K.; Liu, F.; Deng, P. Localized outlying and boundary data detection in sensor networks. *IEEE Trans. Knowl. Data Eng.* **2007**, *19*, 1145–1157.
14. Breunig, M.M.; Kriegel, H.P.; Ng, R.T.; Sander, J. LOF: Identifying density-based local outliers. In Proceedings of the 2000 ACM SIGMOD International Conference on Management of Data, Dallas, TX, USA, 15–18 May 2000; Volume 29, pp. 93–104.
15. Sheela, B.V.; Dasarathy, B.V. OPAL: A new algorithm for optimal partitioning and learning in non parametric unsupervised environments. *Int. J. Parallel Program.* **1979**, *8*, 239–253.
16. Eskin, E. Anomaly detection over noisy data using learned probability distributions. In Proceedings of the International Conference on Machine Learning, Citeseer, Stanford, CA, USA, 29 June–2 July 2000.
17. Eskinand, E.; Stolfo, S. Modeling system call for intrusion detection using dynamic window sizes. In Proceedings of DARPA Information Survivability Conference and Exposition, Anaheim, CA, USA, 12–14 June 2001.
18. Dereszynski, E.W.; Dietterich, T.G. Spatiotemporal models for data-anomaly detection in dynamic environmental monitoring campaigns. *ACM Trans. Sens. Netw. (TOSN)* **2011**, *8*, 3.
19. Bahrepour, M.; van der Zwaag, B.J.; Meratnia, N.; Havinga, P. Fire data analysis and feature reduction using computational intelligence methods. In *Advances in Intelligent Decision Technologies*; Springer: Berlin/Heidelberg, Germany, 2010; pp. 289–298.
20. Phua, C.; Lee, V.; Smith, K.; Gayler, R. A comprehensive survey of data mining-based fraud detection research. *arXiv* **2010**, arXiv:1009.6119. Available online: https://arxiv.org/ftp/arxiv/papers/1009/1009.6119.pdf (access on 29 July 2017).
21. Aqeel-ur-Rehman; Abbasi, A.Z.; Islam, N.; Shaikh, Z.A. A review of wireless sensors and networks' applications in agriculture. *Comput. Stand. Interfaces* **2014**, *36*, 263–270.
22. Misra, P.; Kanhere, S.; Ostry, D. Safety assurance and rescue communication systems in high-stress environments: A mining case study. *IEEE Commun. Mag.* **2010**, *48*, 11206229.
23. García-Hernández, C.F.; Ibarguengoytia-Gonzalez, P.H.; García-Hernández, J.; Pérez-Díaz, J.A. Wireless sensor networks and applications: A survey. *Int. J. Comput. Sci. Netw. Secur.* **2007**, *7*, 264–273.
24. John, G.H. Robust Decision Trees: Removing Outliers from Databases. In Proceedings of the First International Conference on Knowledge Discovery and Data Mining (KDD'95), Montreal, QC, Canada, 20–21 August 1995; pp. 174–179.
25. Han, J.; Pei, J.; Kamber, M. *Data Mining: Concepts and Techniques*; Elsevier: Amsterdam, The Netherlands, 2011.
26. Ash, J.N.; Moses, R.L. Outlier compensation in sensor network self-localization via the EM algorithm. In Proceedings of the IEEE International Conference on Acoustics, Speech, and Signal Processing, Philadelphia, PA, USA, 23–23 March 2005; Volume 4, pp. iv–749.
27. Yin, F.; Zoubir, A.M.; Fritsche, C.; Gustafsson, F. Robust cooperative sensor network localization via the EM criterion in LOS/NLOS environments. In Proceedings of the 2013 IEEE 14th Workshop on Signal Processing Advances in Wireless Communications (SPAWC), Darmstadt, Germany, 16–19 June 2013; pp. 505–509.
28. Münz, G.; Li, S.; Carle, G. Traffic anomaly detection using *k-means* clustering. In Proceedings of the GI/ITG Workshop MMBnet, Hamburg, Germany, September 2007.
29. Devi, T.; Saravanan, N. Development of a data clustering algorithm for predicting heart. *Int. J. Comput. Appl.* **2012**, *48*, doi:10.5120/7358-0095.
30. Brochu, E.; Cora, V.M.; De Freitas, N. A tutorial on Bayesian optimization of expensive cost functions, with application to active user modeling and hierarchical reinforcement learning. *arXiv* **2010**, arXiv:1012.2599. Available online: https://arxiv.org/pdf/1012.2599.pdf (access on 30 June 2017).
31. Bishop, C.M. *Pattern Recognition and Machine Learning*; Springer: Berlin/Heidelberg, Germany, 2006.

32. Intel Lab Data. Available online: http://db.csail.mit.edu/labdata/labdata.html (accessed on 30 August 2017).
33. Mostafaei, H.; Montieri, A.; Persico, V.; Pescapé, A. A sleep scheduling approach based on learning automata for WSN partial coverage. *J. Netw. Comput. Appl.* **2017**, *80*, 67–78.
34. Zhao, Q.; Nakamoto, Y.; Yamada, S.; Yamamura, K.; Iwata, M.; Kai, M. Sensor Scheduling Algorithms for Extending Battery Life in a Sensor Node. *IEICE Trans. Fundam. Electron. Commun. Comput. Sci.* **2013**, *E96-A*, 1236–1244.
35. Zhao, Q.; Nakamoto, Y. Algorithms for Reducing Communication Energy and Avoiding Energy Holes to Extend Lifetime of WSNs. *IEICE Trans. Inf. Syst.* **2014**, *E97-D*, 2995–3006.
36. Zhao, Q.; Nakamoto, Y. Topology Management for Reducing Energy Consumption and Tolerating Failures in Wireless Sensor Networks. *Int. J. Netw. Comput.* **2016**, *6*, 107–123.

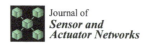

Journal of
*Sensor and
Actuator Networks*

Article

Development of Intelligent Core Network for Tactile Internet and Future Smart Systems

Abdelhamied A. Ateya [1,2], **Ammar Muthanna** [1,*], **Irina Gudkova** [3], **Abdelrahman Abuarqoub** [4],
Anastasia Vybornova [1] and **Andrey Koucheryavy** [1]

[1]   Telecommunication Networks and Data Transmission, The Bonch-Bruevich State University of
     Telecommunication, 193232 Sankt-Peterburg, Russia; a_ashraf@zu.edu.eg (A.A.A.);
     a.vybornova@gmail.com (A.V.); akouch@mail.ru (A.K.)
[2]   Electronics and Communications Engineering, Zagazig University, Ash Sharqia Governorate 44519, Egypt
[3]   Applied Probability and Informatics, Peoples' Friendship University of Russia (RUDN University),
     117198 Moskva, Russia; gudkova_ia@pfur.ru
[4]   Faculty of Information Technology, Middle East University Amman, 383 Amman 11831, Jordan;
     Aabuarqoub@meu.edu.jo
*   Correspondence: ammarexpress@gmail.com; Tel.: +7-952-210-4486

Received: 31 October 2017; Accepted: 11 December 2017; Published: 2 January 2018

Abstract: One of the main design aspects of the Tactile Internet system is the 1 ms end-to-end latency, which is considered as being the main challenge with the system realization. Forced by recent development and capabilities of the fifth generation (5G) cellular system, the Tactile Internet will become a real. One way to overcome the 1 ms latency is to employ a centralized controller in the core of the network with a global knowledge of the system, together with the concept of network function virtualization (NFV). This is the idea behind the software defined networking (SDN). This paper introduces a Tactile Internet system structure, which employs SDN in the core of the cellular network and mobile edge computing (MEC) in multi-levels. The work is mainly concerned with the structure of the core network. The system is simulated over a reliable environment and introduces a round trip latency of orders of 1 ms. This can be interpreted by the reduction of intermediate nodes that are involved in the communication process.

Keywords: Tactile Internet; 5G; latency; NFV; SDN; MEC

---

1. Introduction

Tactile Internet is expected to be a novel approach in the human-to-machine (H2M) communication by moving from the content delivery to the skill-set delivery. The main application that is supported by the Tactile Internet system will be the haptic communication in real time [1]. It will be a revolution in the area of information and communication technology with enormous applications in many fields [2]. Powered by the 5G cellular network, Tactile Internet will provide a way for human to transfer their tough and actuation in real time form.

Tactile Internet is one of the main use cases of the near future 5G cellular system, as announced by International Telecommunication Union (ITU) [3]. Through the Tactile Internet, physical habits will be communicated remotely. The construction of the Tactile Internet system can be viewed as three main parts as presented in Figure 1 [4]. The network part connects the master and the slave parts through a huge infrastructure of fiber cables and network elements. Here, we consider this part to enable live time communication between transmitter and receiver by means of employing modern technologies throughout the cellular network.

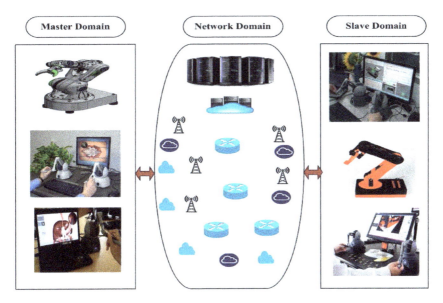

Figure 1. General view of Tactile Internet System.

Designing Tactile Internet system and realizing it meets some challenges that are presented in [5]. The main challenge is the 1 ms end-to-end latency. The end-to-end latency differ from the user plane latency and can be defined as the time duration starts from the transmission of a small data packet from the transmitter's application layer and ends by the reception of the data by the receiver's application layer, including the response feedback that is dedicated by the communication process [6]. Thus, the end-to-end latency depends on the number of network nodes that are involved in the communication process. In order to reduce the round trip latency and achieve the 1 ms latency requirement for the Tactile Internet system, the number of network nodes involved in the communication process should be reduced and bring them as near as possible to the user equipment. This is can be achieved by employing software defined networking (SDN), network function virtualization (NFV), and mobile edge computing (MEC) with the 5G cellular system.

SDN, NFV, and MEC technologies provide powerful solutions for the challenges that are associated with the design of 5G cellular system and Tactile Internet system, specially the 1 ms latency. Thus, the academia and the industry pay a great attention to the research and development in these areas. In today's cellular networks, the network services are handled by means of various network functions that are connected in static manner [7]. Thus, it is not easy to add new services, this is because the cost, energy and integration difficulties of hardware required. To overcome these problems NFV and SDN are developed.

NFV provides fixed network functions by means of software run on a virtualized environment, which increases the flexibility of the overall system. NFV employs virtualization technologies on programmable hardware, such as storage devices, general purpose servers, and switches to separate the software implementation of network functions from the dedicated hardware. In another word, NFV set up the network functions by means of software virtualization techniques on commodity hardware [8]. Several projects are launched, for developing open source, commercial solutions, and standardizations for NFV. The most important projects are the Service Programming and Orchestration for Virtualized Software Networks (SONATA) project and Management and Orchestration (MANO) project. SONATA is constructed with a vision of increasing the programmability and flexibility of 5G cellular system. It aims to make the service platforms easier and modular to be suitable for the requirements of the different service providers. Also, it stands with the network function orchestration and provides a development model for the developers [9]. MANO is an open source project that was developed by European Telecommunications Standards Institute (ETSI) [10].

SDN is a new approach that provides a dynamic and cost effective network structure by the physical separation of data forwarding plane and control plane. The control plane is the network part that gives the appropriate decision to handle traffic [11–13]. The data plane is the other part of the network, which forward traffic in respond to the control plane. The control signal moves from the control plane to the data plane by means of an open standard interface protocol, such as OpenFlow protocol and ForCES protocol [14]. SDN allows for the network operator to configure, control, and manage the network through customized software known as application programming interfaces (APIs). SDN is mainly presented to simplify the network hardware and increase the network flexibility [15].

Dawn of the software networks is supported by the recent development in NFV and SDN technologies. NFV and SDN technologies are not reliant on each other, but they complete each other [16]. Both technologies arise the advantage of employing inexpensive programmable hardware. The early generations of SDN technology were corresponded with data centers, campus networks, and private networks. By the time that SDN find its way to the core of cellular networks. On the other hand, NFV aims to replace the Middleboxes that are used in cellular networks from hardware appliance to software running on commodity hardware (i.e., less expensive general server hardware).

Employing SDN and NFV provides a way for performing the recent important concept of network slicing. The network slice may be viewed as a group of network functions worked together with a specific radio access technology (RAT) to achieve a certain use case of the network [17]. In another word, a network slice is a way of supporting communication service by means of a special connection. Network slicing allows network operator to set up multiple logical networks (each for a certain use case) on the same physical infrastructure [18].

One way to improve the cellular network efficiency is to offload network operations to cloud units that are employed at the edge of the cellular system. This is the idea behind the recent paradigm launched by the cellular network operators and known as MEC. MEC is the way of carrying cloud computing capabilities to the edge of the cellular network one hop away from the user equipment. European Telecommunications Standards Institute (ETSI) is one of the leading organizations in the research of MEC and the standardization of this technology. The latest progress in MEC platforms and their cellular uses are summed in [19]. The main benefit of employing MEC in cellular networks is the reduction of end to end system latency. Moreover, it provides a higher system bandwidth and reduces the network congestion by providing away for offloading data.

In this paper, we introduce a network structure for the Tactile Internet system employs SDN at the core of the network and enable NFV. The system uses MEC in multilevel hierarchical. In (Section 2, the related works to the proposed system is discussed. In Section 3, the system structure is proposed. In Section 4, the system is simulated over a reliable environment. Finally, Section 5 gives the conclusion.

2. Related Works

Moving from traditional Evolved Packet Core networks to next generation of cellular systems requires the involvement of a smart controller at the core of the network. The controller manages all of the operations inside the network. In this part, we present the main works that are concerned with the development of a centralized controller for delay sensitive networks. We analyze each work and provide similarities and differences between each work and our system.

In [20], the authors present a SoftCell cellular system that enables the system operator to achieve service policies at high levels. The proposed system reduces the forwarding table's size and aggregates traffic in multiple dimensions at various switches in the network. The system employs an access switches at the base stations, which are software switches. Access switches can classify packets that have arrived at the base station and handle the required state and bandwidth. SoftCell employs the components of the traditional Evolved Packet Core cellular network with a controller at the core network with certain functions. The controller installs the switch rules and implements the signaling rules that are used between hosts. The system is suggested for deployment to the core of LTE existing networks. The system improves the flexibility and scalability of the LTE cellular system. The main problem with the system is the capability of the core network controller and it still mainly depends on the gateways (SGW, PGW) at the core network.

Recently, there are a number several approaches speak about employing SDN at the core network of cellular system. These are the most relates works. In [21], the problems and transport challenges to realize the 5G system. The authors suggested a structure for the core network based on SDN and employ the edge computing. In [22], a network coding is developed and employed with SDN to reduce Latency in 5G cellular system. The network coding is achieved through a software router that acts as a virtual network function. The main problem with the system is that they did not consider the MEC; however, they mainly concerned with the coding and SDN. The system is mainly introduced for 5G and the Internet of Things [23–25].

In [26], an optimized framework for a virtual network is introduced to reduce end-to-end delay in LTE-A cellular networks. A central controller is employed in the core network and used mainly for slicing the physical resources. The authors employ Virtual Network Embedding (VNE) algorithm to map the virtualized networks on substrate network. The system model consists of destination edge routers and only single gateway. The edge router is responsible for the mobility management based on a distributed mobility management (DMM) scheme that is applied to the system. The system mainly concerned with the path optimization and network virtualization. The system achieves better latency performance and increases the user mobility. MEC is not involved in the structure and the system may be seen as a modification for the LTE-A cellular system.

In [27], a 5G based SDN architecture is introduced, with the dense deployment of small cells. Employing small cell concept raises the challenge of frequent handover and the latency dedicated with the handover process. Authors provide a system structure to overcome these challenges by using SDN controller at the core network. Another main function of the controller is the allocation of radio access resources and overcoming challenges that are associated with the deployment of multiple radio access technologies. The system is mainly concerned with the problem of latency of the handover process. SDN controller defines three types of programmed interfaces that make the system able to predict the user is movement, and thus handle the handover process in less time.

Each work of the previous works employs a controller at the core network for certain functions. All of these functions provide system with a high efficiency in terms of bit rate and latency. Since the main requirement of the Tactile Internet system is the ultra-low latency, intelligent controller should be deployed at the core of the network to achieve the desired latency.

3. System Structure

Tactile Internet system requires a very high availability and reliability, and ultra-low latency. This put high constraints on system components in terms of context, content, and mobility. Tactile Internet system requires an end-to-end latency of millisecond. This contains both the transmission delay (including reaction transmission (feedback)) and the processing delay. The time between stimulation and response should be in one millisecond. In another word, the end-to-end latency should be less than the human reaction time [28]. In this work, we provide a frame work for the Tactile Internet system, which can solve the problem of millisecond latency and achieves other requirements from the Tactile Internet system.

Our Tactile Internet system may be generally viewed as a three layer system that is based on the proposed 5G system structure, as suggested by Next Generation Mobile Networks (NGMN) [6]. As illustrated in Figure 2, the three layer system is based on the three main technologies; MEC, SDN, and NFV. The whole structure is based on the 5G cellular system, which decouples the hardware and software, and provides an APIs to facilitate the control and management of the system.

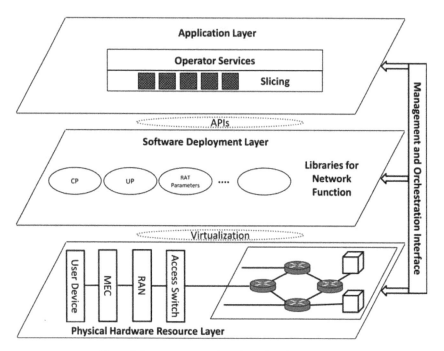

Figure 2. System structure viewed as a three layer system.

The first layer is the physical hardware resource layer, which includes the cellular network infrastructure (5G/Tactile user devices, fiber cables, cloud units, and networking nodes).

User devices may be a master robot or a 5G smart phone that have enough capabilities to be configured in the network [29]. The master robot is a haptic device that represents the human interface system. Haptic device has the ability to translate the human input to a haptic input by means of coding techniques [30]. Using haptic devices users can feel and touch objects in remote environments and also can control them.

Cloud units are employed at the edge of the network based on the concept of MEC. We built a multi-level cloud based Tactile Internet system in [5,31], which can be used as the cloud part in this layer. The multi-level cloud system moves from the idea of centralized cloud to the heterogeneous distributed cloud units. Cloud units are employed in levels, the first level includes Micro-clouds with small storage and processing capabilities connected to each cellular base station (eNB) [5]. The second level employs more efficient cloud units with higher processing and storage capabilities, known as Mini-clouds. Each Mini-cloud unit connects and controls a group of Micro-cloud units through a very high speed fiber connections. The final level of cloud units is the main cloud unit with powerful storage and processing capabilities centered at the core network. Main cloud unit connects, controls, and monitors all Mini-cloud units connected to the core network. Also it acts as the gateway to the huge central cloud units that are employed faraway. Figure 3 illustrates the different levels of cloud units [5].

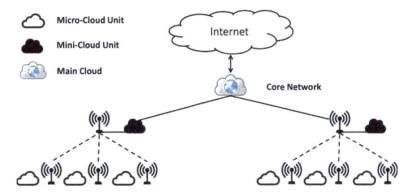

Figure 3. Multi-level cloud layers for Tactile Internet system.

Introducing multi-level cloud units to the Tactile Internet infrastructure, achieves variety of benefits that can be summarized in the following points [31]:

1- provides the offloading for the workload of the end user,
2- reduces the traffic load flow to the core network,
3- achieves better efficiency in terms of network congestion,
4- provides new services by accessing the network parameters through the BS,
5- provides higher security, and
6- reduces the end-to-end latency.

Reducing the end-to-end latency is achieved by reducing the communication path, as the cloud is one hop away from the user's equipment. The time passed in the core of the network has not existed, as there is no data passed to the core network.

The second layer is the software deployment layer, which maintains libraries for all of the functions that are needed in the network. These libraries are software functions and modules that can be used in the desired location in the network. Also, the radio access parameters and other configuration parameters of the network are located in this layer. The final layer is the application layer, which defines the services and applications that are required by system operators.

The three layers of the system are connected through the system management and orchestration interface. This interface is responsible for managing the operation of the first two layers based on the business application in the higher layer. The management and control tasks of the interface are performed through APIs. The management and orchestration interface is connected to the first layer through APIs to perform, the system configuration and monitoring of status and performance. Also, the software and parameters of the second layer can be fetched at any time by the managing interface through APIs. The link between the application layer and the management and orchestration interface allows the interface to perform network slicing for each application or map it to an existing slice [6].

In order to perform these critical and various tasks, the management and orchestration interface employs SDN/NFV technologies. SDN technology is one way that is used to overcome the problem of one millisecond round trip delay concerned with the Tactile Internet system and the future 5G cellular system. Moreover, SDN provides efficient solutions for achieving network flexibility and efficiency. The core network of cellular network will be based on SDN technology [32]. SDN works based on the separation of the data plane and the control plane. The two plans are linked through the OpenFlow interface protocol.

Figure 4 illustrates the end-to-end structure of our proposed Tactile Internet system. The end-to-end system structure consists of user devices, RAN (eNBs), cloud units, access switches,

OpenFlow switches, Middleboxes, and, finally, SDN controller. Each base station (eNB) is connected to the network through an access switch, which powerfully performs packet classification on traffic from user devices. The access switches is software switches such as Open vSwitch [33].

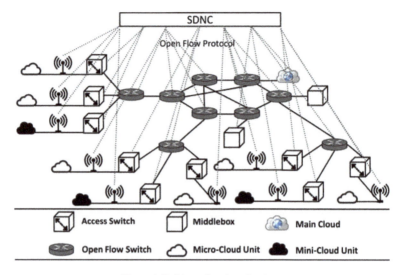

Figure 4. End-to-end system structure.

The whole network is connected through OpenFlow switches that manage data packets and forward traffic based on their flow tables. Middleboxes are commodity hardware that represents a way for the network operators to add extra functionalities, such as firewall and network address translation. The major requirements of the functions and services that are introduced by these Middleboxes are the efficient use of resources and the system protection from attacks. All of these elements represent the data plane of the network.

The last part of the system is the central controller (SDNC), which represents the control plane of the network. By means of programming and control logic, SDNC can execute functions and operations in the control plane. SDNC maintains the global information of the edge and core network devices include; OpenFlow switches, access switches, Middleboxes, RAN, and cloud units. SDNC manages and controls the edge and core network devices mentioned through the OpenFlow protocol. Table 1 contains some of the existing controllers that can be used as an SDNC with the OpenFlow protocol.

Functionally, switches that are used in the tactile system can be viewed as a packet forwarding devices with single or multiple flow tables [34]. Two types of switches are deployed in the OpenFlow based network, pure switches, and hybrid switches. Pure switches support only OpenFlow and fully depended on the SDNC. In the other side, hybrid switches, which are more commercial, have the ability to support OpenFlow with the traditional operations and protocols.

OpenFlow protocol is the signaling standard used for the communication between SDNC and OpenFlow switches. In other words, the instructions from SDNC to other network devices are transferred through the OpenFlow protocol [35]. Each OpenFlow node communicates with the SDNC via a secured OpenFlow channel. OpenFlow switches build their forwarding tables and build the packet processing rules based on the instructions delivered from the SDNC via the OpenFlow protocol. These instructions are deduced from the flow table received from the SDNC. The flow table can be viewed as a set of flow entries. Each of these entries holds a set of instructions to the node [36].

There are only three types of exchanged messages between SDNC and OpenFlow switches that are legalized by the OpenFlow protocol. The first kind is the controller-to-switch messages. This type refers to all messages initiated and moved from the controller to any switch, for the issues that are related to Handshaking, configuring the switch, checking status of the switch, and even modifying the switch. A summary of all available controller-to-switch messages supported by OpenFlow 1.4 are collected in Table 2, with the fields and entities of each one [37].

The second type represents all messages transferred from the switch to the SDNC; these messages are referred to as asynchronous messages. Table 3 summarizes all of the asynchronous messages used be OpenFlow 1.4; also, the function and structure of these messages are pointed [37]. The third type is the message exchanged in both directions between SDNC and a switch. These messages are referred to as symmetric messages and have various forms and functions. One of the main symmetric messages is the echo request/response messages that are used by the switch or the SDNC to check latency and measure bandwidth. Another important symmetric message is the error messages that are used to report a connection problem. Error messages are mainly used by the switch to report a request failure.

SDNC improve system performance in many terms, such as system latency and user's mobility. One important aspect to reduce the round trip latency is to reduce the number of intermediate nodes that are involved in the communication process and this is introduced by employing SDNC. Moreover, SDNC can foresee the user's mobility as it has access to all features of the user device (including; device type, location, billing information, etc.), which improves the critical radio access processes, such as handover. In other words, employing SDNC reduces the round trip latency, achieves handover process easily, and also reduces the handover latency.

On way to illustrate the benefits of our system is to compare it with the latest traditional Evolved Packet Core cellular network [38]. In the traditional Evolved Packet Core networks, all data traffic flow through the Evolved Packet Core network including the Packet data Gateway (PGW) and the Serving Gateway (SGW). This represents a load on these gateways and leads to an increase in round trip latency. Unlike the traditional systems, our proposed system employs SDN, which removes this barrier and reduces the round trip latency by reducing the number of intermediate nodes that are involved in the communication process.

Figure 5 illustrates this comparison between two systems. While, in Figure 5b, the two eNBs belong to the same Mini-cloud unit, but in Figure 5c, the two eNBs belong to different Mini-cloud units. Another important aspect is that the SDN structure allows and facilitates adding or changing network functions, which is not offered by the traditional systems. Moreover, network slicing can be done through the SDNC which will be the main feature of the Tactile Internet and 5G systems.

Summing up, the advantage of the proposed structure can be summarized in the following points:

1- the system is more flexible, as routing can be established easily through SDNC,
2- the system is reliable as it relay on the open flow protocol and other standardized technologies,
3- the network function virtualization can be easily implemented powered by the use of SDNC,
4- the requirements for achieving a certain quality of service (QoS) of the system can be supported by SDN. As the system can define and implement new rules through SDN switches and Middleboxes and
5- the system provides higher scalability than traditional packet core networks. This is because the SDNC takes into account the control process only and not involved in data flow.

Table 1. Features of available open source software defined networking (SDN) controllers.

Controller	Implementation Language	Developer	Year of Release	Review
NOX [39]	C++/Python	Nicira	2008	- The first SDN controller. - considered as network operating system than being a controller.
Maestro [40]	Java	Rice University	2011	- Allows applications to access and modify the network state. - considered as network operating system than being a controller. - Multi-thread platform. - Portable and scalable.
POX [41]	Python	Nicira	2013	- become more common than the old NOX. - Modern controller that enables rabid development and prototyping.
Beacon [42]	Java	Stanford University	2013	- Dynamic and cross-platform. - used to increase productivity of developers. - enables the start and stop of applications and introducing newer ones.
Floodlight [43]	Java	Big Switch Networks	2013	- One of the leading SDN controllers. - Hybrid controller that can support both OpenFlow and non OpenFlow networks. - High performance multi-thread controller.
OpenDaylight [44]	Java	OpenDaylight Foundation	2013	- efficient for any size networks. - provides various commercial use cases. - Main concern is the network programmability.
IRIS [45]	Java	ETRI	2014	- Built on Beacon. - Simpler architecture. - reconfigure some features in Floodlight.
ONOS [46]	Java	Open Network Operating System project	2014	- ONOS stands for Open Network Operating System. - Main concern is the scalability and the availability. - has various commercial applications.
DEFO [47]	Java	DEFO project	2015	- Stands for Declarative and Expressive Forwarding Optimizer. - Increase the connectivity. - Provides scalability and high response.

Table 2. Controller-to-Switch messages supported by OpenFlow.

Message Type	Message Structure	Message	Purpose	Reply
Handshake	- ofp_header - (no body)	OFPT_FEATURES_REQUEST	Used by the controller to identify the switch and its features.	OFPT_FEATURES_REPLY: - ofp_header - pad - n_buffers - n_tables-datapath_id - auxiliary_id
Switch configuration	- ofp_header - (no body)	OFPT_GET_CONFIG_REQUEST	Used by the controller to set the configuration parameter of the switch.	OFPT_GET_CONFIG_REPLY: - ofp_header - flags - miss_send_len
	- ofp_header - table_id - pad - config	OFP_TABLE_MOD	Used by the controller to perform the dynamic state configuration of a switch.	
Modify state messages	- ofp_header - cookie - cookie_mask - table_id - command - idle_timeout - hard_timeout - priority - buffer_id - out_port - out_group - flags - importance - ofp_match	OFPT_FLOW_MOD	Used by the controller to modify a flow table.	No main response message.
	- ofp_header - command - type - pad - group_id - ofp_bucket	OFPT_GROUP_MOD	Used by the controller to modify a group table.	

Table 2. *Cont.*

Message Type	Message Structure	Message	Purpose	Reply
	- ofp_header - port_no - pad - hw_addr - pad2 - config - mask	OFPT_PORT_MOD	Used by the controller to modify the properties of a port.	
	- ofp_header - command - flags - meter_id	OFPT_METER_MOD	Used by the controller to modify a meter and a virtual meter.	
	- ofp_header - type - flags - pad - body	OFPT_MULTIPART_REQUEST	Used by the controller to encode large requests and replies messages that can't be sent in one message.	OFPT_MULTIPART_REPLY: - ofp_header - type - flags - pad - body
	- ofp_header - (no body)	OFPMP_DESC (Request)	Used by the controller to request information about the switch (i.e., switch manufacturer, information about the used software and serial number).	OFPMP_DESC (Reply): - mfr_desc - hw_desc - sw_desc - serial_num - dp_desc
Multipart messages	- table_id - pad - out_port - out_group - pad2 - cookie - cookie_mask - ofp_match	OFPMP_FLOW (Request)	Used by the controller to request information about flow entries.	OFPMP_FLOW (Reply): - length - table_id - pad2 - duration_sec - duration_nsec - pad - priority - ofp_match - idle_timeout - hard_timeout - flags - importance - cookie - packet_count - byte_count

Table 2. *Cont.*

Message Type	Message Structure	Message	Purpose	Reply
	- table_id - pad - out_group - pad2 - cookie - cookie_mask - ofp_match	OFPMP_AGGREGATE (Request)	Used by the controller for the information aggregation of multiple flow entries.	OFPMP_AGGREGATE (Reply): - packet_count - byte_count - flow_count - pad
	- ofp_header (no body)	OFPMP_TABLE (Request)	Used by the controller to get main information about the tables.	OFPMP_TABLE (Reply): - table_id - pad - active_count - lookup_count - matched_count
	- ofp_header (no body)	OFPMP_TABLE_DESC (Request)	Used by the controller to get the current tables configuration of a switch.	OFPMP_TABLE_DESC (Reply): - length - table_id - pad - config - properties
	- port_no - queue_id	FPMP_QUEUE_STATS (Request)	Used by the controller to get the queue information of one or more port.	FPMP_QUEUE_STATS (Reply): - length - queue_id - pad - duration_sec - tx_packets-tx_bytes - tx_errors - port_no - duration_nsec
	- group_id - pad	OFPMP_GROUP (Request)	Used by the controller to get information about one or more groups.	OFPMP_GROUP (Reply): - length - group_id - pad - packet_count - ref_count - pad2 - byte_count - duration_sec - duration_nsec

35

Table 2. *Cont.*

Message Type	Message Structure	Message	Purpose	Reply
	- ofp_header - (no body)	OFPMP_PORT_DESCRIPTION (Request)	Used by the controller to get knowledge of all ports support OpenFlow.	OFPMP_PORT_DESCRIPTION(Reply): - port_no - length - pad-hw_addr - pad2 - name - config - state
	- meter_id - pad	OFPMT_METER (Request)	Used by the controller to request meter statistics.	OFPMT_METER (Reply): - meter_id - pad - byte_in_count - length - flow_count - duration_nsec - packet_in_count - duration_sec
Packet-out message	- ofp_header - buffer_id - in_port-pad - actions_len - ofp_action_header - data	OFPT_PACKET_OUT	Used by the controller when intended to send a packet out.	No main answer.
Barrier message	- ofp_header - (no body)	OFPT_BARRIER_REQUEST	Used by the controller to ask for the completed operations.	OFPT_BARRIER_REPLY
Role request message	- ofp_header - role - pad - generation_id	OFPT_ROLE_REQUEST	Used by the controller to change its role.	OFPT_ROLE_REPLY (if no errors occur) - ofp_header - role - pad - generation_id

Table 3. Asynchronous Messages supported by OpenFlow.

Message type	Message Structure	Message	Purpose
Packet-in message	- ofp_header-data - reason - cookie-table_id - total_len - ofp_match-buffer_id-pad	OFPT_PACKET_IN	Used by the switch to inform controller with packet received.
Flow removed message	- ofp_header - cookie - reason - priority-table_id - ofp_match - idle_timeout - duration_sec - hard_timeout - packet_count - byte_count - duration_nsec	OFPT_FLOW_REMOVED	Used by the switch to notify the controller with deleted flow entries.
Port status message	- ofp_header – reason - pad - ofp_port desc	OFPT_PORT_STATUS	Used by the switch to notify the controller with the ports added, removed or modified.
Controller role status message	- ofp_header - role - reason - pad - generation_id	OFPT_ROLE_STATUS	Used by the switch to change the controller role.
Table status message	- ofp_header - reason - pad - ofp_table_desc table	OFPT_TABLE_STATUS	Used by the switch to inform controller with the change of table status.

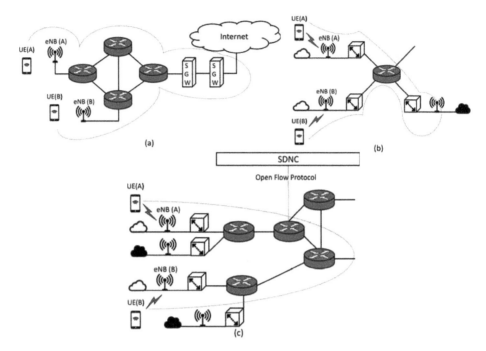

Figure 5. (a) Evolved Packet Core cellular network; (b) First case of the proposed system; (c) Second case of the proposed system.

4. Simulation and Results

In this section, the proposed structure for the Tactile Internet system is simulated over a reliable environment, and the results are discussed.

4.1. Simulation Environment and Experiment Set Up

There are a number of efficient simulation environments and frameworks that are used to simulate and evaluate the performance and attributes of SDN and MEC based networks. One of the most efficient, reliable, and powerful frameworks is the CloudSim environment and its related extension projects. CloudSim is a Java based simulation framework that enables simulation, experimentation, and modeling for cloud based networks [48]. CloudSimSDN is a Java based simulation framework that is built on top of CloudSim [49]. This framework is developed mainly for simulation purposes of SDN and cloud based systems.

In CloudSimSDN, the SDNC is programmable and it allows for the testing of VM management policies and workload scheduling algorithms [50]. Furthermore, the centralized controller is responsible for dynamically managing resources in data centers. Based on [49], the authors prove that CloudSimSDN simulator provides much features and facilities with better or at least the same performance as Mininet simulation environment. Also, it gives the ability for the modifications and extensions.

We consider two simulation cases with the topology illustrated in Figure 5b,c. In the first case, the two hosts belongs two different base stations (eNBs), but the two eNBs are connected to the same Mini-cloud. In the second case, the two hosts are in different cells and the cells are connected to different Mini-cloud units. The round trip delay is considered to be the performance of our system. The simulation process is repeated multi-times, with different bandwidth for each time but with the data size is the same in each case. All important simulation parameters used are illustrated in Table 4.

Table 4. Simulation parameters.

Simulation Parameter	Value
OpenFlow Switch processing delay	5 μs
SDN Controller processing delay	0.5 μs
Arrival rate of the Micro-cloud unit λi	15
The communication latency inside the cellular cell	100 μs
Bandwidth	Variable
Micro-cloud RAM, Storage	1024 Mb, 1 Gb
Mini-cloud RAM, Storage	2048 Mb, 5 Gb

4.2. Simulation Results and Analyses

Figures 6 and 7 illustrate the results for the first and the second simulation cases. From simulation results, the round trip delay is decreased with the increase of the system bandwidth. For the second case, the round trip delay is higher than that of the first case, this is because the core network controller is not involved in the communication process as the Mini-cloud unit manages and performs the communication process. Based on [6,51] the user bit rate for the future 5G cellular system will range from 1 Gbps to 10 Gbps. For the least expected bit rate (1 Gbps), the proposed tactile system affords a round trip delay of 0.95 ms for the first simulation case and 1.22 ms for the second case. Moreover, as the bit rate is raised above 1 Gbps the round trip delay gets below the previous values which make the proposed structure get ride off the challenge of 1 ms round trip latency.

Based on the 3GPP release 13, the LTE system achieves round trip latency of 16 ms for the 100 Mbps bit rate and 8 ms for 1 Gbps based on release 15 [52,53]. Thus, the proposed system can improve the latency efficiency and provides a way for Tactile Internet realization. When compared to the traditional Evolved Packet Core network based on the 3GPP release 15, the proposed system achieves 88% reduction of the round trip latency for the first case and 84% for the second case, which is the worst.

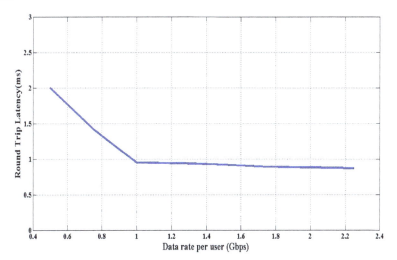

Figure 6. Simulation results for the first case.

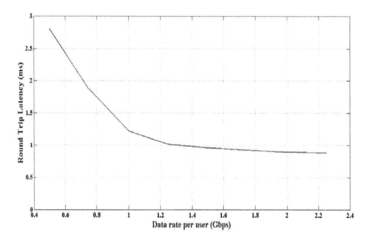

Figure 7. Simulation results for the second case.

5. Conclusions

SDN, NFV, and MEC technologies are solutions to overcome the challenges associated with the realization of Tactile Internet system, especially the 1 ms round trip latency. Employing SDN at the core network of cellular system reduces the latency and efficiently improves the system performance. This is because SDNC can efficiently manage and establish an efficient and flexible routing path between any two end points. Thus, it can reduce the number of intermediate nodes that are involved in communication process. The proposed structure for the Tactile Internet system, which employs SDN at the core of the network and multi-level cloud units, poses a round trip latency of orders of ms. Thus, this structure is helpful and effective for building the Tactile Internet system.

Acknowledgments: The publication was financially supported by the Ministry of Education and Science of the Russian Federation (the Agreement number 02.a03.21.0008). The authors are grateful to the Middle East University, Amman, Jordan for the financial support granted to cover the publication fee of this research article.

Author Contributions: Abdelhamied A. Ateya and Ammar Muthanna built the network model and perform the simulation process. Irina Gudkova and Abdelrahman Abuarqoub analyze the existing methods and the issues related to the OpenFlow protocol. Anastasia Vybornova and Andrey Koucheryavy wrote the paper and revise the whole work.

Conflicts of Interest: The authors declare no conflict of interest.

References

1. Aijaz, A. Towards 5G-enabled tactile internet: Radio resource allocation for haptic communications. In Proceedings of the 2016 IEEE Wireless Communications and Networking Conference (WCNC), Doha, Qatar, 3–6 April 2016; pp. 1–6.
2. Simsek, M.; Aijaz, A.; Dohler, M.; Sachs, J.; Fettweis, G. 5G-enabled tactile internet. *IEEE J. Sel. Areas Commun.* **2016**, *34*, 460–473. [CrossRef]
3. *ITU-T Technology Watch Report—The Tactile Internet*; International Telecommunication Union: Paris, France, 2014.
4. Maier, M.; Chowdhury, M.; Rimal, B.P.; van, D.P. The tactile internet: Vision, recent progress, and open challenges. *IEEE Commun. Mag.* **2016**, *54*, 138–145. [CrossRef]
5. Ateya, A.A.; Vybornova, A.; Kirichek, R.; Koucheryavy, A. Multilevel cloud based Tactile Internet system. In Proceedings of the 19th International Conference on Advanced Communication Technology (ICACT), Bongpyeong, Korea, 19–22 February 2017; pp. 105–110.
6. Alliance, N.G.M.N. *5G White Paper*; Next Generation Mobile Networks: Frankfurt, Germany, 2017.

7. Liu, Y.; Liu, G. User-centric wireless network for 5G. In *5G Mobile Communications*; Springer International Publishing: Cham, Switzerland, 2017; pp. 457–473.
8. Han, B.; Gopalakrishnan, V.; Ji, L.; Lee, S. Network function virtualization: Challenges and opportunities for innovations. *IEEE Commun. Mag.* **2015**, *53*, 90–97. [CrossRef]
9. Karl, H.; Dräxler, S.; Peuster, M.; Galis, A.; Bredel, M.; Ramos, A.; Martrat, J.; Siddiqui, M.S.; van Rossem, S.; Tavernier, W.; et al. DevOps for network functionvirtualisation: An architectural approach. *Trans. Emerg. Telecommun. Technol.* **2016**, *27*, 1206–1215. [CrossRef]
10. Blanco, B.; Fajardo, J.O.; Giannoulakis, I.; Kafetzakis, E.; Peng, S.; Pérez-Romero, J.; Trajkovska, I.; Khodashenas, P.S.; Goratti, L.; Paolino, M.; et al. Technology pillars in the architecture of future 5G mobile networks: NFV, MEC and SDN. *Comput. Stand. Interfaces* **2017**, *54*, 216–228. [CrossRef]
11. Kirichek, R.; Vladyko, A.; Paramonov, A.; Koucheryavy, A. Software-defined architecture for flying ubiquitous sensor networking. In Proceedings of the 2017 19th International Conference on Advanced Communication Technology (ICACT), Bongpyeong, Korea, 19–22 February 2017; pp. 158–162.
12. Hammoudeh, M.; Newman, R. Information extraction from sensor networks using the Watershed transform algorithm. *Inf. Fusion* **2015**, *22*, 39–49. [CrossRef]
13. Abuarqoub, A.; Hammoudeh, M.; Adebisi, B.; Jabbar, S.; Bounceur, A.; Al-Bashar, H. Dynamic clustering and management of mobile wireless sensor networks. *Comput. Netw.* **2017**, *117*, 62–75. [CrossRef]
14. Athmiya, N.S.; Shobha, K.R.; Sarimela, V. Feasibility study and implementation of openflow based SDN controller for tactical scenario. In Proceedings of the IEEE International Conference on Recent Trends in Electronics, Information & Communication Technology (RTEICT), Bangalore, India, 20–21 May 2016; pp. 789–794.
15. Muthanna, A.; Masek, P.; Hosek, J.; Fujdiak, R.; Hussein, O.; Paramonov, A.; Koucheryavy, A. Analytical evaluation of D2D connectivity potential in 5G wireless systems. In Proceedings of the International Conference on Next Generation Wired/Wireless Networking, St. Petersburg, Russia, 26–28 September 2016; Springer International Publishing: Cham, Switzerland, 2016; pp. 395–403.
16. Shariat, M.; Gutierrez-Estevez, D.M.; Vijay, A.; Safjan, K.; Rugeland, P.; Silva, I.; Lorca, J.; Widmer, J.; Fresia, M.; Li, Y.; et al. 5G radio access above 6 GHz. *Trans. Emerg. Telecommun. Technol.* **2016**, *27*, 1160–1167. [CrossRef]
17. Jiang, M.; Condoluci, M.; Mahmoodi, T. Network slicing management & prioritization in 5G mobile systems. In Proceedings of the 22th European Wireless Conference European Wireless (VDE), Oulu, Finland, 18–20 May 2016; pp. 1–6.
18. An, X.; Zhou, C.; Trivisonno, R.; Guerzoni, R.; Kaloxylos, A.; Soldani, D.; Hecker, A. On end to end network slicing for 5G communication systems. *Trans. Emerg. Telecommun. Technol.* **2017**, *28*. [CrossRef]
19. Satyanarayanan, M. The Emergence of Edge Computing. *Computer* **2017**, *50*, 30–39. [CrossRef]
20. Jin, X.; Li, L.E.; Vanbever, L.; Rexford, J. Softcell: Scalable and flexible cellular core network architecture. In Proceedings of the Ninth ACM Conference on Emerging Networking Experiments and Technologies, Santa Barbara, CA, USA, 9–12 December 2013; pp. 163–174.
21. Iovanna, P.; Ubaldi, F. SDN solutions for 5G transport networks. In Proceedings of the 2015 International Conference on Photonics in Switching (PS), Florence, Italy, 22–25 September 2015; pp. 297–299.
22. Szabo, D.; Gulyas, A.; Fitzek, F.H.; Lucani, D.E. Towards the tactile internet: Decreasing communication latency with network coding and software defined networking. In Proceedings of the 21th European Wireless Conference European Wireless, Budapest, Hungary, 20–22 May 2015; pp. 1–6.
23. Hammoudeh, M.; Newman, R. Interpolation techniques for building a continuous map from discrete wireless sensor network data. *Wirel. Commun. Mob. Comput.* **2013**, *13*, 809–827. [CrossRef]
24. Abuarqoub, A.; Abusaimeh, H.; Hammoudeh, M.; Uliyan, D.; Abu-Hashem, M.A.; Murad, S.; Al-Jarrah, M.; Al-Fayez, F. A survey on internet of things enabled smart campus applications. In Proceedings of the International Conference on Future Networks and Distributed Systems, Cambridge, UK, 19–20 July 2017.
25. Hammoudeh, M. Putting the lab on the map: A wireless sensor network system for border security and surveillance. In Proceedings of the International Conference on Internet of things and Cloud Computing, Cambridge, UK, 22–23 March 2016.
26. Chochlidakis, G.; Friderikos, V. Low latency virtual network embedding for mobile networks. In Proceedings of the 2016 IEEE International Conference on Communications (ICC), Kuala Lumpur, Malaysia, 22–27 May 2016; pp. 1–6.

27. Wang, K.; Wang, Y.; Zeng, D.; Guo, S. An SDN-based architecture for next-generation wireless networks. *IEEE Wirel. Commun.* **2017**, *24*, 25–31. [CrossRef]

28. Aijaz, A.; Simsek, M.; Dohler, M.; Fettweis, G. Shaping 5G for the Tactile Inter-net. In *5G Mobile Communications*; Springer International Publishing: Cham, Switzerland, 2017; pp. 677–691.

29. Chih-Lin, I.; Han, S.; Xu, Z.; Sun, Q.; Pan, Z. 5G: Rethink mobile communications for 2020+. *Phil. Trans. R. Soc. A* **2016**, *374*. [CrossRef] [PubMed]

30. Pance, A.; Webb, U.; Mayo, S.A.; Apple Inc. Haptic Feedback Device. U.S. Patent 9,710,061, 18 July 2017.

31. Ateya, A.A.; Vybornova, A.; Samouylov, K.; Koucheryavy, A. System model for multi-level cloud based tactile internet system. In Proceedings of the International Conference on Wired/Wireless Internet Communication, St. Petersburg, Russia, 21–23 June 2017; Springer: Cham, Switzerland, 2017; pp. 77–86.

32. Sahoo, K.S.; Mohanty, S.; Tiwary, M.; Mishra, B.K.; Sahoo, B. A comprehensive tutorial on software defined network: The driving force for the future internet technology. In Proceedings of the International Conference on Advances in Information Communication Technology & Computing, Bikaner, India, 12–13 August 2016; p. 114.

33. Open vSwitch. Available online: http://openvswitch.org (accessed on 20 September 2017).

34. Taleb, T.; Samdanis, K.; Mada, B.; Flinck, H.; Dutta, S.; Sabella, D. On multi-access edge computing: A survey of the emerging 5G network edge architecture & orchestration. *IEEE Commun. Surv. Tutor.* **2017**. [CrossRef]

35. Open Networking Foundation (ONF). Available online: https://www.opennetworking.org/ (accessed on 10 October 2017).

36. Karakus, M.; Durresi, A. Quality of Service (QoS) in software defined networking (SDN): A survey. *J. Netw. Comput. Appl.* **2017**, *80*, 200–218. [CrossRef]

37. OpenFlow v1.4 Specification White Paper. Available online: https://www.opennetworking.org/images/stories/downloads/sdn-resources/onf-specifications/openflow/openflow-spec-v1.4.0.pdf (accessed on 12 December 2017).

38. Basta, A.; Kellerer, W.; Hoffmann, M.; Hoffmann, K.; Schmidt, E.D. A virtual SDN-enabled LTE EPC architecture: A case study for S-/P-gateways functions. In Proceedings of the 2013 IEEE SDN for Future Networks and Services (SDN4FNS), Trento, Italy, 11–13 November 2013; pp. 1–7.

39. Gude, N.; Koponen, T.; Pettit, J.; Pfaff, B.; Casado, M.; McKeown, N.; Shenker, S. NOX: Towards an operating system for networks. *ACM SIGCOMM Comput. Commun. Rev.* **2008**, *38*, 105–110. [CrossRef]

40. Ng, E.; Cai, Z.; Cox, A.L. *Maestro: A System for Scalable Openflow Control*; TSEN Maestro-Technical Report TR10-08; Rice University: Houston, TX, USA, 2010.

41. NOXrepo.org. Available online: https://github.com/noxrepo/ (accessed on 1 October 2017).

42. Erickson, D. The beacon openflow controller. In Proceedings of the Second ACM SIGCOMM Workshop on Hot Topics in Software Defined Networking, Hong Kong, China, 16 August 2013; pp. 13–18.

43. Project Floodlight: Open Source Software for Building Software-Defined Networks. Available online: http://www.projectfloodlight.org/floodlight/ (accessed on 25 September 2017).

44. OpenDaylight. Available online: http://www.opendaylight.org/ (accessed on 25 September 2017).

45. OpenIRIS Project. Available online: https://github.com/openiris/IRIS/wiki (accessed on 5 October 2017).

46. Onosproject. Available online: https://onosproject.org/software/ (accessed on 7 October 2017).

47. Hartert, R.; Vissicchio, S.; Schaus, P.; Bonaventure, O.; Filsfils, C.; Telkamp, T.; Francois, P. A Declarative and Expressive Approach to Control Forwarding Paths in Carrier-Grade Networks. In Proceedings of the ACM SIGCOMM Computer Communication Review, London, UK, 17–21 August 2015; Volume 45, pp. 15–28. Available online: https://sites.uclouvain.be/defo/#publications (accessed on 7 October 2017).

48. Kumar, R.; Sahoo, G. Cloud computing simulation using CloudSim. *arXiv*, 2014.

49. Son, J.; Dastjerdi, A.V.; Calheiros, R.N.; Ji, X.; Yoon, Y.; Buyya, R. Cloudsimsdn: Modeling and simulation of software-defined cloud data centers. In Proceedings of the 2015 15th IEEE/ACM International Symposium on Cluster, Cloud and Grid Computing (CCGrid), Shenzhen, China, 4–7 May 2015; pp. 475–484.

50. CloudSimSDN Project. Available online: https://github.com/jayjmin/cloudsimsdn (accessed on 12 December 2017).

51. Zheng, K.; Zhao, L.; Mei, J.; Dohler, M.; Xiang, W.; Peng, Y. 10 Gb/s hetsnets with millimeter-wave communications: Access and networking-challenges and protocols. *IEEE Commun. Mag.* **2015**, *53*, 222–231. [CrossRef]

52. Arenas, J.; Dudda, T.; Falconetti, L. Ultra-Low Latency in Next Generation LTE Radio Access. In Proceedings of the SCC 2017 11th International ITG Conference on Systems, Communications and Coding, Hamburg, Germany, 6–9 February 2017; pp. 1–6.
53. Lauridsen, M.; Gimenez, L.C.; Rodriguez, I.; Sorensen, T.B.; Mogensen, P. From LTE to 5G for Connected Mobility. *IEEE Commun. Mag.* **2017**, *55*, 156–162. [CrossRef]

Journal of
Sensor and Actuator Networks

Article

Using Sensors to Study Home Activities [†]

Jie Jiang [1,*], Riccardo Pozza [2], Kristrún Gunnarsdóttir [1], Nigel Gilbert [1] and Klaus Moessner [2]

1   Centre for Research in Social Simulation, University of Surrey, Guildford GU2 7XH, UK;
    k.gunnarsdottir@surrey.ac.uk (K.G.); n.gilbert@surrey.ac.uk (N.G.)
2   5G Innovation Centre, University of Surrey, Guildford GU2 7XH, UK; r.pozza@surrey.ac.uk (R.P.);
    k.moessner@surrey.ac.uk (K.M.)
*   Correspondence: jie.jiang@surrey.ac.uk; Tel.: +44-148-368-3965
†   This paper is an extended version of our paper published in Jiang, J.; Pozza, R.; Gunnarsdóttir, K.;
    Gilbert, N.; Moessner, K. Recognising Activities at Home: Digital and Human Sensors. In Proceedings of the
    International Conference on Future Networks and Distributed Systems, Cambridge, UK, 19–20 July 2017;
    ACM: New York, NY, USA, 2017; ICFNDS'17, pp. 17:1–17:11.

Received: 1 November 2017; Accepted: 13 December 2017; Published: 16 December 2017

Abstract: Understanding home activities is important in social research to study aspects of home life, e.g., energy-related practices and assisted living arrangements. Common approaches to identifying which activities are being carried out in the home rely on self-reporting, either retrospectively (e.g., interviews, questionnaires, and surveys) or at the time of the activity (e.g., time use diaries). The use of digital sensors may provide an alternative means of observing activities in the home. For example, temperature, humidity and light sensors can report on the physical environment where activities occur, while energy monitors can report information on the electrical devices that are used to assist the activities. One may then be able to infer from the sensor data which activities are taking place. However, it is first necessary to calibrate the sensor data by matching it to activities identified from self-reports. The calibration involves identifying the features in the sensor data that correlate best with the self-reported activities. This in turn requires a good measure of the agreement between the activities detected from sensor-generated data and those recorded in self-reported data. To illustrate how this can be done, we conducted a trial in three single-occupancy households from which we collected data from a suite of sensors and from time use diaries completed by the occupants. For sensor-based activity recognition, we demonstrate the application of Hidden Markov Models with features extracted from mean-shift clustering and change points analysis. A correlation-based feature selection is also applied to reduce the computational cost. A method based on Levenshtein distance for measuring the agreement between the activities detected in the sensor data and that reported by the participants is demonstrated. We then discuss how the features derived from sensor data can be used in activity recognition and how they relate to activities recorded in time use diaries.

Keywords: sensors; time use diaries; activity recognition; time series; Internet of Things; social research

1. Introduction

Social researchers take a great interest in household practices, among other things, family dynamics and child-rearing (e.g., [1,2]), practices around meals [3], sleep [4], assisted living arrangements and mobile health solutions (e.g., [5,6]), homeworking [7] and energy-related practices [8]. Existing social research methods are both qualitative and quantitative, and often some combination of the two are used for pragmatic and constructivist purposes [9].

Qualitative methods are used to acquire rich in-depth data. Observations and open-ended interviews are particularly effective in capturing the meanings participants attach to various aspects of their everyday lives and relations (e.g., [10]). Quantitative methods such as questionnaires and surveys capture qualitative information in formalised ways for computational processing, and are widely used in large scale studies on demographics, household economics and social attitudes (e.g., [11,12]). Time-use diaries are also used to log activity sequences [13], and to seek evidence of life changes and social evolution [14]. Efforts to harmonise time use surveys across Europe have delivered guidelines (HETUS) [15] on activity coding for analysing the time use data, but interviews and observations are commonly used to cross-validate what goes on, and to calibrate and amplify the meaning of the diary evidence, including the use of activity sensors and video cameras [16].

Sensor-generated data are becoming widely available and the topic of activity recognition [17] has thrived in recent years with applications in areas such as smart homes and assisted living. Researchers have investigated activity recognition methods using data obtained from various types of sensors, for instance, video cameras [18], wearables [19] and sensors embedded in smartphones [20]. Such rich contextual information has been used in various activity specific studies. For example, Williams et al. [4] discuss the use of accelerometers to study people's sleep patterns. Amft and Tröster [21] study people's dietary behaviour by using inertial sensors to recognise movements, a sensor collar for recognising swallowing and an ear microphone for recognising chewing. Wang et al. [22] help in detecting elderly accidental falls by employing accelerometers and cardiotachometers.

Numerous algorithms have been proposed for general activity recognition in the literature, most of which are based on the assumption that by sensing the environment it is possible to infer which activities people are performing. Dynamic Bayesian Networks (e.g., [23]), Hidden Markov Models (e.g., [24]) and Conditional Random Fields (e.g., [25]) are popular methods due to their ability to recognise latent random variables in observing sequences of sensor-generated data. Other approaches rely on Artificial Neural Networks (e.g., [26]). A more detailed discussion will be given in Section 2.

To evaluate the adequacy of inferences about activities derived from sensor data, records of what activities are taking place from direct observation can be used to obtain the so-called "ground truth". In the literature, there are three main types of approaches. The first relies on video cameras to record what participants are doing during an experiment. For example, Lin and Fu [23], use multiple cameras and floor sensors to track their participants. Although the data quality can be guaranteed in a controlled lab, this method is very intrusive and difficult to deploy in an actual home. A second common way of establishing ground truth is by asking participants to carry out a predefined list of tasks, again, in a controlled environment. For example, Cook et al. [27] ask their participants to carry out scripted activities, predetermined and repeatedly performed. Both of these methods correspond with social research methods, such as questionnaires, surveys and interviews, in generating what Silverman calls "researcher-provoked" data [28]. The outcomes may suffer the bias introduced by the researchers in provoking participants' activities as opposed to observing them without interference. The third type of approach relies on human annotators to label sensor-generated data manually. For example, Wang et al. [29] conducted a survey with their participants to have a self-reported record of their main activities, and compared it to the annotated data based on video recordings. This type of approach relies heavily on the annotator's knowledge of participants' activities and their understanding of participants' everyday practices, but may also be challenged by discrepancies between the research-provoked survey and video data and non-provoked sensor-generated data.

In this study, we consider two data sources. The first is "digital sensors" that generate activity data based on activity recognition derived from sensor-generated environment data (referred to as sensor data or sensor-generated data in the rest of the paper). The second is "human sensors" that generate activity data from participants' self-reported time-use diaries (referred to as time use diary or self-reported data in the rest of the paper). To make inferences from sensor data about human activities, it is first necessary to calibrate the sensor data by matching the data to activities identified by the self-reported data. The calibration involves identifying the features in the sensor data that correlate best with the self-reported activities. This in turn requires a good measure of the agreement between the activities detected from sensor-generated data and those recorded in self-reported data.

To illustrate how this can be done, we conducted a trial in three residential houses, collecting data from a set of sensors and from a time use diary recorded by the occupant (human sensor) from each house over four consecutive days. The sensors captured temperature, humidity, range (detecting movements in the house), noise (decibel levels), ambient light intensity (brightness) and energy consumption. For activity recognition, we adopt an unsupervised learning approach based on a Hidden Markov Model, i.e., only sensor-generated data are used to fit the model, which allows the model to discover the patterns by itself rather than fitting the model with unreliable labels from the time use diaries. We apply mean shift clustering [30] and change points detection [31] for extracting features. To reduce computational cost, we adopt a correlation-based approach [32] for feature selection. To compare the data generated by the two types of sensors, we propose a method for measuring the agreement between them based on the Levenshtein distance [33].

The contributions of this paper are three-fold. First, we present a new data collection framework for recognising activities at home, i.e., a mixed-methods approach of combining computational and qualitative types of non-provoked data: sensor-generated and time use diary. Secondly, we investigate the application of several feature extraction and feature selection methods for activity recognition using sensor-generated data. Thirdly, we propose an evaluation method for measuring the agreement between the sensor-supported activity recognition algorithms and the human constructed diary. Compared to our previous work [34], this paper has the following extensions: (1) we add an illustration of the trial setup procedure and discuss the design of the procedure; (2) we use a larger data set of three households and investigate three more activity types; (3) we demonstrate the use of feature selection in activity recognition to harness the exploration of feature combinations; and (4) we further the analysis of results by triangulating with evidence from household interviews.

The rest of the paper is organised as follows. In Section 2, we discuss related work. In Section 3, we give an introduction to the home settings. Thereafter, in Section 4, we describe the data collected for this study, including both the sensor data and the time use diary data. In Section 5, we show how features are extracted and selected and introduce our activity recognition algorithm. In Section 6, we present the metric for evaluating agreement between activities recognised by the sensor-generated data and what is reported by the participant, and give an analysis of the results based on the evidence gathered from household interviews. Finally, we conclude our work with some possible extensions in Section 7.

2. Related Work

In this section, we discuss the works that have been recently published in the area of automated activity recognition in home-like environments in terms of the sensors they use, the activities they detect, and the recognition methods they adopt or propose.

Early works (e.g., [23,35]) were concerned with designing frameworks for providing services based on the prediction of resident action. For example, Lin and Fu [23] leveraged K-means clustering and domain knowledge to create context out of raw sensor data and combined this with Dynamic Bayesian Networks (DBNs) to learn multi-user preferences in a smart home. Their testbed allows location tracking and activity recognition via cameras, floor sensors, motion detectors, temperature and light sensors in order to recommend services to multiple residents, such as turning on TV or lights in various locations or playing music.

More recently, the CASAS smart home project [36] enabled the detection of multi-resident activities and interactions in a testbed featuring motion, temperature, water and stove (ad-hoc) usage sensors, energy monitors, lighting controls and contact detectors for cooking pots, phone books and medicine containers. Using the testbed, Singla et al. [37] applied Hidden Markov Models (HMMs) to perform real-time recognition of activities of daily living. Their work explores seven types of individual activities: filling medication dispenser, hanging up clothes, reading magazine, sweeping floor, setting the table, watering plants, preparing dinner, and 4 types of cooperative activities: moving furniture, playing checkers, paying bills, gathering and packing picnic food. Validated against the same data set, Hsu et al. [25] employed Conditional Random Fields (CRFs) with strategies of iterative and decomposition inference. They found that data association of non-obstructive sensor data is important to improve the performance of activity recognition in a multi-resident environment. Chiang et al. [38] further improved the work in [25] with DBNs that extend coupled HMMs by adding vertices to model both individual and cooperative activities.

The single-occupancy datasets from CASAS also attracted many researchers. For example, Fatima et al. [39] adopted a Support Vector Machine (SVM) based kernel fusion approach for activity recognition and evaluated it on the Milan2009 and Aruba datasets. Fang et al. [40] evaluated the application of neural network for activity recognition based on a dataset of two volunteers. Khrishnan and Cook [41] evaluated an online sliding-window based approach for activity recognition on a dataset of three single-occupancy houses. The authors showed that combining mutual information based weighting of sensor events and adding past contextual information to the feature leads to better performance. To analyse possible changes in cognitive or physical health, Dawadi et al. [42] introduced the notion of activity curve and proposed a permutation-based change detection in activity routine algorithm. The authors validated their approach with a two-year smart home sensor data. In these works, different kinds of sensors were used such as temperature and light sensors, motion and water/stove usage sensors. The recognised activities range from common ones such as eating and sleeping to more specific ones like taking medication.

ARAS [43] is a smart home data set collected from two houses with multiple residents. The two houses were equipped with force sensitive resistors, pressure mats, contact sensors, proximity sensors, sonar distance sensors, photocells, temperature sensors, and infra-red receivers. Twenty-seven types of activities were labelled such as watching TV, studying, using internet/telephone/toilet, preparing/having meals, etc. With the ARAS dataset, Prossegger and Bouchachia [44] illustrated the effectiveness of an extension to the incremental decision tree algorithm ID5R, which induces decision trees with leaf/class nodes augmented by contextual information in the form of activity frequency.

With a mission of elderly care, the CARE project [45] has carried out research on automatic monitoring of human activities in domestic environments. For example, Kasteren et al. [46] investigated HMMs and CRFs for activity recognition in a home setting and proposed to use Bluetooth headsets for data annotation. Fourteen state-change sensors were placed on the doors, cupboards, refrigerator and toilet flush. Seven types of activities were annotated by the participants themselves, including sleeping, having breakfast, showering, eating dinner, drinking, toileting and leaving the house. Two probabilistic models, HMM and CRF, were investigated for activity recognition. Kasteren et al. [24] provided a summary of probabilistic models used in activity recognition and evaluated their performance on datasets of three households with single occupant. Further work by Ordonez et al. [47] evaluated transfer learning with HMMs on a dataset of three houses with the same setting of sensor deployment and labelled activity types, showing potential of reusing experience on new target houses where little annotated data is available.

Besides probabilistic models, neural network models are becoming popular in recognising human activities. For example, Fan et al. [26] studied three neural network structures (Gated Recurrent Unit, Long Short-Term Memory, Recurrent Neural Network) and showed that a simple structure that remembers history as meta-layers outperformed recurrent networks. The sensors they used include grid-eye infrared array, force and noise sensors as well as electrical current detectors. For their model training, the participants performed scripted activities in a home testbed: eating, watching TV, reading books, sleeping and friends visiting. Singh et al. [48] showed that Long Short-Term Memory classifiers outperformed probabilistic models such as HMM and CRF when raw sensor data was used. Laput et al. [49] proposed a general-purpose sensing approach with a single sensor board that is capable of detecting temperature, humidity, light intensity and colour, motion, sound, air pressure, WiFi RSSI, magnetism (magnetometer) and electromagnetic inference (EMI sensor). The sensors were deployed in five different locations including a kitchen, an office, a workshop, a common area and a classroom. For activity recognition, a supervised approach based on SVM and a two-stage clustering approach with AutoEncoder were used. The authors showed the merit of the sensor features with respect to their contribution to the recognition of 38 types of activities.

While several other approaches exist for activity recognition and capture, they mostly employ only wearable sensors (i.e., see [19] for a recent survey), and thus cannot be applied in multi-modal scenarios of smart-home settings with fixed, unobtrusive and ambient sensors. In addition, due to the time-series nature of activity recognition in the home environment, supervised algorithms not incorporating the notion of temporal dependence might lead to poor performance in activity recognition, so such works are not reviewed here.

Time use diaries are widely used for collecting activity data. To validate time use diaries, Kelly et al. [16] tested the feasibility of using wearable cameras. Participants were asked to wear a camera and at the same time keep a record of time use over a 24-hour period. During an interview with each participant afterwards, the visual images were used as prompts to reconstruct the activity sequences and improve upon the activity record. No significant differences were found between the diary and camera data with respect to the aggregate totals of daily time use. However, for discrete activities, the diaries recorded a mean of 19.2 activities per day, while the image-prompted interviews revealed 41.1 activities per day. This raises concerns of using the data collected from time use diaries for training activity recognition models directly.

In this work, we use a suite of fixed sensors. For activity recognition, we build our model based on HMMs. In particular, we investigate the use of mean shift clustering and change points detection techniques for feature extraction. A correlation-based feature selection method is applied to reduce computational cost. Our work differs from similar studies in that we adopt a mixed-methods approach for the problem of recognising activities at home, and we evaluate its effectiveness using a formal framework.

3. Experiment Setting

For this work, we installed a suite of sensors in three households. The data collected by the sensors were encrypted and sent to a central server over the Internet.

3.1. Sensor Modules

We used six types of sensor modules, as summarised in Table 1.

Table 1. Sensor Modules.

	Sensor Modules	Measurement
	Temperature sensor	°C
	Humidity sensor	%
Sensor Box	Light Sensor	$\frac{\mu W}{cm^2}$
	Ranging sensor	*cm*
	Microphone	*dB SPL*
	Energy monitor	*watts*

The first five sensor modules are encapsulated in a sensor box, as shown in Figure 1a, coordinated by a Seeeduino Arch-Pro [50]. The temperature and humidity sensor HTU21D [51] is managed via an I2C interface and sampled periodically by the client application deployed on the ARM core. An Avago ADPS-9960 light sensor [52] , also managed via an I2C interface, is used to sample ambient light measured in $\frac{\mu W}{cm^2}$. The GP2Y0A60SZ ranging sensor from Sharp [53] is an analog sensor with a wide detection range of 10 cm to 150 cm, which is sampled via a 12 bit ADC and converted through the manufacturer's calibration table. Finally, the MEMS Microphone breakout board INMP401 [54] is used to sample noise levels in the environment via an ADC and the values are converted to decibels (dB SPL).

The other sensor module used in this work is a commercial electricity monitoring kit from CurrentCost [55], as shown in Figure 1b. It features a current transformer (CT) clamp, a number of individual appliance monitors (IAMs) and a transmitter to measure the energy consumption in watts of the whole house as well as the individual appliances.

(a)   (b)

Figure 1. Sensor Modules: (**a**) Sensor Box; and (**b**) Electricity Monitor.

Compared to the works discussed in Section 2, the sensor modules used for this work require little effort on part of the participants.

3.2. Demonstration and Installation

For each household, we first set up an interview with the participants, in which we demonstrate the workings of the sensor platform to demystify the experiment, e.g., to show what kinds of data are collected, and what can be seen in the data. Figure 2 shows the interface of our sensor data collection and visualisation platform. Participants can interact with the sensors, e.g., turn electrical equipment on and off, move in front or make loud noise around a sensor box, breathe on it, etc., and see in real time the changes of corresponding sensor readings.

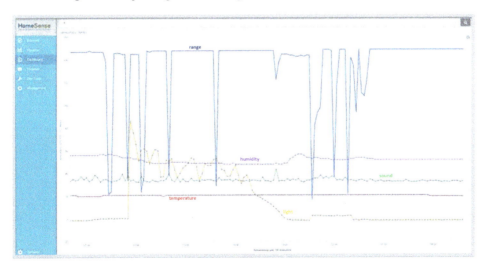

Figure 2. Demonstration Interface.

Thereafter, we ask the participants to give a tour of their house and explain what goes on at different times in different rooms, who is involved, and so on. However, they are free to omit any room or area of the house. A sketch of the floor plan with markings of potential places for installing sensors is produced in the meantime.

After the interview, another appointment is made for sensor installation. During the installation, the participants guide the researchers around the house and negotiate the location for placing the sensors.

3.3. Trial Households

Three trial households are included in the experiment presented here, each with a single occupant. Table 2 shows the house composition and the sensor deployment.

Table 2. Sensors installed in each trial home.

Household	Rooms	Sensor Boxes (Location Installed)	Electricity Monitors (Appliances Attached)
1	Master bedroom	Next to bed	
	Guest bedroom	Next to bed	Teasmade
	Kitchen	Entrance; Food preparation area	Washing machine; Microwave; Kettle
	Living room with dining space	Entrance; Sitting area	TV
	Living room	Sitting area	
	Hallway	On the wall	
2	Bedroom	Next to bed	
	Kitchen	Cooking area	Washing machine; Kettle, Toaster, Bread maker
	Living room with dining space	Dining area; Sitting area	TV; Ironing/Vacuum
	Living room	Sitting area	Laptop
	Study	Book shelf	
	Hallway	On the wall	
3	Bedroom	Next to bed	
	Kitchen	Food preparation area; Cooking area	Washing machine; Kettle, Toaster
	Dining room combined with study	Sitting area; Next to desktop computer	Desktop computer
	Living room	Sitting area	
	First utility room	Near entrance	
	Second utility room	Near entrance	
	Hallway	On the wall	Vacuum cleaner

For all the three houses, there was at least one sensor installed in each room, except bathrooms which do not have electrical outlets in the UK. The number of sensor boxes installed in each room depends on the size of the room. The locations where the sensor boxes were installed were meant to cover as much as possible of the room space but were sometimes constrained by the availability of power supply. A selection of more commonly used home appliances were attached to individual energy monitors. Their energy consumption as well as the total consumption for each of the households were also recorded.

4. Data Sets

In the experiment, two types of data were collected, sensor-generated data and time use diaries. The time use diaries cover a period of four consecutive days for all three households between June and July 2017 from 6:00 a.m. on the first day until 5:50 a.m. on the last day. The sensor-generated data set covers an extended period from 6:00 p.m. on the previous day of the starting date (time use diary) and to 12:00 p.m. of the last day (time use diary). The reason for such an extension is to incorporate the relevant signals before and after the recorded time use which will be illustrated in Section 5.1.

4.1. Sensor-Generated Data

The sensor-generated data consists of readings from the six types of sensor modules as shown in Table 1.

The data from sensor boxes were collected around every three seconds. An example reading from a sensor box is shown as follows:

{"Box_ID": 123, "Timestamp": 2016-12-13 09:00:00, "Temperature": 20,
"Humidity": 50, "Sound": 45, "Range": 100, "Light": 583}

For *range*, the lowest values among samples at 1000 Hz within each period of three seconds was collected, i.e., the distance to the nearest object that has been detected in the period of three seconds. This is to minimise the number of false negative detections which may happen when only collecting samples at a point of time every three seconds. Noise level (sound) is derived from an on-device conversion of air pressure changes (sampling at around 1000 Hz) to decibels (dB). The readings from all the other sensor modules are sampled once every three seconds.

The data from electricity monitors (IAMs) was collected around every six seconds. An example reading from an IAM is shown as follows:

{"IAM_ID": 123, "Timestamp": 2016-12-13 09:00:00, "Watts": 100}

The sensor boxes can capture various environmental changes but not all the changes are caused by human activities. For example, the weather can be an important factor influencing temperature and humidity. By carefully modelling the changes, we may be able to distinguish those caused by human activities from those caused by external factors as they differ in terms of magnitude and frequency.

Table 3 shows the statistics about the total number of readings of the sensor-generated data used in this work with respect to the three households.

Table 3. Sensor Data Set Statistics.

Household	Sensor Boxes	Energy Monitors	Total
1	$1,052,439 \times 5$	$353,487$	$5,615,682$
2	$918,374 \times 5$	$356,310$	$4,948,180$
3	$1,183,008 \times 5$	$298,397$	$6,213,437$

The multiplier 5 in the second column indicates that each reading from a sensor box consists of five data attributes corresponding to the five sensor modules as shown in Table 1.

4.2. Time Use Diary

During the four days of the experiment, the occupant from each household was asked to keep a diary of time use based on the HETUS model [15]. The participants were asked to update the diary at 10-minute intervals except sleeping and keep track of the 10 minutes interval using their own preferred method, e.g. setting up a timer. The diary was paper-based and the participants were given instructions on how to fill the diary using pens and shorthand. For example, an arrow can be used to mark an activity that takes longer than 10 minutes. However, given the heavy workload of filling such a diary, it is very likely that the participants may not have strictly followed the guidelines, as will be further illustrated in Section 6.1.

Table 4 gives a partial sample of what is recorded: the participant specifies for every 10 minutes what he or she has been doing primarily (and possibly secondarily) in which location/room (possibly with the assistance of or involving devices). For each household, there is at least one activity recorded by the occupant at each of the 10 minutes slots over the course of four days, which produces in total 576 data points from the diary.

Table 4. Time use diary example.

Time	Primary Activity	Secondary Activity	Location	Devices
08:00–08:10	Preparing meal	Listening to radio	Kitchen	Kettle, Radio
08:10–08:20	Eating	Watching TV	Living room	TV
⋮	⋮	⋮	⋮	⋮
18:00–18:10	Preparing meal	——	Kitchen	Oven
18:10–18:20	Preparing meal	——	Kitchen	Oven

In this study, we focus on seven types of home activities that have been recorded in the time use diaries: *sleeping, preparing meal, making hot drink* (tea or coffee), *eating* (breakfast, lunch or dinner), *watching TV, listening to radio*, and *doing laundry*. It has to be noted that these are not the only activities the participants reported in their diaries. These seven activity types are selected because they were reported by the occupants from all the three households and occur at a relatively higher frequency or last for a relatively longer time. Table 5 shows a summary of how many times each type of activity occurred and their duration in each household.

Table 5. Number of occurrences and time spent for each type of activity in the data set.

Activity	Household 1		Household 2		Household 3	
	Number of Occurrences	Percentage of Time	Number of Occurrences	Percentage of Time	Number of Occurrences	Percentage of Time
Sleeping	5	36.94%	5	31.08%	5	40.28%
Preparing meal	8	2.08%	10	2.78%	7	3.47%
Making hot drink	13	2.26%	11	1.91%	2	0.52%
Eating	10	4.17%	8	3.65%	8	3.30%
Watching TV	13	16.15%	2	1.39%	/	/
Listening to radio	/	/	15	10.42%	6	17.88%
Doing Laundry	1	0.17%	6	1.04%	2	2.43%

Household 1 does not have a radio while the occupant had the TV turned on a lot of the time. Household 3 does not have a TV while the occupant had the radio turned on a lot of the time. Notice that for each household the total percentage of time designated to the seven activity types does not sum up to 100% because other activities carried out by the occupants are not listed in the table.

4.3. Data Reliability

In this section, we analyse the reliability of sensor-generated data in parallel form via the Pearson correlations between readings from each pair of sensors that are of the same type and placed in the same room (see Table 2). Table 6 summaries the correlations.

Table 6. Pearson correlation between the readings from pairs of sensors placed in the same room.

Sensor Reading	Temperature	Humidity	Light	Range	Sound
Household 1 (kitchen)	0.94	0.75	0.90	0.56	0.88
Household 1 (living/dining room)	0.93	0.89	0.95	0.21	0.86
Household 2 (living/dining room)	0.49	0.62	0.85	0.33	0.57
Household 3 (kitchen)	0.90	0.92	0.97	0.29	0.80
Household 3 (dining room/study)	0.83	0.90	0.71	0.20	0.57

It can be seen that sensor readings from the same type of sensor in the same room have a strong correlation except for the readings from all pairs of ranging sensors and the pair of temperature sensors in Household 2 (living/dining room). The relatively low correlations between ranging sensors may relate to the fact that: (1) ranging sensors have a limited sensing capability (up to 150 cm); and (2) one of our guidelines of installing sensors is to cover as much room space as possible, i.e., ranging sensors (sensor boxes) are placed to capture movements in different parts of the room. Therefore, it is expected that only one of the ranging sensors is triggered at any given time. As for the pair of temperature sensors, the relatively low correlation may be due to their positions in the room, i.e., one of the sensor boxes is placed near the window and the other is placed away from the window.

In Section 6, we will further discuss inter-rater/observer reliability by means of the agreement between sensor-generated data and human recorded time use diary.

5. Recognising Activities

Sensor-generated data provides a digital means of looking into the life of a household. Such data in itself does not tell directly what is taking place but it provides rich contextual information drawn from the aggregate of environmental variables. Our objective in this section is to investigate what kinds of features can be drawn from the sensor-generated data and how such features can be used for activity recognition.

5.1. Feature Extraction

Activities give rise to changes in sensor readings. For example, when cooking, the *temperature* may rise in the kitchen because of the heat emitted from the hob, *humidity* levels go up and *range* readings may fluctuate intensively because of the physical movements involved. These types of changes in the sensor-generated data are essential to better understand the context of activities and to recognise their occurrence.

There are two types of patterns in the sensor readings observed in our experiments. The first type is clusters, i.e., absolute values of sensor readings appear naturally in clusters. For example, the readings of the ranging sensor are either the maximum value during periods when nothing comes in and out of range or distinctly much smaller values. The second type relates to the distribution changes of sensor readings along the time dimension, thus taking into account both time dependency and value changes between sensor readings.

Accordingly, we investigate the application of three methods for extracting features from sensor-generated data. The first, *mean shift* [30], aims at clustering the readings of sensor data into different value bands. The second method, *change points detection* [31], aims at finding meaningful points of change in the sequences of sensor-generated data. The third method, *change points gap detection*, which is based on the second method, aims at identifying the length of stable periods of readings in sensor-generated data. In our experiment setting, we apply these three feature extraction methods upon the re-sampled data, which is detailed in the next section.

5.1.1. Re-Sampling

To align with the time use diary and synchronise the data from the different sensors (sensor box and energy monitors), we re-sample the sensor data with bins of 10 minutes. Re-sampling is done using the maximum values for temperature, humidity, brightness, noise level, and the minimum values for range. To cover the time use diary and give buffers for feature extraction, we re-sample and use the sensor data from 6:00 p.m. on the day before the period of the time use diary to 12:00 p.m. on the day after that. The re-sampling results 685 data points (observations) for each sensor.

5.1.2. Mean Shift

Mean shift is a non-parametric clustering method that does not require prior knowledge of the number of clusters. It is based on an iterative procedure that shifts each data point to its nearest local mode, by updating candidates for centroids to be the mean of the data points within its neighbourhood [30].

Given a set of data points S in a n-dimensional Euclidean space X, mean shift considers these data points as sampled from some underlying probability density function and uses a kernel function for estimating the probability density function. In this work, we chose to use a flat kernel K with a bandwidth h, as defined below:

$$K(x) = \begin{cases} 1 & \text{if } \|x\| \leq h, \\ 0 & \text{otherwise.} \end{cases}$$

The sample mean at $x \in X$ is

$$m(x) = \frac{\sum_{s \in S} K(s-x)s}{\sum_{s \in S} K(s-x)}$$

The difference $m(x) - x$ is called mean shift and the mean shift algorithm is the procedure of repeatedly moving data points to the sample means until the means converge. In each iteration, s is updated by $m(s)$ for all $s \in S$ simultaneously. As a result, all the data points are associated with a centroid/cluster. Applying this procedure to the re-sampled raw sensor readings, each data point in the re-sampled dataset is represented by the index of its associated cluster. The implementation is based on python scikit-learn [56].

As an example, the lower parts of Figures 3 and 4 show the results of features extracted via the mean shift clustering algorithm. The data depicted in the upper parts of the two figures are from range and noise-level readings in the living room (with dining space) of Household 1. The readings for range generate two clusters with indices of 0 and 1. A straightforward explanation is that the cluster with index 0 represents the times when no movements are detected in the room and the cluster with index 1 represents the times when movements are detected. As for the noise level, four clusters are generated with indices of 0, 1, 2, and 3, in which the cluster with index 0 represents the times when the kitchen is relatively quiet while the other three clusters represent increasingly higher levels of noise.

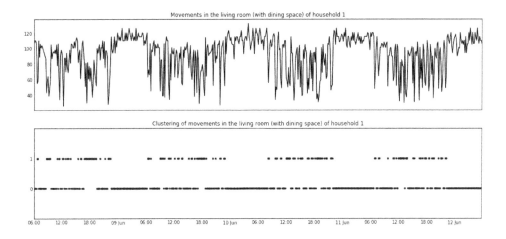

Figure 3. Mean shift clustering of range readings from a sensor box in the living room (with dining space) of Household 1.

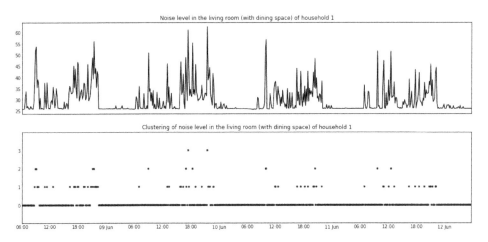

Figure 4. Mean shift clustering of noise-level readings from a sensor box in the living room (with dining space) of Household 1.

5.1.3. Change Points Detection

Change points detection is a method of estimating the times at which the statistical properties of a sequence of observations change [31].

Given a sequence of data, $x_{1:n} = (x_1, \ldots, x_n)$, a change is considered to occur when there exists a time $\tau \in \{1, \ldots, n-1\}$ such that the statistical properties of $\{x_1, \ldots, x_\tau\}$ differ from that of $\{x_{\tau+1}, \ldots, x_n\}$, e.g., in *mean* or *variance*. In the case of multiple changes, a number of change points $\tau_i, i \in \{1, \ldots, m\}$ are identified, that split the sequence of data into $m+1$ segments.

The parameters of the change points distribution are estimated via maximum likelihood by minimising the following cost function:

$$\sum_{i=1}^{m+1} [\mathcal{C}(x_{(\tau_{i-1}+1):\tau_i})] + \beta f(m)$$

where $\mathcal{C}$ is a cost function for assuming a change point at τ_i in the time series data and $\beta f(m)$ is a penalty function to avoid over fitting (i.e., too many change points).

For our sensor data, we focus on detecting the changes of *mean* in the sensor readings. A manual setting is used for the penalty function so that the number of change points can be adjusted. The change points detection algorithm is the pruned exact linear time (PELT) [57] which is computationally efficient and provides an exact segmentation. By applying the change points detection algorithm upon the re-sampled data, we obtain a sequence of 1s and 0s, where "1" represents the presence of a change point and "0" as absence. The implementation is based on the R package introduced in [58].

As an example, Figures 5 and 6 show the change points detected from the temperature and humidity readings in the kitchen of Household 2. The change points are indicated by the vertical grey lines.

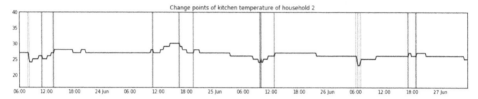

Figure 5. Change points of temperature readings from a sensor box in the kitchen of Household 2.

Figure 6. Change points of humidity readings from a sensor box in the kitchen of Household 2.

5.1.4. Change Point Gaps

Change points detected in sensor signals indicate changes in the home environment, which may be caused by human activities. While the time periods during which no change of sensor signal is detected may on the other hand indicate the lasting of some activities. For instance, when the house is asleep we can expect a long gap between changes that are detected in electricity consumption and brightness in the house, i.e., from the time of going to bed to getting up, as shown in Figures 7 and 8. Therefore, the length of gaps between change points can also be a useful feature to identify occurrences of activities. Given a sequence $X = (x_1, \ldots, x_n)$ where $x_i = 1$ represents the presence of a change point and $x_i = 0$ represents the absence of a change point, the length of gaps between change points with respect to x_i is calculated as follows:

$$gap\_cp(x_i) = \begin{cases} k - j & \text{if } x_i = 0, \\ 0 & \text{otherwise.} \end{cases}$$

where $j < i < k, x_j = x_k = 1, \forall l \in \{j+1, \ldots, k-1\} : x_l = 0.$

In the experiment, we apply the above gap detection to the change points inferred from each type of sensor reading.

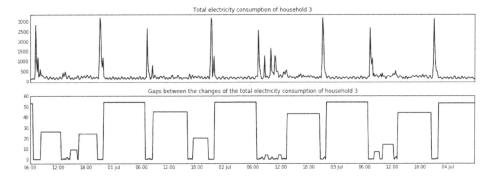

Figure 7. Gaps between change points in the electricity readings from the CT clamp connected to the electricity main of Household 3.

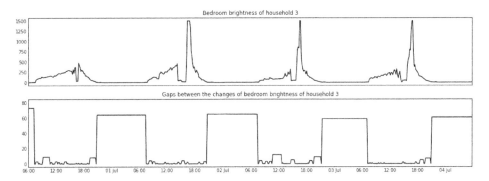

Figure 8. Gaps between change points in the brightness readings from the sensor box in the bedroom of Household 3.

Figure 7 shows big gaps between changes in the total energy consumption, indicated by the width and height of the bars, detected between midnight and early morning every night. A similar and aligned pattern can be found in the brightness of the bedroom as shown in Figure 8.

In this section, we presented three kinds of features (mean-shift clustering, change points, and gaps between change points) that can be extracted from the sensor-generated data, which expands the number of data values in each observation by three times. That is, for Household 1, there are 140 features extracted from the sensor readings of eight sensor boxes and six energy monitors; for Household 2, there are 123 features extracted from the sensor readings of seven sensor boxes and six energy monitors; and, for Household 3, there are 150 features extracted from the sensor readings of nine sensor boxes and five energy monitors. After feature extraction, we truncate the feature data points in the extended periods to match the time use diary. This reduces the number of feature data points from 685 to 576 for each type of sensor reading. The series of feature data points is at the frequency of one per 10 minutes.

5.2. Feature Selection

For different types of activities, some features are more relevant than the others. Given the size of the feature sets, it is intractable to evaluate all the possible subsets of the features. To this end, a feature selection process is necessary for finding a subset of features that can effectively describe the data while reducing irrelevant or highly-correlated inputs [59]. In this work, we adopt the approach proposed in [32], which is based on the heuristic that takes into account the usefulness of individual features for predicting the class labels along with their inter-correlations. A formalisation of the heuristic is given by [60]:

$$Merit_S = \frac{k\overline{r_{cf}}}{\sqrt{k + k(k-1)\overline{r_{ff}}}}$$

where $Merit_S$ represents the heuristic "merit" of a feature subset S containing k features, $\overline{r_{cf}}$ is the mean feature-class correlation ($f \in S$), and $\overline{r_{ff}}$ is the average feature-feature inter-correlation. The numerator indicates how predicative of the class a group of features is, while the denominator indicates how much redundancy there is within the group.

Following the proposal in [32], the metric of symmetrical uncertainty [61] is used for calculating feature-feature and feature-class correlations. Symmetrical uncertainty is based on the concept of information gain [62] while compensating for its bias towards attributes with more values and normalising its values to the range from 0 to 1.

As an example, Figures 9 and 10 show the feature-feature correlations between the sensor readings (temperature and range) of the two sensor boxes installed in the kitchen of Household 1, and the feature-class correlation between the sensor readings of electricity consumption and seven activity types in Household 3. The prefixes, $MS\_$, $CP\_$ and $Gap\_CP\_$, represent the feature extracted via the mean shift clustering, the change points detection, and the gaps between the detected change points. We can see in Figure 9 that the features extracted from the temperature readings of the two sensor boxes have much higher correlations than that of the features extracted from the range readings. That is, the temperature readings from the two sensor boxes have high redundancy, and thus it is likely that the feature selection algorithm will only keep one of them. In Figure 10, we can see that there is a strong correlation between the occurrences of laundry activity and the features based on the readings of the energy monitor attached to the washing machine. Therefore, for recognising laundry activity, such features should be kept.

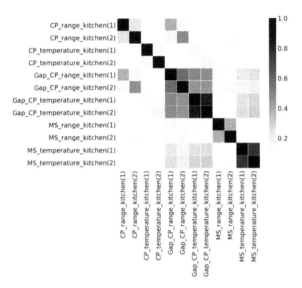

Figure 9. Correlations between the features of temperature and range readings from two sensor boxes installed in the kitchen of Household 1.

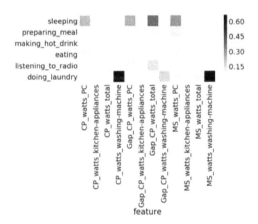

Figure 10. Correlations between the activities recorded by the occupant from Household 3 and the features of electricity consumption.

In the experiment, we run the feature selection algorithm upon the data from each combination of households and activities. The implementation is based on the python package scikit-feature [63]. As a result, an "optimal" subset of features is returned per activity type per household. Since the feature selection algorithm is based on correlation rather than prediction results directly, their performance is not guaranteed. Thus, we evaluate all the prefixes of the feature array returned by the feature selection algorithm in the task of activity recognition and find the best subset in terms of the agreement between the recognition results and the time use diaries.

5.3. Recognition Method

Hidden Markov models (HMMs) have proven to be effective in modelling time series data [64]. They are a good fit for recognising activities from sensor-generated data in the sense that they are capable of recovering a series of latent states from a series of observations.

An HMM is a Markov model whose states are not directly observable but can be characterised by a probability distribution over observable variables. In our case, the hidden states correspond to the activities performed by the participant and the observations correspond to the sensor readings. There are two assumptions in HMMs, as illustrated in Figure 11. The first is that the hidden state y_t depends only on the previous hidden state y_{t-1}. The second is that the observation x_t depends on the hidden state y_t.

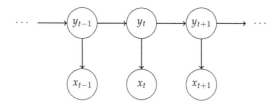

Figure 11. Graphical representation of a Hidden Markov Model.

An HMM is specified using three probability distributions: (i) the initial state probability distribution; (ii) the transition probability of moving from one hidden state to another; and (iii) the emission probability of a hidden state generating an observation. The parameters of these three probability distributions can be estimated by maximising the joint probability:

$$P(y, x) = P(y_1)P(x_1|y_1) \prod_{t=2}^{T} P(y_t|y_{t-1})P(x_t|y_t)$$

For each type of activity in each household, we built HMMs using the feature sets selected by the method presented in Section 5.2. We parameterize the HMMs with two hidden states (either an activity is occurring or not occurring) and multinomial emissions since input features are discrete values. When fitting HMMs to the data, we do not prescribe the labels for the hidden states. Thus, the activity labels (indicting whether an activity is occurring or not) in the time use diaries are randomly assigned to the hidden states by HMM fitting algorithm. For each type of activity, we evaluate both possible assignments of activity labels to the two hidden states of HMMs. This allows the HMMs to discover the patterns by itself rather than fitting models with unreliable labels from the time use diaries. In this way, the application of HMM is unsupervised as the model is fitted only with sensor-generated data.

For each of the seven types of activity shown in Table 5, we fitted the HMMs n times with each subset of features returned by the feature selection algorithm explained in Section 5.2 using randomised initial states. The implementation is based on python hmmlearn [65]. Only the model with the highest agreement is considered as the one recognising the designated activities. Other HMMs with lower agreement may detect other non-relevant activities or not even activities. In this work, we use $n = 1000$ which is manually tuned.

In the next section, we describe how to evaluate the agreement between HMM models and time use diaries, i.e., how sequences of hidden states returned by the HMMs are related to the sequences of activities recorded in the time use diary.

6. Agreement Evaluation

6.1. Evaluation Metric

In the previous section, we introduced the activity recognition framework. By fitting a HMM to the data generated by the sensors, sequences of hidden states can be extracted. In this section we illustrate how to evaluate the agreement between state sequences generated by the HMMs and the activity sequences recorded in the time use diary, which provides a quantification of inter-rater/observer reliability.

A time use diary may contain misreports in several ways. First, the start and end time of individual activities may not be accurately recorded, i.e., either earlier or later than the actual occurrence. This is called *time shifting*. Secondly, there might be activities that occurred but were not recorded, which are *missing values*. Pairwise comparison like precision and recall may exaggerate the dis-similarity introduced by such noise. Thus, we need an agreement evaluation metric that is able to alleviate the effect.

A suitable metric for this task is the Levenshtein distance (LD), a.k.a., edit distance [33] which has been widely used for measuring the similarity between two sequences. It is defined as the minimum sum of weighted operations (insertions, deletions and substitutions) needed to transform one sequence into the other. Compared to the pair-wise evaluation framework upon sequence data, LD based method can deal with the aforementioned problems of misreports. However, it is more computation intense.

Formally, given two sequences s and q, the Levenshtein distance between these two sequences $D_{s,q}(|s|, |q|)$ is defined by:

$$
D_{s,q}(i,j) = \begin{cases}
D_{i0} = \sum_{k=1}^{i} w_{del}(s_k) & \text{for } 1 \le i \le |s| \\
D_{0j} = \sum_{k=1}^{j} w_{ins}(q_k) & \text{for } 1 \le j \le |q| \\
\min \begin{cases}
D_{s,q}(i-1,j) + w_{del}(s_i) \\
D_{s,q}(i,j-1) + w_{ins}(q_j) & \text{for } 1 \le i \le |s|, 1 \le j \le |q|. \\
D_{s,q}(i-1,j-1) + 1_{(s_i \ne q_j)} w_{sub}(s_i, q_j)
\end{cases}
\end{cases}
$$

where $1_{(s_i \ne q_j)}$ is an indicator function that equals 0 when $s_i = q_j$ and equals 1 otherwise. The three lines in the *min* bracket correspond to the three operations transforming s into q, i.e., deletion, insertion and substitution. w_{del}, w_{ins} and w_{sub} are respectively the costs associated with the deletion, insertion and substitution operations.

The inputs to the function of Levenshtein distance, in our case, are two sequences of labels with respect to a type of activity. One is generated by the HMMs and the other is the corresponding activity labels recorded in the time use diary. The elements of both sequences are composed of two values: "0" indicating the absence of the activity and "1" indicating the presence of the activity. In our agreement evaluation, we attempt to minimise the difference introduced by slight time shifting and mis-recording of activities. For these reasons, we set the costs of the three types of operations w_{del}, w_{ins} and w_{sub} as follows. For substituting "1" with "0", the cost is set to 0.7; for substituting "0" with "1", the cost is set to 1.0. This gives less penalty to cases of false positive than to cases of false negative, i.e., the agreement is lower when the activities recorded in the time use diaries are not recognised from the sensor data. The costs of inserting and deleting '0' are set to 0.4. This is to reduce the penalty introduced by time shifting. We set the cost of inserting and deleting '1' to 100 to disable these two operations. The output is the minimum cost of the operations that are needed to transform predicated sequences to the ones recorded in time use diaries and lower values indicate higher agreements. The implementation is based on the python package weighted-levenshtein [66].

The costs of deletion, insertion and substitution are used to differentiate their influence upon the perceived agreement. The absolute difference between these costs will be investigated in future work.

6.2. Results and Analysis

In this section we discuss the results from applying the aforementioned activity recognition method to the collected data and compare them to the interview data of the corresponding households. Table 7 lists the set of features that achieves the best agreement in terms of the Levenshtein distance (LD) between the activity sequences generated by the HMMs and that recorded in the time use diary.

Table 7. Feature sets achieve best agreement with respect to the seven types of activities.

Household	Activities	Feature Sets	LD
1	Sleeping	(MS_light_living/dining-room, Gap_CP_light_bedroom)	11.9
	Preparing meal	(MS_watts_total, MS_watts_microwave)	6.0
	Making hot drink	(MS_watts_kitchen-appliances)	5.1
	Eating	(MS_watts_total)	17.0
	Watching TV	(MS_watts_TV)	16.6
	Doing laundry	(MS_watts_washing-machine)	0.7
2	Sleeping	(CP_light_kitchen(1), CP_light_bedroom, MS_temperature_living/dining-room(2))	16.7
	Preparing meal	(MS_watts_kitchen-appliances)	11.2
	Making hot drink	(MS_sound_kitchen(1))	11.6
	Eating	(MS_watts_kitchen-appliances, MS_range_living/dining-room(2))	11.0
	Watching TV	(MS_watts_TV)	4.8
	Listening to radio	(CP_range_hallway, MS_watts_kitchen-appliances, MS_range_bedroom)	37.3
	Doing laundry	(CP_watts_total, CP_watts_kitchen-appliances, CP_watts_washing-machine)	12.1
3	Sleeping	(Gap_CP_range_living-room)	5.9
	Preparing meal	(MS_range_kitchen(2), MS_watts_PC)	26.1
	Making hot drink	(CP_humidity_second-utility, CP_temperature_kitchen(2), CP_humidity_bedroom)	1.7
	Eating	(MS_range_kitchen(2), CP_temperature_dining-room/study(1))	16.0
	Listening to radio	(MS_sound_living-room)	37.2
	Doing laundry	(MS_watts_washing-machine, CP_watts_washing-machine)	2.6

For the sleeping activity of Household 3, the best agreement is achieved by the feature capturing the gaps between the changes of movements in the living room. According to the interview data, we know that the living room is the geographical centre of the house, i.e., the passage to transit between kitchen, dining/study area and the sleeping area. The occupant keeps busy at home and spends a lot of time in the dining/study area and the living area.

For the activity of making hot drink, the feature identifying humidity changes in the utility room and bedroom of Household 3 is contained in the subset of features that achieves the best agreement. A further investigation of the time use diary shows that when making coffee in the kitchen in the mornings the occupant shaves in the bathroom which is located next to the utility room and bedroom. The humidity change in this case is very likely caused by the humid bathroom.

The overlaps between the subsets of features that achieve the best agreement in recognising activities of preparing meal and eating show the close relation between the two types of activities. This demonstrates that sensor insensitive activities may be recognised via sensor readings from their causal/correlated activities. In this case, the recognition of preparing meal can help recognise eating.

For the laundry activity, since we have an energy monitor attached to the washing machine of each household, it is expected that using the features capturing the energy consumption of the washing machine would achieves the best agreement. However, for Household 2, the feature subset that achieves the best agreement also contains the changes of the energy consumption of the kitchen appliances as well as that of the total energy consumption. A further investigation of the time use diary shows that when doing laundry the occupant quite often cooks or makes coffee around the same time. However, among the three households, the agreement between the HMM and the time use diary for laundry activity in Household 2 is the lowest, which may indicate the possibility of misreport or that the reported laundry activities involve other elements, such as sorting, hanging out, folding, etc.

Among the seven types of activities, *listening to radio* has the lowest agreement (the largest value in LD) between the detection from the sensor-generated data and the records in the time use diaries. In case of Household 2, the time use diary tells us that the occupant listens to radio in the bedroom while getting up, in the kitchen while preparing meals and in the dining area when having meals. Similarly, the occupant in Household 3 listens to radio in the kitchen when preparing meal and in the living room when relaxing. In both cases, the occupant is using more than one device for listening to radio in more than one place.

For illustration, we plot the comparison of each type of activity detected from the sensor data and that recorded in the time use diaries (Figures 12–18). In each figure, the upper part shows the state sequences generated by an HMM using the specific set of features, and the lower part shows the activity sequences recorded in the time use diary (TUD). The black bins represent the time slices when a particular activity is detected/recorded.

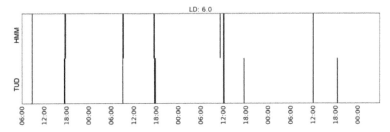

Figure 12. Recognising the activity of preparing meal in Household 1 with feature set (MS_watts_total, MS_watts_microwave).

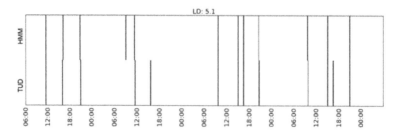

Figure 13. Recognising the activity of making hot drink in Household 1 with feature set (MS_watts_kitchen-appliances).

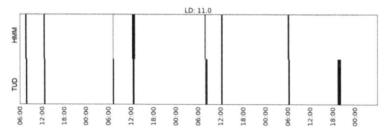

Figure 14. Recognising the activity of eating in Household 2 with feature set (MS_watts_kitchen-appliances, MS_range_living/dining-room(2)).

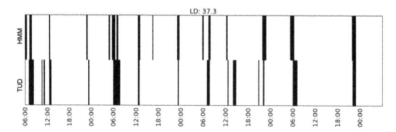

Figure 15. Recognising the activity of listening to radio in Household 2 with feature set (CP_range_hallway, MS_watts_kitchen-appliances, MS_range_bedroom).

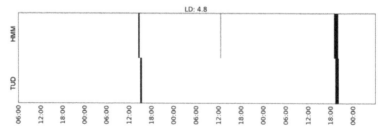

Figure 16. Recognising the activity of watching TV in Household 2 with feature set (MS_watts_TV).

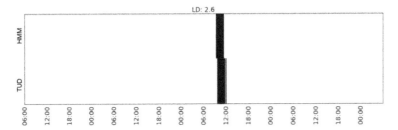

Figure 17. Recognising the activity of doing laundry in Household 3 with feature set (MS_watts_washing-machine, CP_watts_washing-machine).

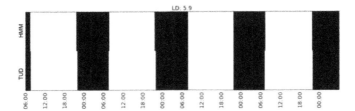

Figure 18. Recognising the activity of sleeping in Household 3 with feature set (Gap_CP_range_living-room).

The activity durations generated by the HMMs mostly overlap with those recorded in the time use diary, with some local shifts along the time line. The only exception in these seven plots is the activity of listening to radio in Household 2, which suggests that the features being used are not sufficient enough to distinguish the occurrences of such activities. In some cases, radio is used as background, which does not necessarily constitute the activity of listening to the radio.

7. Conclusions

In this paper, we presented a mixed-methods approach for recognising activities at home. In particular, we proposed a metric for evaluating the agreement between the predicted activities from models trained by the sensor data and the activities recorded in a time use diary. We also investigated ways of extracting and selecting features from sensor-generated data for activity recognition.

The focus of this work is not on improving the recognition performance of particular models but to present a framework for quantifying how activity recognition models trained by sensor-generated data can be evaluated on the basis of their agreement with activities recorded in time use diaries. We demonstrate the usefulness of this framework by an experiment involving three trial households. The evaluation results can provide evidence about which types of sensors are more effective for detecting certain types of activities in a household. This may further help researchers in understanding the occupant's daily activities and the contexts in which certain activities occur. The agreement between the sensor-generated data and the time use diary may also help to validate the quality of the diary.

This is an on-going research, investigating the use of digital sensors for social research, using household practices as a testbed. As this is written, we are in the process of collecting data from three types of households: single occupant, families with children and ≥ 2 adults. There are several directions to consider for extending this work. We are adding a wearable wristband sensor to the setting to detect the proximity of participants to each sensor box via Bluetooth RSSI (received signal strength indicator). Such data will give us a more accurate reading of presence and co-presence of particular occupants in different parts of their home, while also helping us in obtaining more accurate start and end times of certain activities. We will continue to investigate other activity recognition methods and feature selection techniques. In addition, we are interested in employing post and assisted labelling mechanisms, for example, by asking participants to assign an agreement score to the activity sequences generated by our activity recognition models. In this way, another layer of agreement can be added to the evaluation.

Acknowledgments: The authors thank William Headley for the design and manufacture of the sensor box (also known as desk egg). The work was carried out as part of the "HomeSense: digital sensors for social research" project funded by the Economic and Social Research Council (grant ES/N011589/1) through the National Centre for Research Methods.

Author Contributions: All authors participated in refining the initial study. Jie Jiang and Riccardo Pozza designed the experiments; Jie Jiang performed the experiments and analysed the data; and Kristrún Gunnarsdóttir orchestrated the fieldwork and contributed materials. All authors discussed enhancements, results and implications, wrote the manuscript and commented on it at all stages.

Conflicts of Interest: The authors declare no conflict of interest. The founding sponsors had no role in the design of the study; in the collection, analyses, or interpretation of data; in the writing of the manuscript, and in the decision to publish the results.

References

1. Ruppanner, L. *Contemporary Family Issues*; Oxford University Press: Oxford, UK, 2015.
2. Atkinson, R.; Jacobs, K. *House, Home and Society*; Palgrave: London, UK, 2016.
3. Gattshall, M.L.; Shoup, J.A.; Marshall, J.A.; Crane, L.A.; Estabrooks, P.A. Validation of a survey instrument to assess home environments for physical activity and healthy eating in overweight children. *Int. J. Behav. Nutr. Phys. Act.* **2008**, *5*, 1–13.
4. Williams, S.J.; Coveney, C.; Meadows, R. 'M-apping' sleep? Trends and transformations in the digital age. *Sociol. Health Illn.* **2015**, *37*, 1039–1054.
5. López, D.; Sánchez-Criado, T. Analysing Hands-on-Tech Care Work in Telecare Installations. Frictional Encounters with Gerontechnological Designs. In *Aging and the Digital Life Course*; Prendergast, D., Garattini, C., Eds.; Berghahn: New York, NY, USA, 2015; Chapter 9.
6. Mort, M.; Roberts, C.; Callen, B. Ageing with telecare: care or coercion in austerity? *Sociol. Health Illn.* **2013**, *35*, 799–812.
7. Sullivan, O.; Gershuny, J. Change in Spousal Human Capital and Housework: A Longitudinal Analysis. *Eur. Sociol. Rev.* **2016**, *32*, 864–880.
8. Pierce, J.; Schiano, D.J.; Paulos, E. Home, Habits, and Energy: Examining Domestic Interactions and Energy Consumption. In Proceedings of the SIGCHI Conference on Human Factors in Computing Systems CHI '10, Atlanta, GA, USA, 10–15 April 2010; pp. 1985–1994.
9. Shannon-Baker, P. Making Paradigms Meaningful in Mixed Methods Research. *J. Mixed Methods Res.* **2016**, *10*, 319–334.
10. Ganong, L.; Coleman, M. Qualitative research on family relationships. *J. Soc. Person. Relatsh.* **2014**, *31*, 451–459.
11. British Social Attitudes Survey (33rd ed.). Available online: http://www.bsa.natcen.ac.uk/latest-report/british-social-attitudes-33/introduction.aspx (accessed on 30 March 2017).
12. Office for National Statistic (UK). Available online: https://www.ons.gov.uk/ (accessed on 30 March 2017).
13. Chenu, A.; Lesnard, L. Time Use Surveys: A Review of their Aims, Methods, and Results. *Eur. J. Sociol.* **2006**, *47*, 335–359.
14. Gershuny, J.; Harms, T.A. Housework Now Takes Much Less Time: 85 Years of US Rural Women's Time Use. *Soc. Forces* **2016**, *95*, 503–524.
15. European Communities. *Harmonised European Time Use Surveys: 2008 Guidelines*; Eurostat Methodologies and Working Papers; Population and social conditions; European Communities: Luxembourg, 2009.
16. Kelly, P.; Thomas, E.; Doherty, A.; Harms, T.; Burke, O.; Gershuny, J.; Foster, C. Developing a Method to Test the Validity of 24 Hour Time Use Diaries Using Wearable Cameras: A Feasibility Pilot. *PLOS ONE* **2015**, *10*, 1–15.
17. Benmansour, A.; Bouchachia, A.; Feham, M. Multioccupant Activity Recognition in Pervasive Smart Home Environments. *ACM Comput. Surv.* **2015**, *48*, 34:1–34:36.
18. Poppe, R. A survey on vision-based human action recognition. *Image Vis. Comput.* **2010**, *28*, 976–990.

19. Lara, O.D.; Labrador, M.A. A Survey on Human Activity Recognition using Wearable Sensors. *IEEE Commun. Surv. Tutor.* **2013**, *15*, 1192–1209.

20. Shoaib, M.; Bosch, S.; Incel, O.D.; Scholten, H.; Havinga, P.J. A Survey of Online Activity Recognition Using Mobile Phones. *Sensors* **2015**, *15*, 2059–2085.

21. Amft, O.; Tröster, G. Recognition of dietary activity events using on-body sensors. *Artif. Intell. Med.* **2008**, *42*, 121–136.

22. Wang, J.; Zhang, Z.; Li, B.; Lee, S.; Sherratt, R.S. An enhanced fall detection system for elderly person monitoring using consumer home networks. *IEEE Trans. Consum. Electron.* **2014**, *60*, 23–29.

23. Lin, Z.H.; Fu, L.C. Multi-user Preference Model and Service Provision in a Smart Home Environment. In Proceedings of the 2007 IEEE International Conference on Automation Science and Engineering, Scottsdale, AZ, USA, 22–25 September 2007; pp. 759–764.

24. van Kasteren, T.L.M.; Englebienne, G.; Kröse, B.J.A. Human Activity Recognition from Wireless Sensor Network Data: Benchmark and Software. In *Activity Recognition in Pervasive Intelligent Environments*; Chen, L.; Nugent, C.D.; Biswas, J.; Hoey, J., Eds.; Atlantics Press: Amsterdam, The Netherland, 2011; pp. 165–186.

25. Hsu, K.C.; Chiang, Y.T.; Lin, G.Y.; Lu, C.H.; Hsu, J.Y.J.; Fu, L.C., Strategies for Inference Mechanism of Conditional Random Fields for Multiple-Resident Activity Recognition in a Smart Home. In *Trends in Applied Intelligent Systems, Proceedings of the 23rd International Conference on Industrial Engineering and Other Applications of Applied Intelligent Systems, Cordoba, Spain, 1–4 June 2010*; García-Pedrajas, N., Herrera, F., Fyfe, C., Benítez, J.M., Ali, M., Eds.; Springer: Berlin/Heidelberg, Germany, 2010; pp. 417–426.

26. Fan, X.; Zhang, H.; Leung, C.; Miao, C. Comparative study of machine learning algorithms for activity recognition with data sequence in home-like environment. In Proceedings of the 2016 IEEE International Conference on Multisensor Fusion and Integration for Intelligent Systems (MFI), Baden-Baden, Germany, 19–21 September 2016, pp. 168–173.

27. Cook, D.J.; Crandall, A.; Singla, G.; Thomas, B. Detection of Social Interaction in Smart Spaces. *Cybern. Syst.* **2010**, *41*, 90–104.

28. Silverman, D. *Interpreting Qualitative Data: Methods for Analyzing Talk, Text and Interaction*, 3rd ed.; SAGE Publications: Thousand Oaks, CA, USA, 2006.

29. Wang, L.; Gu, T.; Tao, X.; Chen, H.; Lu, J. Recognizing multi-user activities using wearable sensors in a smart home. *Pervasive Mob. Comput.* **2011**, *7*, 287 – 298.

30. Cheng, Y. Mean Shift, Mode Seeking, and Clustering. *IEEE Trans. Pattern Anal. Mach. Intell.* **1995**, *17*, 790–799.

31. Picard, D. Testing and estimating change-points in time series. *Adv. Appl. Probab.* **1985**, *17*, 841 – 867.

32. Hall, M.A.; Smith, L.A. Feature Selection for Machine Learning: Comparing a Correlation-Based Filter Approach to the Wrapper. In Proceedings of the Twelfth International Florida Artificial Intelligence Research Society Conference, San Francisco, CA, USA, 1–5 May 1999; AAAI Press: Palo Alto, CA, USA, 1999; pp. 235–239.

33. Levenshtein, V.I. Binary codes capable of correcting deletions, insertions, and reversals. *Cybern. Control Theory* **1966**, *10*, 707–710.

34. Jiang, J.; Pozza, R.; Gunnarsdóttir, K.; Gilbert, N.; Moessner, K. Recognising Activities at Home: Digital and Human Sensors. In Proceedings of the International Conference on Future Networks and Distributed Systems ICFNDS '17, Cambridge, UK, 19–20 July 2017; ACM: New York, NY, USA, 2017; pp. 17:1–17:11.

35. Cook, D.J.; Youngblood, M.; Heierman, E.O.; Gopalratnam, K.; Rao, S.; Litvin, A.; Khawaja, F. MavHome: An agent-based smart home. In Proceedings of the First IEEE International Conference on Pervasive Computing and Communications, Fort Worth, TX, USA, 23 26 March 2003; pp. 521–524.

36. Cook, D.J.; Schmitter-edgecombe, M.; Crandall, A.; Sanders, C.; Thomas, B. Collecting and Disseminating Smart Home Sensor Data in the CASAS Project. In Proceedings of the CHI Workshop on Developing Shared Home Behavior Datasets to Advance HCI and Ubiquitous Computing Research, Boston, MA, USA, 4–9 April 2009.

37. Singla, G.; Cook, D.J.; Schmitter-Edgecombe, M. Recognizing independent and joint activities among multiple residents in smart environments. *J. Ambient Intell. Humaniz. Comput.* **2010**, *1*, 57–63.

38. Chiang, Y.T.; Hsu, K.C.; Lu, C.H.; Fu, L.C.; Hsu, J.Y.J. Interaction models for multiple-resident activity recognition in a smart home. In Proceedings of the 2010 IEEE/RSJ International Conference on Intelligent Robots and Systems, Taipei, Taiwan, 18–22 October 2010; pp. 3753–3758.

39. Fatima, I.; Fahim, M.; Lee, Y.K.; Lee, S. A Unified Framework for Activity Recognition-Based Behavior Analysis and Action Prediction in Smart Homes. *Sensors* **2013**, *13*, 2682–2699.

40. Fang, H.; He, L.; Si, H.; Liu, P.; Xie, X. Human activity recognition based on feature selection in smart home using back-propagation algorithm. *ISA Trans.* **2014**, *53*, 1629–1638.

41. Krishnan, N.C.; Cook, D.J. Activity Recognition on Streaming Sensor Data. *Pervasive Mob. Comput.* **2014**, *10*, 138–154.

42. Dawadi, P.N.; Cook, D.J.; Schmitter-Edgecombe, M. Modeling Patterns of Activities Using Activity Curves. *Pervasive Mob. Comput.* **2016**, *28*, 51–68.

43. Alemdar, H.; Ertan, H.; Incel, O.D.; Ersoy, C. ARAS human activity datasets in multiple homes with multiple residents. In Proceedings of the 2013 7th International Conference on Pervasive Computing Technologies for Healthcare and Workshops, Venice, Italy, 5–8 May 2013; pp. 232–235.

44. Prossegger, M.; Bouchachia, A., Multi-resident Activity Recognition Using Incremental Decision Trees. In Proceedings of the Third International Conference ICAIS 2014 Adaptive and Intelligent Systems, Bournemouth, UK, 8–10 September 2014; Bouchachia, A., Ed.; Springer: Cham, Switzerland, 2014; pp. 182–191.

45. Kröse, B.; Kasteren, T.V.; Gibson, C.; Dool, T.V.D. Care: Context awareness in residences for elderly. In Proceedings of the Conference of the International Society for Gerontechnology, Pisa, Italy, 21–25 June 2008.

46. van Kasteren, T.; Noulas, A.; Englebienne, G.; Kröse, B. Accurate Activity Recognition in a Home Setting. In Proceedings of the 10th International Conference on Ubiquitous Computing UbiComp '08, Seoul, Korea, 21–24 September 2008; pp. 1–9.

47. Nez, F.J.O.; Englebienne, G.; de Toledo, P.; van Kasteren, T.; Sanchis, A.; Kröse, B. In-Home Activity Recognition: Bayesian Inference for Hidden Markov Models. *IEEE Pervasive Comput.* **2014**, *13*, 67–75.

48. Singh, D.; Merdivan, E.; Psychoula, I.; Kropf, J.; Hanke, S.; Geist, M.; Holzinger, A. Human Activity Recognition Using Recurrent Neural Networks. In *Machine Learning and Knowledge Extraction: First IFIP TC 5, WG 8.4, 8.9, 12.9, Proceedings of the International Cross-Domain Conference, CD-MAKE 2017, Reggio, Italy, 29 August–1 September 2017*; Holzinger, A.; Kieseberg, P., Tjoa, A.M., Weippl, E., Eds.; Springer: Berlin, Germany, 2017; pp. 267–274.

49. Laput, G.; Zhang, Y.; Harrison, C. Synthetic Sensors: Towards General-Purpose Sensing. In Proceedings of the 2017 CHI Conference on Human Factors in Computing Systems, Denver, CO, USA, 6–11 May 2017; ACM: New York, NY, USA, 2017; pp. 3986–3999.

50. Seeeduino Arch-Pro. Available online: https://developer.mbed.org/platforms/Seeeduino-Arch-Pro (accessed on 30 March 2017).

51. SparkFun Humidity and Temperature Sensor Breakout—HTU21D. Available online: https://www.sparkfun.com/products/retired/12064 (accessed on 30 March 2017).

52. SparkFun RGB and Gesture Sensor—APDS-9960. Available online: https://www.sparkfun.com/products/12787 (accessed on 30 March 2017).

53. Pololu Carrier with Sharp GP2Y0A60SZLF Analog Distance Sensor. Available online: https://www.pololu.com/product/2474 (accessed on 30 March 2017).

54. SparkFun MEMS Microphone Breakout—INMP401 (ADMP401). Available online: https://www.sparkfun.com/products/9868 (accessed on 30 March 2017).

55. Current Cost—Individual Appliance Monitor (IAM). Available online: http://www.currentcost.com/product-iams.html (accessed on 30 March 2017).

56. Pedregosa, F.; Varoquaux, G.; Gramfort, A.; Michel, V.; Thirion, B.; Grisel, O.; Blondel, M.; Prettenhofer, P.; Weiss, R.; Dubourg, V.; et al. Scikit-learn: Machine learning in Python. *J. Mach. Learn. Res.* **2011**, *12*, 2825–2830.

57. Killick, R.; Fearnhead, P.; Eckley, I.A. Optimal Detection of Changepoints with a Linear Computational Cost. *J. Am. Stat. Assoc.* **2012**, *107*, 1590–1598.

58. Killick, R.; Eckley, I.A. Changepoint: An R package for changepoint analysis. *J. Stat. Softw.* **2014**, *58*, 1–19.

59. Guyon, I.; Elisseeff, A. An Introduction to Variable and Feature Selection. *J. Mach. Learn. Res.* **2003**, *3*, 1157–1182.

60. Ghiselli, E.E. *Theory of Psychological Measurement*; McGraw-Hill: New York, NY, USA, 1964.

61. Press, W.H.; Flannery, B.P.; Teukolski, S.A.; Vetterling, W.T. *Numerical Recipes in C*; Cambridge University Press: Cambridge, UK, 1988.

62. Quinlan, J.R. *Programs for Machine Learning*; Morgan Kaufmann: Burlington, MA, USA, 1993.

63. Li, J.; Cheng, K.; Wang, S.; Morstatter, F.; Trevino, R.P.; Tang, J.; Liu, H. Feature Selection: A Data Perspective. *arXiv* **2016**, arXiv:1601.07996.

64. Zucchini, W.; MacDonald, I.L. *Hidden Markov Models for Time Series: An Introduction Using R*; CRC Press: Boca Raton, FL, USA, 2009.

65. Hmmlearn. Available online: http://hmmlearn.readthedocs.io/ (accessed on 30 March 2017)

66. Weighted-Levenshtein. Available online: http://weighted-levenshtein.readthedocs.io/ (accessed on 30 March 2017)

 Journal of
Sensor and
Actuator Networks

Article

Wearable-Based Human Activity Recognition Using an IoT Approach

Diego Castro *, William Coral , Camilo Rodriguez, Jose Cabra and Julian Colorado

Department of Electronics, School of Engineering, Pontificia Universidad Javeriana,
Cr. 7 No. 40-62 Bldg. Jose Gabriel Maldonado, Bogota 110111, Colombia; william.coral@gmail.com (W.C.);
crodriguez_r@javeriana.edu.co (C.R.); jcabra@javeriana.edu.co (J.S.); coloradoj@javeriana.edu.co (J.C.)
* Correspondence: diegocastro@javeriana.edu.co

Received: 30 September 2017 ; Accepted: 17 November 2017; Published: 24 November 2017

Abstract: This paper presents a novel system based on the Internet of Things (IoT) to Human Activity Recognition (HAR) by monitoring vital signs remotely. We use machine learning algorithms to determine the activity done within four pre-established categories (lie, sit, walk and jog). Meanwhile, it is able to give feedback during and after the activity is performed, using a remote monitoring component with remote visualization and programmable alarms. This system was successfully implemented with a 95.83% success ratio.

Keywords: e-health; human activity recognition (HAR); Internet of Things (IoT); rule tree classifier; C4.5; Bayesian classifier

1. Introduction

The Internet of Things, IoT, is a new concept in which all sensing objects can be connected to the internet to have remote and constant access to its measurements (data). This access allows for taking action in a faster way, with better results and much more data involved [1,2]. The data that compose these kinds of systems can go from temperature [3], outdoor location [4], indoor location [5], storage stock, humidity or other industry related variables [6]. In short, any sensor that can be connected to the Internet makes part of an IoT paradigm [7].

In such a way, classical applications of pervasive computing can be upgraded to an IoT scheme for an activity recognition application: Human Activity Recognition (HAR). These applications, in their classical approach, have been researched, evaluated and developed to the point that several commonly available products have HAR systems built in. This can be seen on some fitness trackers, references [8,9], which have HAR systems built into the mobile applications of their manufacturer. These applications usually register and analyze daily and sleep activity [10]. The HAR system consists of sensing the person's positioning and movement, performing a feature extraction and a classification of those features to decide which activity was performed in a pre-selected list of activities [11–13]. The HAR systems have several methods to perform recognition, the most common one being an artificial vision assisted system [14,15]. This kind recognition can be seen in commercial products such as the Microsoft Kinect™ [16]. Despite the many benefits and high popularity, in both usability and research, of vision assisted HAR, it presents several disadvantages for subjects such as accuracy, coverage and cost. Another method that can overcome these challenges are on-body sensors systems or wearable assisted HAR [17]. This kind of approach relies on wearable sensors present throughout the body, which help to perform the recognition [18]. This method can either require that the subject wear one [19,20] or more [21] for pre-established periods of time. Some systems even require that the device(s) have to be permanently worn by the person [22]. These devices could be those within another device such as a smartphone [23,24].

J. Sens. Actuator Netw. **2017**, *6*, 28

In this paper, we present a more detailed and novel version of an HAR-IoT system that employs a single device with occasional usage, as seen in [20] presented at the International Conference on Future Networks and Distributed Systems (ICFNDS) 2017. This system is intended to be used by patients with chronic heart diseases, patients that have their health status in a non-critical condition but still need constant monitoring. The presented system focuses on the daily routine, activity and physical therapy that each patient must have as part of their recuperation process. Although an IoT approach needs a security analysis [25,26], our approach to the IoT does not rely on a wireless sensor network (WSN) [27], the data information is not sensitive to outside listeners [28] and, as previously stated, the focus of the paper is to validate the presented approach to HAR-IoT systems.

The HAR-IoT system uses a specialized hardware for vital signs monitoring including embedded heart, respiration and body acceleration sensors. The activity recognition was implemented using a classifier that uses the information gathered by this hardware. Two different methods were implemented for the classifiers: Bayes [29] and C4.5 [30]. An (IoT) cloud based component was integrated [31,32] to perform different tasks, such as: remote consultation [33], feedback and therapy control for both duration and quality [34] or even an online classification service [35]. This component also grants remote access to the data and configurable alerts for the activity done, if needed. This paper presents a novel interaction between a traditional HAR system and an IoT system with a different approach to the classical feature extraction in an HAR system, which resulted in a 95.83% success ratio with a notable small training data set.

This work will be presented as follows: in Section 2, the system architecture is explained and complemented with the system description in Section 3. Section 4 focuses on explaining the feature extraction method and the classifier information. The experiments and results are presented in Section 5, and, finally, the conclusions are shown in Section 6.

2. System Architecture

The proposed system is composed of two main modules: a traditional HAR system that can be implemented on any mobile and non-mobile device, and an e-health application of any recognition or surveillance system used in a health care related subject. These modules work independently, but the novelty of the approach lays with the increase of availability and decrease response times.

2.1. HAR Systems

An HAR system is a specific application of pattern recognition and expert systems. This recognition works in two phases: a training phase and a recognition phase. Although both have similar steps, the training phase has a priori information of the activities done and the recognition phase uses the knowledge of the training phase to have accurate recognition. This means that the recognition phase is highly dependent on the training phase success.

2.1.1. Learning/Training Phase

The learning or training phase is the first phase of any recognition algorithm. This phase is in charge of establishing the relations between the data and the activities. It has three main steps (Figure 1):

1. Data collection: The data collection step conducts the data acquisition from all the sensors available for the system. The sensor available will be dependent on the kind of device that the recognition is built for. This step needs an activity log of every activity performed detailing the time, the type and duration. The training phase must consider all possible activities, needing all to be performed, preferably, in an aleatory manner without a correlation in activity, duration or any other factor that might be involved in the recognition. It is important to note that the data collection is done without any signal processing as all processing and analysis is done during the feature extraction step.

2. Feature extraction: The feature extraction step has several possibilities depending on the kind of sensors and variables types that are involved during the data collection step. There can be structural features and statistical features. The structural features are those that try to find interrelation or correlation between the signals. This also means that the signal can fit a previously defined mathematical function to the current state of the variables. The statistical feature extraction performs a transformation on the signal using statistical information. These features could be the mean of the signal, standard deviation, correlation, etc. The most common transformations performed are the Fourier and Wavelet transforms. During this step, it is common to perform signal processing to eliminate noise, reduce the range of the signal or perform other kinds of processing to better extract the relevant features for each activity.

3. Learning: The learning or the final step of the training phase is the development of a recognition model that is learned from the data set, the activity log and the relevant features to properly recognize any activity. This step is highly dependent on the training data set, which is the reason for the strict methodology and rigorous logging on the data collection step. There are many recognition models that can go from a rule tree based on signal parameters, neural networks, statistical base algorithms or fuzzy logic, each one having their advantages and disadvantages. Based on the complexity, response time and available resources, the model must be selected to best fit the system demands.

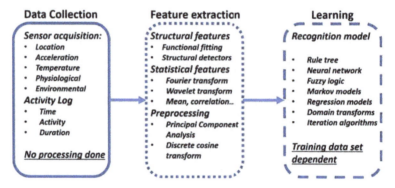

Figure 1. Learning process of an HAR system.

2.1.2. Recognition Phase

The recognition phase is the final phase of an HAR system. It does the recognition of the activity performed using the training phase result. The recognition phase has three main steps (Figure 2):

1. Data collection: The data collection step does the data acquisition of all the sensors available for the recognition. The sensor available will be dependent on the kind of device that the recognition is built for. Unlike the learning phase, there is not any prior knowledge of the activities performed, so there is no need, either choice, to have an activity log. It is important to note that the data collection is done without any signal processing, as all processing and analysis is done during the feature extraction step.

2. Feature extraction: The feature extraction step has several possibilities according to the kind of sensors and variable types that are involved during the data collection step. There can be structural features and statistical features. The structural features are those that try to find interrelation or correlation between the signals. This also means that the signal can fit a previously defined mathematical function to the current state of the variables. The statistical feature performs transformation on the signal using statistical information. This could be using the mean of the signal, standard deviation, correlation, etc. The most common transformations performed are

the Fourier and Wavelet transforms. During this step, it is common to perform signal processing to eliminate noise, reduce the range of the signal or perform other kinds of processing to better extract the relevant features for each activity.

3. Recognition: The recognition or the final step of the training phase is the inference of the activity performed using the gathered data and extracted features on the previous steps using the recognition model of the training phase. This step decides which of the possible activities were done with a percentage of accuracy, which depends on the recognition model. This step is the most time-consuming part of any HAR system and, according to the selected model and available resources, this time and accuracy change.

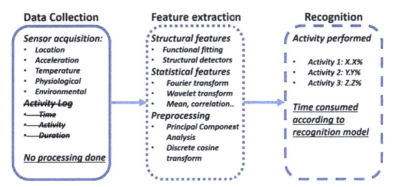

Figure 2. Recognition process of an HAR system.

2.2. E-Health Applications

An IoT solution gathers information from the available sensors, people and/or electronic devices. If the data source, application, user or place of implementation are related to the healthcare industry, it is called an e-health solution. These kinds of applications provide a novel approach to the healthcare system, which bring new and better services such as constant monitoring of patients and remote consultation services. All of these services provide a faster and reliable healthcare industry with almost zero waiting time, changing the classical approach of the healthcare system from a reactive service to a preemptive industry.

In this project, the main focus is to improve the healthcare services that take care of patients for which their health status is not in a critical condition, but they still need constant monitoring. To better understand the proposed solution, it is necessary to discuss and understand the general scheme of a remote patient service, especially home remote patient monitoring. The general architecture of a remote patient service (Figure 3) includes a variety of sensor and/or medical devices to measure relevant variables of the patient that include but are not limited to:

*   Heart Rate.
*   Respiration rate.
*   Weight.
*   Oxygen saturation.
*   Posture.

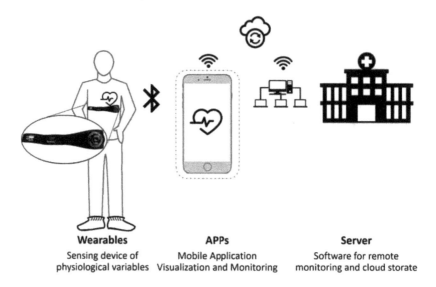

| **Wearables** | **APPs** | **Server** |
| Sensing device of physiological variables | Mobile Application Visualization and Monitoring | Software for remote monitoring and cloud storate |

Figure 3. Basic scheme in an e-health system.

According to the signal properties and signal availability, the data is transmitted via the Internet to a database. Inside the database, the data can be constantly analyzed, displayed or even take action, usually in the form of alarms, to give a better healthcare service. The constant availability of the data implies a full time monitoring of the relevant data of the patient, which makes it easier to detect an abnormality on the patient. This also means that the medical record of the patient gets a huge amount of data, opening the possibility of performing a more integral and objective medical diagnosis. This will reduce the cost service, improve the recuperation time and will improve the efficiency on the healthcare system overall.

The lower cost service is associated with the fact that the patient will assume the high expenses related to it, accommodation and infrastructure related costs. There is also a reduction in staffing cost, as the remote monitoring implicates that the qualified personnel for the care services does not need to be present at the patient location, and one person can be in charge of the tracking of more than one patient at a time, with the help of the data analytics of the system. In addition, at their homes, the patient's recuperation process can be accelerated, as a remote care service greatly minimizes the exposure of the patient to others' diseases, comparing this scenario to a classical hospitalization environment.

Having the patient data in real time will improve any treatment, as the adjustments of the quantity, methodology and other factors of the treatment can be adjusted in the same manner. This follows a paradigm to change from a situational response to a situation prevention and avoid high risk scenarios. This real-time management allows the procedures to be simpler and more efficient. Consequently, there will be great improvement on the quality of life of patients undergoing remote monitoring services, with stress levels lowering because of their home accommodation rather than in a hospital. The implemented solution will be described in further sections.

3. System Description

The goal of this prototype is to implement an HAR-IoT system, which needs to be able to measure physiological variables, have an HAR component that works according to the sensor data, and implement a cloud system for data storage and remote display. Intelligent alarms can be programmed according to different levels following the hospital requirements.

J. Sens. Actuator Netw. **2017**, *6*, 28

The system's block diagram is composed of three main elements (wearable, the smartphone application and the cloud). This diagram is shown in Figure 4:

- Wearable: The selected wearable is the Bioharness (Zaphyr, Annapolis, Maryland, US). This wearable is capable of measuring several physiological variables (for more information, see Section 3.1) and connect to a smartphone via Bluetooth.
- Smartphone application: This application has three main components. The data reception that handles the communication and storage of the raw sensor data of the wearable. The HAR classifier, which recognizes the kind of movement done at that moment using the raw sensor data, a classifier algorithm and a machine learning process. Furthermore, a local visualization is responsible for displaying raw sensor data and the activity recognized.
- Cloud: The cloud component receives all the raw data of the wearable and the activities recognized by the HAR classifier. All the data is stored and can be consulted online using a web browser.

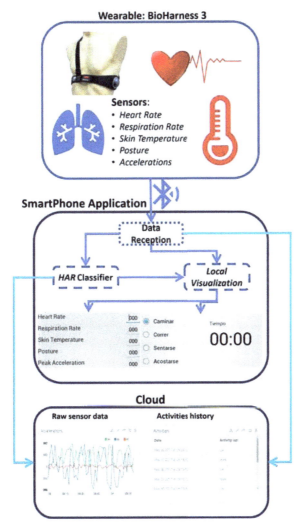

Figure 4. Solution architecture.

3.1. Hardware Component

The selected wearable device (Figure 5) was the Zephyr™ Bioharness 3 model K113045. This is a device that measures physiological variables [36]. It can measure heart rate, heart rate variability, and respiratory rate, it has a built-in accelerometer for posture and several activity analysis. These sensors are embedded on an elastic band that must be worn at chest height and pressured against the skin. The strap design allows it to be used under regular clothes, at any given place such as the work place, home and/or health centers.

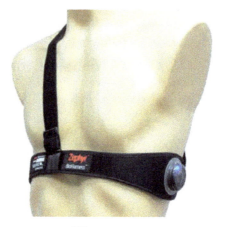

Figure 5. Zephyr™ Bioharness reference K113045.

The Bioharness 3 has a special characteristic that allows the device to not require the use of electrolytic gel nor any adhesive material for its proper operation, unlike other skin-contact devices. The device has an internal storage in which all the physiological data is saved as it performs measurements. When the Bioharness 3 connects via Bluetooth (class 1) to another device, it sends the storage data to the device. If the Bioharness 3 is connected while performing measurements, the data sent is the last measurement done. The strap of the Bioharness is washable and the plastic where all the sensors are can be submerged up to 1 m under water. Table 1 contains the detailed information as provided by the manufacturer.

Table 1. Bioharness 3 specifications.

Parameter	Value
HR Range:	25–240 BPM
BR Range:	4–70 BPM
Acc. Range:	±16 g
Battery type:	Rechargeable Lithium Polymer
Battery Life:	26 h per charge

3.2. Software Component

The software components of the system have two separate environments. The first is a smartphone application to gather, analyze, locally visualize and send the data to the cloud and is implemented for Android devices. The other one is a cloud environment. This allows for remote visualization of the raw data and activity recognition, and can have several configurable alarms.

3.2.1. Smartphone Application

The gathering of data, analysis and patient local interface of the project was implemented in a smartphone application compatible with Android 4.1 or higher. This application, as seen in the block diagram (Figure 4), has the following main functions:

- Data reception: The application has to receive Bioharness information packages using Bluetooth protocol. Then, the system has to discriminate the packages to get all the individual sensors' information.
- HAR classifier: With the raw sensor data, the app uses a classifier algorithm to build a recognition model to estimate the current activity.
- Local visualization: All the latest sensor data can be seen in the mobile screen, in conjunction with the latest recognized activity.

Both the sensor's raw data and the recognized activity is sent to the cloud system using either HTTP or Message Queue Telemetry Transport (*MQTT*) protocols.

3.2.2. Cloud

For the cloud environment, a platform called *Ubidots* was selected, which is a Colombian enterprise that offers cloud services for IoT solutions. This is an integrated solution that covers all necessary services to successfully implement small to medium solutions at a low cost. The services include: data storage (up to 500.000 data points), remote visualization (several widgets), basic data manipulation (basic algebraic operations) and programmable email and Short Message Service *SMS* alarms.

This platform was used to visualize the history of the activities recognized, heart rate, respiration rate, posture and the acceleration values. The alarms were configured for heart rate and respiration having minimum and maximum levels alerts. The last alarm was configured for a maximum level of the peak acceleration (behavior that indicates a fall) (Figure 6).

Figure 6. Example of the data visualization on the cloud service.

4. HAR System

Having the data collected, the next step is to perform the activity recognition. To do this, we performed a two-phase recognition algorithm. The first step is the feature extraction, which uses the raw data to create a set of features that are the input of the second phase: the classification phase.

The classification phase can be either a training step (see Section 2.1) that generates the recognition model or a recognition step that uses the recognition model and the extracted features to determine the activity performed.

4.1. Feature Extraction

The feature extraction is an algorithm that standardizes the raw data set, which reduces the amount of data to process. It performs analysis over the data set, such as structure detection, transformations or statistical functions. This allows the data to be organized in standard forms (mathematical functions) with an emphasis on how well the data explains these standard forms (fit). This process reduces the raw data to a finite and concrete set of aspects of the signal, which reduces the complexity of the recognition model.

For each available sensor, there can be several features that can be extracted and, if not well proposed, the classification problem can become an overdetermined system. To avoid an indeterminate problem, there are several options to decrease the amount of features used in the classification. To select the features and reduction methods appropriate to the problem, it is first necessary to see which data is available. For this project, the available data is:

1. Heart Rate.
2. Respiration Rate.
3. Posture.
4. Three-axis acceleration (X, Y, Z).
5. Peak Acceleration.
6. Electrocardiogram (*ECG*) magnitude.

In this case, most signals are time series measurements with low variability, meaning that the most appropriate feature extraction method is a structure detector without any prior processing [18]. The only exception to this is the three-axis acceleration, as these kinds of signals are too fluctuating and oscillatory to use a structure detection without pre-processing.

To decrease the unwanted behavior of the signal, two methods can be used: a principal component analysis (PCA) or a discrete cosine transform (DCT). Both extract the most relevant information of the signal, and the PCA uses statistical procedures to get a set of linearly uncorrelated variables. On the other hand, DCT uses a only real domain Laplace transform to get the frequency components of the signal. In this case and for this kind of signal, the best results are obtained using PCA over DCT [37].

The structure detection algorithm searches for the best fitting mathematical function for the selected data, a minimization of the mean square error between the data and the function (Equation (1)):

$$\sum_{t=1}^{n}(Y(t) - \widehat{Y}(t))^2 \text{ with } \widehat{Y}(t) = f(Y(t)). \tag{1}$$

The structural detectors, $f(Y(t))$, can be either lineal or nonlineal functions. These functions have different parameters that describe the behavior of the function. Modifying these parameter allows for fitting each signal iteration to a structure with a unique set of parameters. These parameters become the features selected to perform the recognition. To avoid a high cost search in mathematical structures, a few structures were selected. This was done according to the usual behavior and range of the available signals. Table 2 presents the selected mathematical functions from which the algorithm will try to fit the signals. This table also presents the different parameters that describe the functions, their restrictions, characteristics or formulas that define them.

Table 2. Attribute counting: value and probability.

Structure	Formula	Parameters
Linear: Constant	$f(Y(t)) = a$	$a = \frac{1}{n} \sum_{t=1}^{n} Y(t)$
Linear: line	$f(Y(t)) = a + b * t$	$a = \overline{Y} - b * \overline{t}, b = \dfrac{\sum_{t=1}^{n} (t - \overline{t})(Y(t)) - \overline{Y}}{\sum_{t=1}^{n} (t - \overline{t})^2}$ $\overline{Y} = \frac{1}{n} \sum_{t=1}^{n} Y(t), \overline{t} = \frac{1}{n} \sum_{t=1}^{n} t$
Non-Linear: Exponential	$f(Y(t)) = a * |b|^t + c$	$a, b, c \in \Re$
Non-Linear: Sine	$f(Y(t)) = a * Sin(t + b) + c$	$a \in \Re, b \in \Im, c = \overline{Y}$
Non-Linear: Triangle	$f(Y(t)) = \begin{cases} a + b & t \le c \\ a + 2bc - bt & c < t \end{cases}$	$a, b, c \in \Re$
Non-Linear: Trapezoid	$f(Y(t)) = \begin{cases} a + bt & t \le c \\ a + bc & c < t \le d \\ (a + bc + bd) - (bt) & t > d \end{cases}$	$a, b, c, d \in \Re$

The implemented algorithm that performs the feature extraction takes into account the current data set, the parameters of the structure with a priority on the less resource-consuming structures. The serial steps of this algorithm are:

1. Get the current data set.
2. Iterate and execute the linear structural detectors.
3. Calculate the mean square error for the best fitting lineal structures.
4. If the error is high enough, iterate and execute the nonlineal detectors.
5. Calculate the mean square error for the best fitting nonlineal structures.
6. Select the structure with the lowest error.
7. Pass the function parameters as the features to the classifier.

4.2. Classifier

There are several classifier algorithms that could work on an HAR system. The main kind of classifiers are:

- Rule trees: The rule tree, or decision tree is a hierarchy based model, in which all the features are mapped as nodes and each possible value for the feature is presented as a branch. These kinds of classifiers have a computational complexity of $O(\log(n))$, for n features. The most common decision trees models are D3/4/5, CLS, ASSISTANT, CART and C4.5.
- Bayesian methods: The Bayesian methods use conditional probabilities to calculate the likelihood of an event according to a set of features and their probabilities. The most common Bayesian methods are the Bayesian network and the naive Bayes, the later one being a special case that considers all features to be statistically independent of one another.
- Iteration based learning: The iteration based learning (IBL) are methods that learn the similarities and relations between features according to the training data set. These methods rely on high computational resources, large data sets and high storage capacities.
- Support vector machines: Support vector machines (SVM) have been widely used in HAR systems. They are based on several kernel functions that transform all the features to a higher degree space gaining information and relations between the features and the activities.
- Artificial neural networks: The artificial neural networks, (ANN or NN), use a weighted network to perform an analysis of the features and the activities performed. It imitates the neural synapses on biological brains to successfully recognize patters and models.

Following the requirements and constraints of the project, either IBL, SVN or ANN can be used, as the limited resources of the device in which the algorithm will be implemented prevent a successful implementation of these classifiers. Only a rule tree or Bayesian method could be implemented for this project. One algorithm of each kind of classifier was implemented in the mobile device to analyze the performance and the best was implemented in the system.

4.2.1. Rule Tree Classifier

For the rule tree classifiers, the C4.5 algorithm was selected. This algorithm uses different sets of rules according to the training data set, which divide the data set in different sections (gains) following the feature's relation to the activity to be recognized (attribute).

In Figure 7, a small example of this algorithm can be seen. The decision branches are probabilities of the feature to be in a certain location, which are expressed as binary variables. This algorithm has the following process to generate the rule tree:

1. Root calculation: To select a starting point, root node selection, it uses the feature with the highest gain, as it covers the most possible cases with the first iteration.
2. New branch search: The branch selection is done for each new node. It looks at the different features that the node can interact with and evaluates the possibility to recognize an attribute. The highest probability is assigned as a branch.
3. New node selection: After the branch is assigned, the algorithm evaluates the new node probability of attribute selection and selects a feature with the highest chance of attribute recognition.
4. Iteration: Iterate the steps 2 and 3 until the probability of attribute recognition is 1, which means it is the end of a branch. With the end of the branch, a rule is produced and associated with that attribute. If, after the iterations of all possible attributes a branch end has not been found, the starting node changes to the second highest gain.
5. Search through all attributes in the current node: Steps 2–4 are needed to be repeated until all attributes have a rule associated.

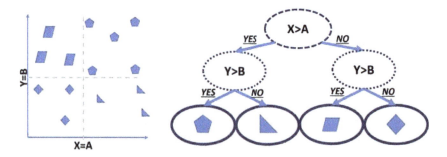

Figure 7. Example of the decision tree of a C4.5 Algorithm.

4.2.2. Bayesian Classifier

For the Bayesian classifier, a Naive Bayes algorithm was selected. This algorithm is based on the conditional probabilities of an activity being performed for each given set of features. It assumes that all features are statistically independent from one another. The algorithm begins by counting and identifying all the features available (attributes) and the activity to be recognized (classes). The rules are generated by using the conditional probability of the attribute for a determined class. This is done for all possible classes (Equation (2)):

$$P(C|x) = \frac{P(C)p(x|C)}{P(x)}. \tag{2}$$

This means attributes times classes number of rules in a single problem. After all rules are calculated, a conditional calculation of the rule for a given set of attributes and class is performed. It selects the higher probability rule to be assigned to the class (Figure 8).

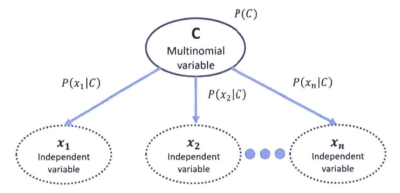

Figure 8. Example of the probability tree of the Bayes algorithm.

4.2.3. Classifier Selection

To test each classifier performance, each classifier was implemented in the target device and was presented with a single binary output problem. The problem consisted of a question: *¿Can I go out to play?*. To solve this, there were four features to evaluate it. Table 3 presents all attributes and the class with the possible values.

Table 3. Classifier's test problems.

Feature/Class	Possible Values
Feature: Outlook	Sunny: Overcast: Rain
Feature: Temperature	Cool: Mild: Hot
Feature: Humidity	Normal: High
Feature: Windy	Strong: Weak
Class: Outcome	Play: No Play

The training data set consisted of 14 samples, with no statistical correlation between instances. With this, each algorithm generated its own set of rules. The resulting rule sets were five rules for a C4.5 algorithm (Figure 9) and 36 for the Naive Bayes algorithm (Figure 10).

As expected, the Naive Bayes algorithm has a much larger rule set because it combines all the features, and then produces a rule with the probability obtained with the number of times found in the training set rule. The rule is maintained even when it does not provide useful information, unlike the C4.5 algorithm, which deletes them. The results of this test concluded that the C4.5 algorithm is the best suited for this project. Because the proposed prototype will have 18 features, the rule set size of the Naive algorithm will be much larger than the one of the C4.5, implicating a less cost efficient algorithm.

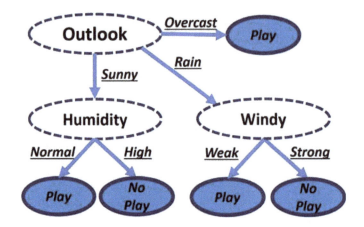

Figure 9. The classifier's test problem: C4.5 rule tree.

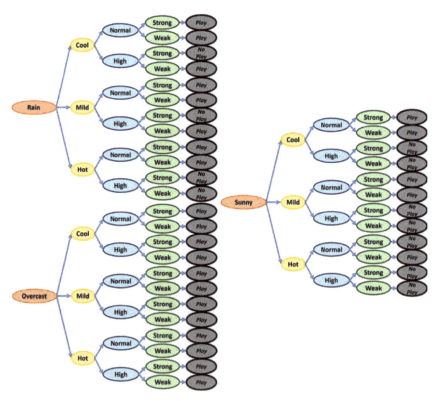

Figure 10. The classifier's test problem: Naive Bayes decision tree.

5. Experiment and Results

This project presents an HAR-IoT system that uses an *Food and Drug Administration* (FDA)-certified strap that measure several physiological variables, in conjunction with an Android application that has a C4.5 classifier and PCA to improve the results and a cloud-based system for remote visualization of the strap raw data and the classifier outcome. In this section, the experiment setup used to validate the system will be described in addition to the results obtained after the experiment being successful.

5.1. Experiment Description

The experiment had two phases: **Learning** and **Recognition**. During the training phase, three different test subjects (students with similar body types, age and weight) were performed several physical activities in a pre-established order (lie, sit, lie, walk, sit, jog, sit, jog and walk) while wearing the Bioharness. Each activity needs to be performed for a time frame of four minutes without changing activity or stopping. This time frames are divided in eight smaller frames that are called windows, which need to be at least 15 s long, as it is the minimum amount of time for the variable detection by the Bioharness. These windows were selected to have twice the amount of time, which is a balance between the length of the activity and the amount of data gathered for each activity. During the whole learning phase, the sensors acquire the data and the classifier generates the rules for the recognition. In addition, all data is available in the cloud to supervise the exercises in a remote location (if needed).

For the feature extraction, a single structure detector was selected: a straight line. This is due to the convergence time, meaning that we obtained two features per signal, and this resulted in size of the resulting matrix being twice the number of signals, in the columns, and the number of time windows, in the rows. As this classifier works only with qualitative values, all probabilities were assigned a qualitative equivalent. Therefore, using the mean values of each feature, a qualitative value can be assigned. If the value is less than the mean, it is assigned as low and high, otherwise.

After the classifier generates the rules (recognition model), the recognition phase can start. During this phase, the prototype will extract, evaluate and detect the user activity based on the recognition model that was found during the learning phase. This phase does not have a time frame and can start or stop at any given time. Finally, for redundancy purposes, a text file with the data recorded from each instance is created.

5.2. Learning Phase Results

The training data set was composed of 74 time windows (Figure 11). As the activities that require more energy could have changes with an exhaustion factor during a prolonged experiment, a recurrent rest was included to have the best and more consistent results (inclusion of sitting periods of time between walking and jogging activities). The learning phase ended with the following qualitative assignments (Table 4).

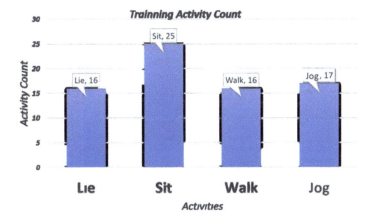

Figure 11. Training data set: activity count.

Table 4. Qualitative assignment.

Feature	# In Low	Low Probability	# In High	High Probability
heart rate 1	62	0.837	12	0.162
heart rate 2	4	0.054	70	0.945
respiratory rate 1	45	0.608	29	0.391
respiratory rate 2	10	0.135	64	0.865
posture 1	17	0.230	57	0.770
posture 2	1	0.013	73	0.986
acceleration peak 1	57	0.770	17	0.229
acceleration peak 2	39	0.527	35	0.473
amplitude ECG 1	58	0.783	16	0.216
amplitude ECG 2	73	0.986	1	0.013
acceleration X 1	3	0.040	71	0.959
acceleration X 2	2	0.027	72	0.973
acceleration Y 1	9	0.122	65	0.878
acceleration Y 2	2	0.027	72	0.973
acceleration Z 1	12	0.162	62	0.837
acceleration Z 2	2	0.027	72	0.973

After the feature extraction phase, the algorithm proceeds generating the rule tree to that specific training data set (Figure 12). For this project, there were 13 rules in total having a single recognition model for the different subjects that were involved during this phase (Table 5).

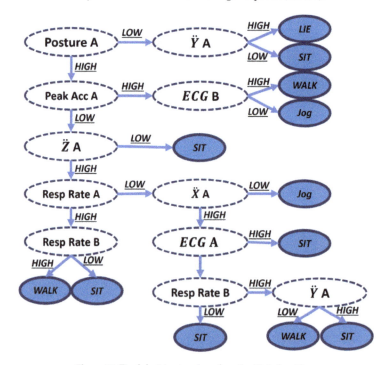

Figure 12. Final decision tree based on the C4.5 algorithm.

Table 5. Final rule set based on the C4.5 algorithm.

R#	Condition	Output
1	Post A=L; Ÿ A=H	Lie
2	Post A=L; Ÿ A=L	Sit
3	Post A=H; PAcc A=L; Ž A=L	Sit
4	Post A=H; PAcc A=L; Ž A= 1; Resp A, ECG A=L; Resp B=H; Ÿ A=H; PAcc B=H	Sit
5	Pos A=H; PAcc A=L; Ž A=1; Resp A=L; Ẍ A=H, ECG A=L; Resp B=H; Ÿ A=H; PAcc B=L	Sit
6	Post A=H; PAcc A=L; Ž A=1; Resp A=L; Ẍ A=H, ECG=L, Resp B=H, AccY A=L	Walk
7	Post A=H; PAcc A=L; Ž A=H; Resp A=L, AccX=L; ECG A=L; Resp B=L	Sit
8	Post A=H; PAcc A=L; Ž A=H; Resp A=L; Ẍ A=H, ECG A=H	Sit
9	Post A=H; PAcc A=L; Ž A=H; Resp A=L; Ẍ A=L	Jog
10	Post A=H; PAcc A=L; Ž A=H; Resp A=H; Resp B=H	Walk
11	Post A=H; PAcc A=L; Ž A=L; Resp A=H; Resp B=L	Sit
12	Post A=H; PAcc A=H; ECG B=L	Jog
13	Post A=H; PAcc A=H; ECG B=H	Walk

During the implementation phase, one of the test subjects was randomly asked to perform a total of 72 activity windows that were recollected. For these 72 windows, in 69 of them, the activity was successfully recognized, with only three that were wrongly classified. The confusion matrix of this implementation is present in Table 6. Likewise, a time series displaying each activity done and its activity recognized can be seen in Figure 13 and the same data in Table 7.

Table 6. Offline confusion table.

	Lie	Sit	Walk	Jog	Total	Error C
Lie	16	0	0	0	16	0
Sit	0	23	1	0	24	0.042
Walk	0	2	14	0	16	0.143
Jog	0	0	0	16	16	0
Total	16	25	15	16	72	
Error O	0	0.08	0.066	0		0.0417

Table 7. Table of results of the implementation phase.

Min:Sec	Activity	Classified	Score
0:00–4:00	Lie	Lie	True
4:30–8:00	Sit	Sit	True
8:30–12:00	Lie	Lie	True
12:30–13:00	Walk	Sit	False
13:30–16:00	Walk	Walk	True
16:30–20:00	Sit	Sit	True
20:30–24:00	Jog	Jog	True
24:30	Sit	Sit	True
25:00	Sit	Walk	False
25:30–28:00	Sit	Sit	True
28:30–32:00	Jog	Jog	True
32:30–36:00	Walk	Walk	True

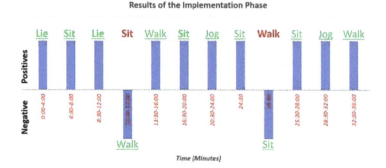

Figure 13. Results of the implementation phase.

6. Conclusions

This project successfully developed and implemented a novel human activity recognition system using a smartphone, the Bioharness 3 and a cloud system. For feature extraction, we used structural functions and, for pre-processing, a PCA algorithm was used. For the classifier, both the C4.5 and the Naive Bayes rules were implemented on the target hardware, but the C4.5 was selected instead of Naive Bayes due to the size of the rule set. The prototype in implementation phase got a score of 95.83% in the classification success. The project can be improved by adding more light-weight algorithms, different structural functions and the usage of more features. As future work, we presented the following path that contributed to the improvement of the presented project:

1. The comparison between the performance using multiple different structural functions: having different structural functions can optimize the resource consumption and decreasing the computational load of the classifier.
2. The broadening of the training data and robustness of the system: the system was implemented as a proof of concept of an HAR-IoT system, with a few users. These kinds of systems to be implemented in a product or in a trial must be trained with a high amount of data sets, as the recognition models should be trained user-independently so the recognition works independently from the subject using it. With our system, the test subjects were students with similar body types, ages and weights, which resulted in a functional system. For the later implementation, the system should have more training data. To improve the classification, another set of features such as mean, variance or percentile could be used along with the features we used to have more information. In addition, another recognition model could be used.
3. The implementation of the classifier on the cloud: The mayor constraint that the system present is the limited hardware available for the classifier. If the cloud resources can be available to perform the classification, more complex and better algorithms can be integrated into the system. There could even be a classifier redundancy system in which both the local application and the cloud system perform classification.

Acknowledgments: This work was supported by the Pontificia Universidad Javeriana (PUJ) in Bogota, Colombia under the project framework Centro de Excelencia y Apropiacion en Internet de las Cosas (CEA-IoT). The authors would like acknowledge the cooperation of all partners within the CEA-IoT and also like to thank all the institutions that supported this work: the Colombian Ministry for the Information and Communications Technology (Ministerio de Tecnologias de la Informacion y las Comunicaciones—MinTIC) and the Colombian Administrative Department of Science, Technology and Innovation (Departamento Administrativo de Ciencia, Tecnología e Innovacion—COLCIENCIAS) through the Fondo Nacional de Financiamiento para la Ciencia, la Tecnologia y la Innovacion Francisco José de Caldas (Project ID: FP44842-502-2015).

J. Sens. Actuator Netw. **2017**, *6*, 28

Author Contributions: Camilo Rodriguez implemented and tested the HAR application and classifiers, and Jose Cabra implemented the cloud and alarm system. Julian Colorado supervised the HAR implementation and testing. Diego Castro wrote, corrected and verified the publications and reports of the project. William Coral supervised, verified, corrected and guided the writing and testing protocol.

Conflicts of Interest: The authors declare no conflict of interest. The founding sponsors had no role in the design of the study; in the collection, analyses, or interpretation of data; in the writing of the manuscript, and in the decision to publish the results.

References

1. Gubbi, J.; Buyya, R.; Marusic, S.; Palaniswami, M. Internet of Things (IoT): A vision, architectural elements, and future directions. *Future Gener. Comput. Syst.* **2013**, *29*, 1645–1660.

2. Roncancio, G.; Espinosa, M.; Perez, M.R. Spectral Sensing Method in the Radio Cognitive Context for IoT Applications. In Proceedings of the 10th IEEE International Conference on Internet of Things (iThings 2017), Exeter, Devon, UK, 21–23 June 2017; pp. 1–6.

3. Cabra, J.; Castro, D.; Colorado, J.; Mendez, D.; Trujillo, L. An IoT approach for Wireless Sensor Networks Applied to E-Health Environmental Monitoring. In Proceedings of the 10th IEEE International Conference on Internet of Things (iThings 2017), Exeter, Devon, UK, 21–23 June 2017; pp. 14–22.

4. Velasquez, N.; Medina, C.; Castro, D.; Acosta, J.C.; Mendez, D. Design and Development of an IoT System Prototype for Outdoor Tracking. In Proceedings of the International Conference on Future Networks and Distributed Systems—ICFNDS '17, Cambridge, UK, 19–20 July 2017; pp. 1–6.

5. Teran, M.; Aranda, J.; Carrillo, H.; Mendez, D.; Parra, C. IoT-based System for Indoor Location using Bluetooth Low Energy. In Proceedings of the IEEE Colombian Conference on Communications and Computing (COLCOM2017), Cartagena, Colombia, 16–18 August 2017; IEEE Xplore Digital Library: Cartagena, Colombia, 2017.

6. Perera, C.; Liu, C.H.I.H.; Jayawardena, S.; Chen, M. A Survey on Internet of Things From Industrial Market Perspective. *IEEE Access* **2014**, *2*, 1660–1679.

7. Ganz, F.; Barnaghi, P.; Carrez, F. Information Abstraction for Heterogeneous Real World Internet Data. *IEEE Sens. J.* **2013**, *13*, 3793–3805.

8. Fitbit. Heart Rate Tracker: Fitbit Charge 2^{TM}. Available online: https://misfit.com/fitness-trackers/ (accessed on 25 November 2017).

9. Misfit. Misfit: Fitness Trackers & Wearable Technology—Misfit.com. Available online: https://www.fitbit.com/home (accessed on 25 November 2017).

10. Liu, C.H. A Survey of Context-Aware Middleware Designs for Human Activity Recognition Communications a Survey of Context-Aware Middleware Designs for Human Activity Recognition. *IEEE Commun. Mag.* **2014**, *52*, 24–31.

11. Sikder, F.; Sarkar, D. Log-sum distance measures and its application to human-activity monitoring and recognition using data from motion sensors. *IEEE Sens. J.* **2017**, *17*, 4520–4533.

12. Wang, Z.; Wu, D.; Chen, J.; Ghoneim, A.; Hossain, M.A. Human Activity Recognition via Game-Theory-Based Feature Selection. *IEEE Sens. J.* **2016**, *16*, 3198–3207.

13. Testoni, A.; Di Felice, M. A software architecture for generic human activity recognition from smartphone sensor data. In Proceedings of the 2017 IEEE International Workshop on Measurement and Networking (M&N), Naples, Italy, 27–29 September 2017; pp. 1–6.

14. Poppe, R. A survey on vision-based human action recognition. *Image Vis. Comput.* **2010**, *28*, 976–990.

15. Mo, L.; Li, F.; Zhu, Y.; Huang, A. Human physical activity recognition based on computer vision with deep learning model. In Proceedings of the IEEE Instrumentation and Measurement Technology Conference, Taipei, Taiwan, 23–26 May 2016.

16. Boufama, B. Trajectory-Based Human Activity Recognition from Videos. In Proceedings of the 3rd International Conference on Advanced Technologies for Signal and Image Processing—ATSIP'2017, Fez, Morocco, 22–24 May 2017; pp. 1–5.

17. Chetty, G.; White, M. Body sensor networks for human activity recognition. In Proceedings of the 2016 3rd International Conference on Signal Processing and Integrated Networks (SPIN), Noida, India, 11–12 February 2016; pp. 660–665.

18. Lara, O.D.; Labrador, M.A. A Survey on Human Activity Recognition using Wearable Sensors. *IEEE Commun. Surv. Tutor.* **2013**, *15*, 1192–1209.

19. Huang, H.; Member, S.; Li, X.; Member, S.; Sun, Y. A Triboelectric Motion Sensor in Wearable Body Sensor Network for Human Activity Recognition. In Proceedings of the 2016 IEEE 38th Annual International Conference of the Engineering in Medicine and Biology Society (EMBC), Orlando, FL, USA, 16–20 August 2016; pp. 4889–4892.

20. Rodriguez, C.; Castro, D.M.; Coral, W.; Cabra, J.L.; Velasquez, N.; Colorado, J.; Mendez, D.; Trujillo, L.C. IoT system for Human Activity Recognition using BioHarness 3 and Smartphone. In Proceedings of the International Conference on Future Networks and Distributed Systems—ICFNDS '17, Cambridge, UK, 19–20 July 2017; pp. 1–7.

21. Yazdansepas, D.; Niazi, A.H.; Gay, J.L.; Maier, F.W.; Ramaswamy, L.; Rasheed, K.; Buman, M.P. A Multi-Featured Approach for Wearable Sensor-based Human Activity Recognition. In Proceedings of the 2016 IEEE International Conference on Healthcare Informatics (ICHI), Chicago, IL, USA, 4–7 October 2016; pp. 423–431.

22. Koskimäki, H.; Siirtola, P. Adaptive model fusion for wearable sensors based human activity recognition. In Proceedings of the 2016 19th International Conference on Information Fusion (FUSION), Heidelberg, Germany, 5–8 July 2016; pp. 1709–1713.

23. Chen, Y.; Shen, C. Performance Analysis of Smartphone-Sensor Behavior for Human Activity Recognition. *IEEE Access* **2017**, *5*, 3095–3110.

24. Siirtola, P.; Röning, J. Recognizing human activities user-independently on smartphones based on accelerometer data. *Int. J. Interact. Multimedia Artif. Intell.* **2012**, *1*, 4–12.

25. Suciu, G.; Suciu, V.; Martian, A.; Craciunescu, R.; Vulpe, A.; Marcu, I.; Halunga, S.; Fratu, O. Big data, internet of things and cloud convergence—An architecture for secure e-health applications. *J. Med. Syst.* **2015**, *39*, 141.

26. Perez, A.J.; Zeadally, S.; Jabeur, N. Investigating Security for Ubiquitous Sensor Networks. *Procedia Comput. Sci.* **2017**, *109*, 737–744.

27. Tomic, I.; McCann, J.A. A Survey of Potential Security Issues in Existing Wireless Sensor Network Protocols. *IEEE Internet Things J.* **2017**, *4662*, 1.

28. Barakovic, S.; Kurtovic, E.; Bozanovic, O.; Mirojevic, A.; Ljevakovic, S.; Jokic, A.; Peranovic, M.; Husic, J.B. Security issues in wireless networks: An overview. In Proceedings of the 2016 XI International Symposium on Telecommunications (BIHTEL), Sarajevo, Bosnia and Herzegovina, 24–26 October 2016; pp. 1–6.

29. Rodrigues, L.M.; Mestria, M. Classification methods based on bayes and neural networks for human activity recognition. In Proceedings of the 12th International Conference on Natural Computation, Fuzzy Systems and Knowledge Discovery (ICNC-FSKD), Changsha, China, 13–15 August 2016; pp. 1141–1146.

30. Nazábal, A.; García-Moreno, P.; Artés-Rodríguez, A.; Ghahramani, Z. Human Activity Recognition by Combining a Small Number of Classifiers. *IEEE J. Biomed. Health Inform.* **2016**, *20*, 1342–1351.

31. Postma-Nilsenová, M.; Postma, E.; Tates, K. Automatic detection of confusion in elderly users of a web-based health instruction video. *Telemed. J. E-Health* **2015**, *21*, 514–519.

32. Armentia, A.; Gangoiti, U.; Priego, R.; Estévez, E.; Marcos, M. Flexibility support for homecare applications based on models and multi-agent technology. *Sensors* **2015**, *15*, 31939–31964.

33. Alkmim, M.B.; Marcolino, M.S.; Figueira, R.M.; Sousa, L.; Nunes, M.S.; Cardoso, C.S.; Ribeiro, A.L. Factors Associated with the Use of a Teleconsultation System in Brazilian Primary Care. *Telemed. J. E-Health* **2015**, *21*, 473–483.

34. Sankaranarayanan, J.; Murante, L.J.; Moffett, L.M. A retrospective evaluation of remote pharmacist interventions in a telepharmacy service model using a conceptual framework. *Telemed. J. E-Health* **2014**, *20*, 893–901.

35. Sun, X.; Kashima, H.; Ueda, N. Large-scale personalized human activity recognition using online multitask learning. *IEEE Trans. Knowl. Data Eng.* **2013**, *25*, 2551–2563.

36. Johnstone, J.A.; Ford, P.A.; Hughes, G.; Watson, T.; Mitchell, A.C.S.; Garrett, A.T. Field Based Reliability and Validity of the Bioharness™ Multivariable Monitoring Device. 2012. Available online: https://www.zephyranywhere.com/system/overview (accessed on 1 September 2017).

37. He, Z.; Jin, L. Activity recognition from acceleration data based on discrete consine transform and SVM. In Proceedings of the IEEE International Conference on Systems, Man and Cybernetics, San Antonio, TX, USA, 11–14 October 2009; pp. 5041–5044.

 Journal of
Sensor and
Actuator Networks

Article

Extended Batches Petri Nets Based System for Road Traffic Management in WSNs †

Youness Riouali , Laila Benhlima and Slimane Bah

AMIPS, Mohammadia School of Engineers, Mohammed V University of Rabat, Rabat 10000, Morocco; laila.benhlima@gmail.com (L.B.); slimane.bah@emi.ac.ma (S.B.)

* Correspondence: youness.riouali@yahoo.fr

† This paper is an extended version of our paper published in Riouali, Y.; Benhlima, L.; Bah, S. Toward a Global WSN-Based System to manage road traffic. In Proceedings of the International Conference on Future Networks and Distributed Systems, Cambridge, UK, 19–20 July 2017.

Received: 1 October 2017; Accepted: 28 November 2017; Published: 4 December 2017

Abstract: One of the most critical issues in modern cities is transportation management. Issues that are encountered in this regard, such as traffic congestion, high accidents rates and air pollution etc., have pushed the use of Intelligent Transportation System (ITS) technologies in order to facilitate the traffic management. Seen in this perspective, this paper brings forward a road traffic management system based on wireless sensor networks; it introduces the functional and deployment architecture of the system and focuses on the analysis component that uses a new extension of batches Petri nets for modeling road traffic flow. A real world implementation of visualization and data analysis components were carried out.

Keywords: road traffic modelling; petri net; architecture; wireless sensor networks (WSN); traffic congestion; traffic management; traffic monitoring

---

1. Introduction

The continous development in highly integrated microelectronics technologies and Information and Communication technology (ICT) have made the wireless sensor networks (WSNs) concept a reality. WSNs, that feature high flexibililty, good scalability and reliability, are emerging as one of the most promising solutions to sense, collect, process and disseminate information from various environmental phenomena. WSN has been widely utilized in various fields including transportation [1], environmental monitoring [2], healthcare [3], battlefield monitoring and surveillance [4], inventory tracking [5], security monitoring [6], civil applications [7,8], and so on. It consists of tiny wireless-capable sensor devices that are battery powered, sense the surrounding environment and have wireless communication, data storage, computation and signal processing capabilities. The data collected from sensor devices is usually sent to a centralized node called sink (or base station) that can act as user interfaces or gateway with other networks [9].

Nowadays, the concept of modern city has emerged to be complex systems that, on one hand invest in human and social capital and in deployment of advanced information and communication technologies, and yet, on the other hand, demand huge quantities of resources and discharge waste into environment [10]; although cities cover only 2.8% of Earth's surface area, they consume 75% of its global resource and produce an equivalent proportion of waste and pollution that leads to a massive negative impacts [11,12].

The world population has continued to grow rapidly and its concentration in cities keeps rising at an ever-faster pace. It has been projected that the total population in urban areas will jump from 3.6 billion to 6.3 billion by 2050, which means approximatively 67% of the world population. This mass urbanization is bringing with it an inescapable tide of issues such as environment pollution, traffic congestion, energy consumption and inefficient transport systems.

Strictly linked to transportation, one of the most critical issues in modern cities is transportation management. Issues such as traffic congestion and high accidents rate affects environment, economies and human health [13], have pushed the use of Intelligent Transportation System (ITS) technologies in order to facilitate the traffic management or planning to do so in the coming years especially in developing countries [14].

The use of WSNs in Intelligent Transportation System applications such as traffic monitoring and traffic light control has been experiencing a rapid growth [15,16].

Traffic road modeling is a crucial element in traffic management [17,18]. It grows unceasingly clear and has attracted considerable attention of both academic researchers and industry practitioners. There are various criteria for categorizing traffic flow models, according to the level of detail, whether they operate in continuous or discrete time (or even event-based), or whether they are deterministic or stochastic [19–21].

Based on the level of detail provided to describe traffic and also the mathematical formulas, Traffic flow can be analyzed macroscopically, microscopically or mesoscopically [22,23]:

Macroscopic models deal with traffic at a high aggregate level. For example, the traffic variables are represented using aggregated characteristics as density, flow rate and velocity.

Microscopic models are based on the explicit consideration of the interactions between individual vehicles within a traffic stream.

Mesoscopic models or kinetic models: The traffic flow is described at an intermediate level of detail. The family of mesoscopic models describes the behavior of individuals in aggregate terms for instance in probability distributions. Thus, traffic is modeled as groups of traffic entities that are governed by flow laws without taking into consideration interactions between individual vehicles.

Petri nets modelling have been approached to study traffic flow at the macroscopic level and we have adopted them as a basis to model the road traffic flow [24].

Petri net are suitable to represent urban traffic systems because they allow representation of states that are distributed, deterministic, concurrent and continuous, and can model shared resources, synchronous and asynchronous communications etc. Moreover, Petri net is a useful formalism for optimizing traffic control and management system. Batch Petri net is an extension of Petri nets; it has been introduced for modelling systems with discrete evolution, continuous evolution and accumulation phenomena. Batch petri nets are proven to be efficient and accurate representation of systems with accumulated continuous elements [25,26]. However, they aren't able to express accurately all rules and situations in traffic applications such as traffic that has to stop when approaching an intersection and give way rules. We have proposed in [24] an extension of Batch Petri nets that generalize the traffic flow modelling, enable the representation of some complex cases and address the issue of improving energy efficiency in road network monitoring since it involves the minimum number of sensors to capture traffic flow and simulate its evolution over time. To exploit this modelling for managing the traffic dynamicity, we have designed a global system based on wireless sensor networks for achieving energy efficiency during traffic flow monitoring and providing an accurate traffic state estimate and prediction of the overall network. In this paper, we present an overview of the system with its functional architecture and a description of the flow in case of a chosen scenario.

This article is an extended and revised version of our earlier conference paper [27]. The main addition with regard to the conference paper consists in presenting an enhanced architecture of WSN-based traffic management system, and containing additional details about the developed prototype.

The rest of the paper is organized as follow. In Section 2, the related works are reviewed. Our solution, WSN-based traffic management system with its functional architecture and components are described in Sections 3 and 4 highlights the data analysis component of the proposed WSN based traffic management including the used model for road traffic flow evolution. Details for the deployment architecture as well as prototype of the system analytics and visualization components are reported in Section 5. Section 6 concludes the paper along with description of the intended future work.

2. Related Work

In [28], a scheme that uses a multi-hop replay wireless sensor network (WSN) to monitor urban transport vehicles has been presented and a traffic monitoring system based on WSN that is applicable to all types of city environment was designed. The nodes are distributed dynamically based on the traffic flow forecasts and their statistical law of mobility in order to monitor the important roads that are easily blocked and find out the time changing law of traffic congestion, and then put focus on monitoring them. The paper proposed the use of gray model in order to forecast the traffic flow. Gray model is simple and doesn't require a huge amount of available data like many other methods. However, one of its disadvantages is that it cannot deal with non-linear structure of data which decreases its efficiency and competitiveness in forecasting road traffic flow on complex networks.

A wireless sensor network based monitoring system has been proposed in [29] with dynamic mathematical model for managing road traffic in important intersections of a city. It aims at reducing congestion by broadcasting the traffic status when it comes to a congested status. Monitoring and calculating the congestion level on the most important intersections is not always a relieable approach since too many cars on intersections is only one reason of traffic congestion. Other causes such as double parking and events that may change traffic dynamics at any place within roads are not taking into consideration.

Nafi et al. [30] presents a Vehicular Ad-hoc Network (VANET) based predictive road traffic management system (PRTMS). PRTMS is simple and uses a modified linear prediction algorithm to estimate traffic intensities at different intersections using a vehicle to infrastructure (V2I) scheme. However, the proposed system architecture, which relies mainly on information received from vehicles and V2I communications requires a significant power resources.

In [31], A traffic congestion detection system was presented that combines vehicle-to-vehicle (V2V), vehicle to infrastructure and infrastructure-to-infrastructure (I2I) connectivity and big data. The system aims at decreasing travel time and reducing CO_2 emissions by allowing drivers to identify traffic jam and change accordingly their routes. The proposed system monitors, processes and stores large amounts of data into a Cassandra table which is one of the open-source distributed NoSQL databases. Through a series of algorithms, a big data cluster identifies vehicular congestion and informs drivers so that they can make real time decisions and avoid it. A weakness of this work is that the system cannot answer queries. For instance, it cannot evaluate the impact of upcoming events such as road works on traffic flow state.

Iwasaki et al. [32] proposed a method for stop line detection using thermal images taken with infrared cameras under different weather conditions. According to the first method, the windshield of a vehicle and its surroundings are used as the target of pattern recognition. The vehicle detection process involves spatio-temporal image processing by computing standard deviations of pixel values, vehicle pattern recognition by using Viola-Jones detector [33,34] that considers the windshield and its surroundings as the target of pattern recognition, and correction procedures for misrecognized vehicles.

Since the vehicle detection accuracy decreases in low temperatures because the temperature of the windshield is usually similar to that of the windshield exterior, Iwasaki et al. proposed a second method, to deal with this limitation, that detects vehicles based on tire thermal energy reflection area on the road surface. The method is based on the idea that the temperature difference between the tires and the road surface is considerably high in cold weather. By combining both methods, the overall vehicle detection accuracy was highly maintained under various environmental conditions and an automatic traffic flow monitoring was achieved by computing the number of vehicles in the target area and the degree of movement of each vehicle.

Another approach proposed in [35] uses vehicles as mobile sensors for sensing the urban traffic and send the reports to a traffic-monitoring center (TMC) for traffic estimation. The so-called probe vehicles (PVs), i.e., taxis and buses that are equipped with the necessary devices to transmit traffic conditions to the TMC at regular time intervals, and floating cars (FCs), such as patrol cars for surveillance, report periodically their speed and location to traffic-monitoring center.

Since PVs cannot cover all roads in most of the time, a Matrix Completion (MC) has been proposed to reconstruct data in empty rows in the collected probe data. In order to facilitate MC based estimation and improve its performance, Du et al. proposed a floating car control algorithms. However, the proposed approach doesn't take into account different sources of traffic data and correlation of road sections.

Based on the previous studies and literature reviews, the challenge of designing a monitoring energy-efficiency system while ensuring the accuracy of traffic flow estimation and prediction remains open.

The system we propose aims at enabling energy-efficient management and providing accurate estimation and prediction of road traffic by:

- Modelling the traffic in order to predict its evolution in accordance with deploying of the minimum number of sensors.
- Estimating vehicles dispatched in a road intersection using statistical models
- Taking into account events for predicting traffic status

3. WSN-Based Traffic Management System (WTMS)

In this section we present functional architecture of our management system. The system takes advantage of WSNs technology, traffic modelling and data learning approaches for dealing with traffic-related challenges and leading to more efficient and safer travels. Before turning to this discussion we introduce an overview of the system.

3.1. Overview of the WTMS

The proposed road traffic management system aims to monitor the road network and proactively provide information about traffic flow. It takes input from various sources, mainly road sensors, and internet to ingest weather and events information such as national celebrations, sportive events (soccer games etc.). Data afforded from vehicles, especially neighboring traffic flow and average speed, can be included in the system's input in order to refine better the output and the final model, and then model the road network and the traffic flow dynamics spatially as well as temporally, and yield to an overall traffic flow of road network.

This allows the cars, buses, taxis to respond to the city's needs on the fly.

Raw data always goes through at least one filter before being delivered to models and estimation algorithms. The output of these models is used in various applications such as adaptive traffic signal control and dynamic route guidance and is sent to third parties for consumption or analysis. Consequently, reliable information can be shareable with the public over internet. For instance, the road users can be informed of the traffic congestion and real time traffic situations through mobile applications.

In the following section we briefly describe the WTMS through its components.

3.2. WTMS Architecture

Our WSN-based Traffic Management System is composed of several components which are: Data Acquisition, Data Preprocessing, Data analysis, Visualization and Reports, System Settings and Administration, Traffic data repositories and finally Applications. All these components use Data Communication component. Figure 1 illustrates the functional architecture of the system. In the next, we describe each component.

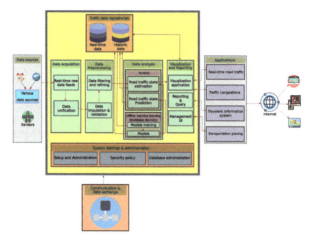

Figure 1. Traffic management system (WTMS) architecture.

3.2.1. Acquisition Component

Data acquisition consists of gathering the raw data and passing it to data preprocessing component. The data can be acquired in different formats and it draws from heterogeneous sources. This component has to ingest all needed information that will be sent to the other components in a unified format. Data acquisition contains two subcomponents:

Real-time raw data feeds

Real time data feeds are collected through sensors. This data includes traffic volume, average speed, roadway conditions. This part of system has to deal with two approaches of data acquisition:

- Pull-based approach: it allows users to selectively acquire and query the data at preferred point in time, within a specific time interval or within a user-defined frequency acquisition.
- Push-based approach: In this approach, data acquisition is executed in regular periods. Data are disseminated proactively through sensors, i.e., the sensors can decide when to send data to a centre node such as a sink.

Adding to roadside sensors, other sources of data can be taken into consideration such as vehicles, especially regarding the movement count estimates, and traffic.

Data unification

Data unification means the integration of data culled from raw sensor data and a variety of other structured of unstructred sources such as scheduled events, weather information, road works etc. and the representation of this heterogeneous data in the same unified format.

3.2.2. Data Preprocessing

This component is responsible for the preparation of raw data for further utilisation and providing the cleaned data; the collected data must undergo a preprocessing step where it must be checked, filtered and completed in order to avoid as much noise as possible and being usable by models. Data preprocessing includes:

Data filtering and refining

Data in real-world contain redundant information. Data filtering and refining is the process of cleaning data by filtering duplications, data that contradicts itself and noise and ensuring data integrity. This is essential for obtaining consistent modeling results.

Data imputation and validation

Due to sensors malfunction, measurements can be erroneous, missed or corrupted. Therefore, some preliminary tasks need to be performed for effeciently analyzing the data such as data imputation and data validation. In this step, imputing missing values and examining data quality and reliability are performed.

3.2.3. Data Analysis

Data analysis aims at turning recieved data into information that guides effective decision making through estimating the current traffic state and traffic flow dynamics evolution over time and space. To this end, Data analysis has two aspects: offline machine learning for knowledge discovery and runtime compenents for applying the knowledge during the execution.

Offline machine learning includes:

Models training

This component carries out the necessary machine learning tools to train models based on new data.

Models

It consists of mathematical equations and parameters that are trained and calibrated, but are improved using additional knowledge.

The runtime part is composed of road traffic state estimation and road traffic state prediction:

Road traffic state estimation

It is the most mandatory component of the system since it transforms multisource traffic data into useful traffic information and provides the basis for additional application and practices. In this subcomponent, we use the generalized nondeterministic batch Petri net formalism to model the road traffic for each segment in one hand. In another hand, the necessary models, when needed, are deployed and executed.

Road traffic state prediction

Given historical information, or driving correlation and dependencies among the road network, this module is performing short and long-term predictions using models that were built offline. We aim at predicting traffic flow from few minutes to several hours ahead.

3.2.4. Visualization and Reports

The output of models can be used for further analysis. Converting models results into well-formed forms for analysis, visualization or end-user information is a real benefit from data analysis component. This can simply enhance decision making. In addition, analyzed data and reports can help traffic planner to make well-informed decisions and interact fast to different traffic situations and evaluate or design transportation facilities. Or on another side, it can enhance the individual traffic participants' navigation.

Visualization applications refer to a web-based tool that provides a holistic view of the overall road network while displaying the emergency events as well such as congestion. Reporting and Query refers to tools that offers traffic reports for advising travelers and traffic managers and planners and allows users to interactively query up-to-date information. Management UI is a set of user interfaces for that enables traffic planners and managers to set up traffic and roads parameters such as road length, maximum velocity and traffic signal cycle lengths and to enhance their interventions through broadcasting notifications and alerts to travelers.

3.2.5. System Settings and Administration

System settings and administration component handles prepares the sensor infrastructure, it allows configuration of sensor data, that are needed for applications, and intervals. It allows displaying and modifying all configurations. This includes security policies, user roles and database administration.

3.2.6. Traffic Data Repositories

It supports the storing of raw traffic data and archiving of historical data for use as needed. The stored data concerns the data aggregated from sensors, the necessary data structure for modelling the traffic flow, the historical data to train the machine learning or statistical models to achieve prediction, etc.

3.2.7. Communication and Data Exchange

This allows the network to communicate the traffic information and exchange data between its various components.

In the next section we will focus on the data analysis component and more precisely on generalized nondeterministic batch Petri net model that we adopt for this system.

4. Road Traffic State Estimation

Road traffic flow is a very complex phenomenon. To approach its dynamic evolution we proposed the generalized nondeterministic batch Petri net [24] since it deals with both continuous and discrete states that characterize traffic flow and allows modeling its behavior along roads for complex cases.

4.1. Background on Triangular Batches Petri Net

In this section, we introduce Petri nets concepts and the theoretical background of our extension of batches Petri nets model.

4.1.1. Petri Nets

In his PhD Thesis, Carl Adam Petri introduced Petri nets in order to represent the global state of a system as composed of a set of local states [36]. Petri nets are both a graphical and mathematical tool for design, modeling and formal analysis of various discrete event systems [37]. Being a graphical tool, it allows to easily represent the different interactions in a complex system such as concurrency, parallelism, synchronization, non-determinism, communication, alternatives and so on by means of only few elements types. Being a mathematical tool, it allows to fomally model these interactions and analyze the properties of the modeled system [38].

A Petri net can be defined as a directed graph that consists of two types of nodes interpreted as places and transitions where an arc can only connect two nodes of different types [39]. Places are drawn as round shapes (circles or eclipses) to model different states of a system. Transitions are depicted as rectangular shapes (rectangles or bars) to represent events or activities that can cause the change of a system state. An arc connects a place to a transition or vice versa, it models the flow of processes through the system and the abstract relationship between a place and a transition. The dynamic behavior of a system is introduced by means of tokens into places where every place holds either zero or more tokens that are graphically appear as solid dots in places. At any given time, the distribution of tokens among the places, termed Petri net marking, determines the current state of the modeled system. A marked Petri net consequently is used to study dynamic behavior of the modeled system.

Formally, a Petri net is quadruplet $N = (P, T, Pre, Post)$ where:

- P and T are, respectively, disjoint non-empty finite sets of places and transitions;
- Pre: $P \times T \rightarrow N$ is the backward incidence matrix, $Post$: $T \times P \rightarrow N$ is the forward incidence matrix.

Over the years, several extensions of the original Petri net model have been developed, we mention in the following paragraph some of them in order to better understand the proposed model in this paper.

4.1.2. Generalized Batch Petri Nets

Hybrid Petri nets (HPN) contain two parts: a discrete part and a continuous part since they include discrete and continuous places and transitions. For instance, in traffic system, traffic lights are modeled as discrete places and transitions and road sections can be modeled by continuous places as can be illustrated in Figure 2.

Figure 2 shows an example of signalized street with its HPN model where $P^C = (p1, p2)$ is the set of continuous places representing the two sections of the road, $P^D = (p4, p5)$ is the set of discrete places that models the signal system switching between red and green. $T^C = (t1, t2, t3)$ is the set of continuous transitions model the limit between two sections and $T^D = (t4, t5)$ is the set of the discrete transitions which represent the delay associated with every section for switching between green and red lights.

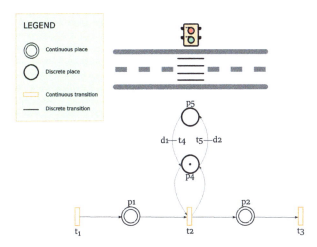

Figure 2. Signalized road and the HPN model.

Batches Petri nets are a modeling tool for systems with accumulation. The new with this extension of HPN is the introduction of batch concept; a batch (β_r) is a group of entities whose movement through a transfer zone (i.e., a portion of road), and is characterized by continuous variables, namely the length, the density, and the head position. Thus, batch places represent the delays on continuous flow and batch transitions behave like continuous transitions are associated with a maximum flow.

4.1.3. The Triangular Batches Petri Net

In the following, some of the main definitions of triangular batches Petri nets are presented.

Definition 1. *The triangular batches Petri net can be defined by the following elements:*
   A triangular batch Petri net is $6 - tuplet$ $N = (P, T, Pre, Post, \gamma, Time)$ where
   P is a non-empty finite set of places partitioned into discrete (P^D), continuous (P^C) and batch places (P^B): $P = P^C \cup P^D \cup P^B$; Continuous places are used to model variables real values; While discrete places are used in modelling variables with integer values; Batch Places are used to model transfer zones whose elements move at the same speed.

J. Sens. Actuator Netw. **2017**, *6*, 30

T is a non-empty finite set of transitions partitioned into discrete (T^D), continuous (T^C) and batch transitions (T^B).

Pre, respectively Post: $(P^D \times T \rightarrow N) \cup ((P^C \cup P^B) \times T \rightarrow R \geq 0)$ are defining the weight of arcs directed from places to transitions and the weight of arcs directed from transitions to places.

$\gamma : P^B \rightarrow \Re^4 \geq 0$ is the batch place function. It associates with each batch place $p_i \in P^B$ the $4-uplet$ of continuous characteristics $g(p_i) = (V_i, d_i^{max}, S_i, \Phi^{max})$ that represents, respectively, a speed, a maximum density, a length and a maximum flow.

Time: it represents the firing delay in case of discrete transitions and the maximal firing flow in case of continuous or batches transitions.

For analysis of Petri net, two notions are needed: Preset and Postset since they are crucial in modelling, respectively, pre-conditions and post-conditions of a system changes.

Definition 2 (Preset and Postset). *Let $m =| P |$ and $n =| T |$ be the number of places and transitions in a TrBPN, respectively. The preset of a place p (resp. of a transition t) is defined as $\cdot p = \{t \in T \mid Post(p,t) > 0\}$ (resp. $\cdot t = \{p \in P \mid Pre(p,t) > 0\}$) and the postset is defined as $\cdot p = \{t \in T \mid Pre(p,t) > 0\}$ (resp. $\cdot t = \{p \in P \mid Post(p,t) > 0\}$).*

Batches are moving at different speeds. For controlling this, the concept of controllable batch is introduced.

Definition 3 (Controllable batch). *Additionally to the three basic characteristics of a batch, a controllable batch $(C\beta_r)$ is characterized also by the speed. $C\beta_r(\tau) = (l_r(\tau), d_r(\tau), x_r(\tau), v_r(\tau)) \in \Re^+ \times \Re^+ \times \Re^+ \times \Re^+$. An instantaneous batch flow of $(C\beta_r)(\tau)$ is given by: $\phi_r(\tau) = v_r(\tau) \cdot d_r(\tau)$.*

The marking of the batch place is a series of batches ordered by their head positions.

The moving of batches and their evolution depend on the state of batch places and are governed by various functions, namely: Creation, Destruction, Merging and splitting.

Definition 4 (Dynamics of controllable batches). *For every batch place, four continuous dynamic functions can change the values of its batches and then change its marking.*

Creation: A controllable batch $C\beta_r(\tau) = (0, d_r(\tau), 0, v_r(\tau))$, is created inside a batch place p_i and added to its marking if its input flow is not null i.e., With

$$d_r(\tau) = \frac{\phi_i^{in}(\tau)}{v_i(\tau)}$$

Destruction: A controllable batch is destroyed, if its length is null i.e., $l_r(\tau) = 0$ and it is not a created batch i.e., $x_r(\tau) \neq 0$, such that $C\beta_r(\tau) = 0$ and removed from the marking.

Merging: A controllable batch is obtained from the fusion of two batched, if they are in contact with the same density and the same speed. Consider the two controllable batches: $(C\beta_r)(\tau) = (l_r(\tau), d_r(\tau), x_r(\tau), v_r(\tau))$ and $C\beta_h(\tau) = (l_h(\tau), d_h(\tau), x_h(\tau), v_h(\tau))$ with $x_r(\tau) = x_h(\tau) + l_r(\tau)$, $v_r(\tau) = v_h(\tau)$ and $d_r(\tau) = d_h(\tau)$, $(C\beta_r)(\tau)$ becomes $(C\beta_r)(\tau) = (l_r(\tau) + l_r(\tau), d_r(\tau), x_r(\tau), v_r(\tau))$ and $C\beta_h(\tau)$ is destroyed $C\beta_h = 0$.

Splitting: A controllable can be split into two batches in contact with same density and the same speed.

The aforementioned models aren't able to express accurately some rules and situations in traffic applications such as priority roads, traffic that has to stop when approaching an intersection. For example, the traffic behavior can change significantly due to the type of intersections whether they are right-of-way or roundabout, the presence of road signs or not. Therefore, taking into consideration non deterministic time based traffic dynamics will lead to improve modelling accuracy and generalization.

J. Sens. Actuator Netw. **2017**, *6*, 30

4.2. Our Extension: Generalized Nondeterministic Batch Petri Net

The batch Petri net that will be presented in this section is based mainly on the same principles as triangular batch Petri net such as triangular fundamental diagram, generalizes the traffic flow modelling and tackles other cases of road networks. We extend the existing formalization to support, on one hand, dependencies between traffic flow dynamics and external conditions, and on the other hand, events that change dynamics at any place within roads.

To illustrate this, consider the following example:

Example 1. *At T-intersection, the batch coming from section S_2 and aiming to turn left, it must give way to the oncoming batch from section S_1. Figure 3 illustrates this giving way case.*

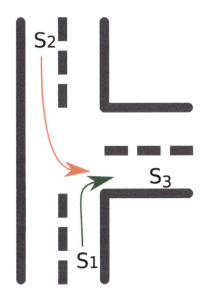

Figure 3. T-intersection with give way rule, as depicted in the example.

By considering the above example and other such situations, the traffic behavior or the batch is not only depending on simple delay times or flow rules but can also depend on more complex uncontrollable events that may even change completely the batch characteristics. In the triangular batches Petri net modeling, these cases and others are not modeled precisely or are not considered; For instance, in the example mentioned above, the batch (coming from S_2) doesn't have necessary the same behavior since the batch can be divided according to the other traffic behaviors (batch coming from S_1); the condition that has to be filled is neither delay time nor flow rule, the traffic has to stop and wait for the way to be clear.

The proposed generalized nondeterministic batch Petri net (GNBPN) seeks to complete Petri net formalism by adding new non-deterministic time based transitions which we call untimed transition in order to formally represent changes that depend on external conditions (i.e., vehicles move at intersections only when the road ahead is empty). This allows us to include uncontrollable events which cannot be fixed in time. Moreover, we enrich the model to take into consideration relationships to previous observed changes at a given station and/or to neighboring roads at the same time; for instance, at fork, splitting a traffic flow into more accurate proportions can depend on temporal and spatial information (presence of an event, roadworks, etc.). The benefit of the added statistical feature is to enhance the firing rule of batch transitions.

Generalized nondeterministic batch Petri net (GNBPN) is defined formally as follows [24]: $(P, T, Pre, Post, C, f, Prio, E)$ Where:

1. *P*, *Pre* and *Post* are respectively the set of places, the pre-incidence and the post-incidence matrices;
2. *T* is a finite set of transitions that are partitioned into the three set of timed (T^t), untimed (T^u) and batch (T^B) transitions $T = T^t \cup T^u \cup T^B$;
3. *C* is the "characteristic function". It associates with every batch place three continuous characteristics $(V_i, d_i^{max}, S_i, N_s)$ that represent respectively speed, maximum density, and length and the total number of segments of the batch place;
4. *f*: is an application that associates a non-negative number to every transition:

    -   if $t_j \in T^t$, then $f(t_j) = d_j$ denotes the firing delay associated with the timed transition expressed in time unit;
    -   if $t_j \in T^B$, then $f(t_j) = \Phi_j$ denotes the maximal firing flow associated with the batch transition expressed in entities/time unit and estimated by statistical models in case of multiple outputs;
        We use the symbol *f* to refer to firing rules of transitions which can depend on both delay times and flow rules.

5. *Prio* is the priority of a transition according to the output flow of a place, $\forall t_j \in T^u$. This priority's feature is added to support non-deterministic time based transitions.

For better understanding of the concept of GNBPN model, we illustrate the primitives of the proposal petri net using the example of T-intersection where the batch, coming from section S_2 and aiming to turn left, must give way to the oncoming batch from section S_1 (Figure 3). The Sections S_1 and S_2 are represented respectively, by batch places p_1, p_2. The intersection is modelled by the batch place p_{21}. While the maximum inputs flow of S_1 and S_2 are modelled by the batch transitions t_1 and t_2.

The give way rule within intersection is modelled by the untimed transition $t23$ representing that vehicles at section $S2$ have to wait until the traffic ahead clears the intersection. Maximum flows Φ_{13}, Φ_{21} and Φ_3 of batch transitions t_{13}, t_{21} and t_3 represent, respectively, the maximum output flow of Sections S_1 and S_2 and the maximum input flow of section S_3. The associated model is shown in Figure 4.

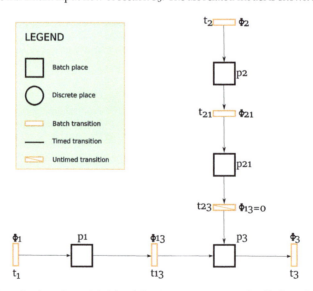

Figure 4. Generalized nondeterministic batch Petri net representation of traffic flow of the use case.

5. Implementation

This section presents a deployment architecture that uses wireless sensor network and then it introduces an implementation of Visualization component and Traffic Modelling and Analytics component of the WTSM.

5.1. Deployment Architecture of WTMS

All nodes in this network are connected directly to a base station or via a relay node if needed and share their data. On another hand base stations model the traffic flow based on the received data and then output the current traffic flow state. Consequently, they send the estimated traffic flow to the Control manager that evaluates all the received traffic flow estimations and provides an overall traffic estimation for the network. Such that, if congestion is detected, the Control manager broadcasts an alarm notification to the authorities in order to take appropriate decision. The system deployment architecture is illustrated in Figure 5.

The proposed system is mainly made up of the following elements:

- *Sensor nodes*: are responsible for detecting traffic flow at points of interest namely the beginning of roads, and sending the real time measurements to the sensor head;
- *Relay nodes*: are intermediate sensor nodes that are used in case the network is wide and a multi-hope communication is needed;
- *Sensor head*: The duty of the sensor head is to aggregate the physical traffic parameters that were captured by sensor nodes like density, velocity and to send the aggregated data to the base station.
- *Base station*: The major purpose of base stations is to model and simulate the received traffic flow in the corresponding region and provide its dynamic evolution over time.
- *Control manager*: provides more coherent traffic flow of the overall road network, while dealing with some of the most common critical situations such as congestion.

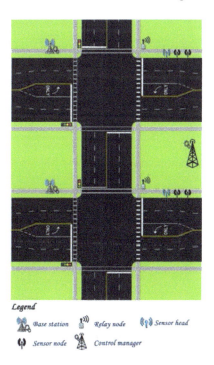

Figure 5. Major components of the proposed architecture.

Following is a simple use case representing the WSN based traffic management system and how it can operate when detecting traffic flow in road network.

The scenario consists of two intersections $IS1$ and $IS2$ where two roads cross each other as depicted in (Figure 6). At least two sensors are positioned preceding every road to detect and transmit the data that consist mainly of velocity, density and length of the entering vehicles. These data are collected in the base station so as to model the traffic flow and estimate its evolution within the network.

Suppose at time T_0, different batches of vehicles are detected within roads R_1 and R_2 (Arrows blue and red) by a set of sensors that are positioned at the beginning of these roads. Sensor S1 will transmit information about velocity, length and density to the corresponding base station BS_1, through the sensor head, where generalized nondeterministic batch Petri modeling will perform and output the traffic flow evolution at every section of roads i.e., the velocity, the length, the density and the time when vehicles will be there. The same process will be carried out for sensor 2 and BS_2. Consequently, a control manager will model the whole network based on the output of every base station.

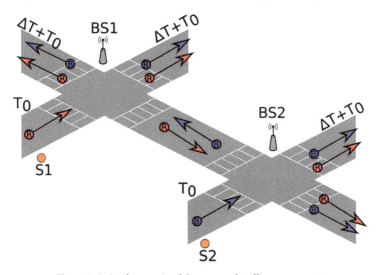

Figure 6. A simple scenario of the proposed traffic management.

5.2. Prototyping

A prototype has been developed in order to implement the data analysis component and more precisely the proposed GNBPN model and check its applicability. To this end, we have proposed a preliminary architecture consisting of the following elements: Web interface, two sensors and a base station.

The web interface is meant to allow the system administrator to save the characterestics of each road within the network mainly its maximum speed, maximum density and length.

The sensors are meant to detect a batch of vehicles and determine its average speed and density.

The base station is meant to execute the batch evolution model GNBPN based on the inserted parameters through the web interface and the detected values received from sensors.

The suggested prototype aims mainly at implementing a simplified version of GNBPN model. This simplified version is used to study the dynamic evolution of a vehicles batch that is moving in a certain section of the road, in order to predict whether congestion may occur at the level of the entire road or not.

To perform the calculations necessary to determine the vehicles batch evolution within a section, the algorithm takes as inputs:

- The characteristics of the vehicles batch, which are:
  - d_b: The density of vehicles batch (veh/km);
  - x_b: The position of vehicles batch;
  - v_b: The speed of vehicles batch (km/h).
- The characteristics of the road R:
  - L_R: The length of the road (km);
  - D_R^{max}: The maximum density (veh/km);
  - V_R: The maximum speed (km/h);
  - Φ_R^{max}: The maximum flow (veh/h).

Once the algorithm is executed, it yields the output vector A which contains four values describing the evolution of the batch, namely:

- t: The travel time needed to reach the end of the road;
- d_b: The updated density of vehicles batch;
- x_b: The updated position of vehicles batch;
- v_b: The updated speed of vehicles batch.

Figure 7 shows the Arduino IDE with a sample of the simplified sketches loaded.

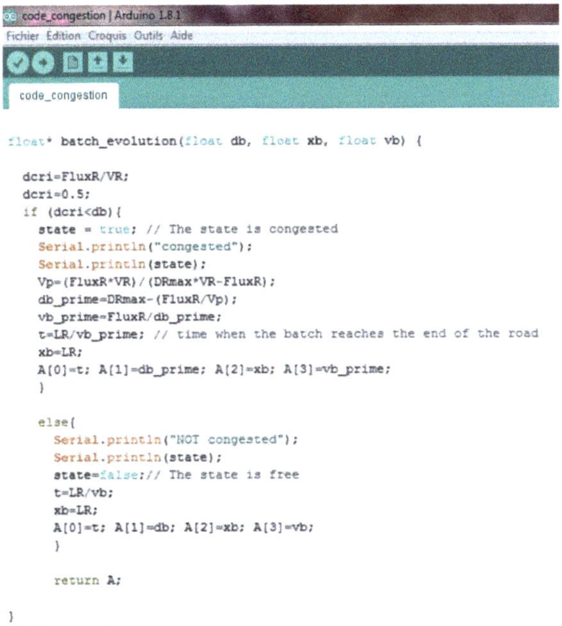
code_congestion | Arduino 1.8.1
Fichier Edition Croquis Outils Aide
code_congestion
float* batch_evolution(float db, float xb, float vb) {
dcri=FluxR/VR;
dcri=0.5;
if (dcri<db){
state = true; // The state is congested
Serial.println("congested");
Serial.println(state);
Vp=(FluxR*VR)/(DRmax*VR-FluxR);
db_prime=DRmax-(FluxR/Vp);
vb_prime=FluxR/db_prime;
t=LR/vb_prime; // time when the batch reaches the end of the road
xb=LR;
A[0]=t; A[1]=db_prime; A[2]=xb; A[3]=vb_prime;
}
else{
Serial.println("NOT congested");
Serial.println(state);
state=false;// The state is free
t=LR/vb;
xb=LR;
A[0]=t; A[1]=db; A[2]=xb; A[3]=vb;
}
return A;
}

Figure 7. screen of the Arduino IDE program with a sample sketches loaded of GNBPN model.

The development of the prototype involved the use of two HC-SR04 ultrasonic sensors for detecting the vehicles batch and sending the measurements to the base station, a MAMP Web Server and an Intel Galileo Gen 2; the intel Galileo Gen 2 development board is used as a base station on the one hand, and as data aggregation platform on the other hand. This board plays the role of sensor head since it performs an aggregation operation over sensor measurements such as aggregating vehicles speed. Also, Intel Galileo Board performs the simplified version of Batches Petri nets algorithm using the aggregated data and the input parameters, that were given through the web interface, to determine whether a congestion will occur or no. Figure 8a shows the used Intel Galileo Gen 2 connected to two HC-SR04 ultrasonic sensors.

(a)   (b)

Figure 8. The main elements of the proposed prototype. (**a**) HC-SR04 ultrasonic sensors with Intel Galileo Gen 2; (**b**) Web Interface for inserting road parameters.

The current deployed version of the model is totally based on installation on Galileo gen 2 boards. The software installation process consists of the following steps:

- Setting up the computer for development with the Galileo Gen 2 board by installing arduino integrated development environment (IDE) software;
- Writing and Uploading the code: Once the code is created, it has to be compiled and uploaded to the Galileo board.

The system contains a web interface as well for inserting the required parameters for the model such as maximum density, maximum speed and maximum length of a road.

Figure 8b shows the web interface screen. The data inserted is thus sent and stored into a XAMPP based database server.

In this work, the HC-SR04 ultrasonic sensors have been chosen to detect vehicles batch and measure its speed and density. They operate on 5 V and provide 2 to 400 cm or 1″ to 10 feet non-contact measurement function with high accuracy and stable readings (up to 3 mm accuracy).

The HC-SR04 ultrasonic sensors consist of a transmitter and a receiver. The transducer transmits eight 40 kHz pulses of ultrasonic pulses which travel through the air until it meets an object that these pulses are reflected back by the object. The waves reflected by the objects and received by the transducer are used to compute the speed and density of vehicles' batch by Intel Galileo Gen 2.

Intel Galileo Gen 2 Development board is powered by intel Quark System-on-Chip (SoC) ×1000 and operating at speed up to 400 MHz. it runs on an embedded Linux Kernel and it ensures saving data on the SD card and transmitting them using internet.

The advantage of using Intel Galileo Gen 2 is the ease of writing Arduino's sketches in order to:

- Obtain the parameters that have already been stored via the web interface into a database
- Interact with sensors for computing cars speed and density
- Perform the simplified version of GNBPN model
- Transmit the result and save it into XAMPP based database server

Figure 9 represents a workflow diagram for the developed prototype.

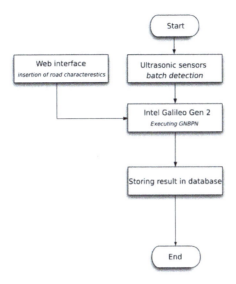

Figure 9. The flow diagram of the developed prototype.

On another hand, based on our GNBPN model and estimation methods, we have developed color-coded visualizer that is used for viewing different segments of road network and estimating traffic evolution on (i) the same segments (temporal prediction) and (ii) related segments (spatial prediction). Different features are taken into consideration such as displaying traffic situations and computing travel times along possible routes for origin-destination pair etc. The visualizer takes the knowledge derived from models and turns it into easy and interpretable accessible visualizations that include near real-time road traffic flow, and road traffic prediction. Interaction with the system can be ensured through mobile applications or web portal (users) and dashboard (managers).

Figure 10 depicts a sample of the visualizer that we have developed. For instance, Figure 10a shows the level of congestion of a section that is characterized by flux, density, length and maximum speed. As for Figure 10b, it is an exploratory example of an event covers a circular geographical area, as well as the affluence that indicates its impact vis-à-vis the sections concerned.

| (a) | (b) |

Figure 10. Illustration of the road network visualizer application. (**a**) The main characteristics of a road section; (**b**) An event occurs in a geographical area.

We have used google map APIs for developing our color-coded visualizer described in the previous section and we have proceeded with customizing it by adding modules for CRUD operations on road segments using Java 8 and MySQL.

J. Sens. Actuator Netw. **2017**, *6*, 30

6. Conclusions

This paper presents a novel wireless sensor networks based system for road traffic management while detailing the deployment and the functional architectures.

The paper exhibits an implementation of two elements of the proposed system: Visualization and data analysis components. We are currently working on various components of the system :

- Implementation of the complete algorithm of our traffic state evolution
- Estimation of intersection turning movements and its implementation
- Using NoSQL database for data storage

Acknowledgments: The authors thank Joel Tankam, Bousseta Ayyoub and Ahmadou Youssef for their great help during the prototype development that contributed to improving the quality of our paper.

Author Contributions: This work is the result of the collective efforts of all authors. Youness Riouali conducted the research and trials. Laila Benhlima and Slimane Bah supervised the research and added their intellectual property and experience into the system. All the authors contributed to revision the paper and provided detailed comments to improve the content of the manuscript.

Conflicts of Interest: The authors declare no conflict of interest.

Abbreviations

The following abbreviations are used in this manuscript:

WSN	Wireless Sensor Network
ITS	Intelligent Transportation System
ICT	Information and Communication technology
VANET	Vehicular Ad-hoc Network
HPN	Hybrid Petri nets
WTMS	WSN-based Traffic Management System

References

1. Losilla, F.; Garcia-Sanchez, A.J.; Garcia-Sanchez, F.; Garcia-Haro, J.; Haas, Z.J. A Comprehensive Approach to WSN-Based ITS Applications: A Survey. *Sensors* **2011**, *11*, 10220–10265.
2. Lazarescu, M.T. Design and Field Test of a WSN Platform Prototype for Long-Term Environmental Monitoring. *Sensors* **2015**, *15*, 9481–9518.
3. Darwish, A.; Hassanien, A.E. Wearable and Implantable Wireless Sensor Network Solutions for Healthcare Monitoring. *Sensors* **2011**, *11*, 5561–5595.
4. Conti, M. *Secure Wireless Sensor Networks: Threats and Solutions*; Advances in Information Security; Springer: New York, NY, USA, 2015.
5. Mason, A.; Al-Shamma'a, A.I.; Shaw, A. Wireless Sensor Network for Intelligent Inventory Management for Packaged Gases. In Proceedings of the 2009 Second International Conference on Developments in eSystems Engineering, Abu Dhabi, UAE, 14–16 December 2009; pp. 413–417.
6. Zhao, F.; Guibas, L. *Wireless Sensor Networks: An Information Processing Approach*; Electronics & Electrical, Morgan Kaufmann: Burlington, MA, USA, 2004.
7. Liu, X.; Cao, J.; Lai, S.; Yang, C.; Wu, H.; Xu, Y.L. Energy efficient clustering for WSN-based structural health monitoring. In Proceedings of the 2011 IEEE INFOCOM, Shanghai, China, 10–15 April 2011; pp. 2768–2776.
8. Giammarini, M.; Isidori, D.; Concettoni, E.; Cristalli, C.; Fioravanti, M.; Pieralisi, M. Design of Wireless Sensor Network for Real-Time Structural Health Monitoring. In Proceedings of the 2015 IEEE 18th International Symposium on Design and Diagnostics of Electronic Circuits Systems, Belgrade, Serbia, 22–24 April 2015, pp. 107–110.
9. Bhattacharyya, S.; Deprettere, E.; Leupers, R.; Takala, J. *Handbook of Signal Processing Systems*; Springer: New York, NY, USA, 2013.
10. Forster, C.A. *Australian Cities: Continuity and Change*; Meridian (Melbourne, Australia), Oxford University Press: Oxford, UK, 2004.

11. Daven, J.; Klein, R. *Progress in Waste Management Research*; Nova Science Publishers: Hauppauge, NY, USA, 2008.

12. Engelbrecht, J.; Booysen, M.J.; van Rooyen, G.J.; Bruwer, F.J. Survey of smartphone-based sensing in vehicles for intelligent transportation system applications. *IET Intell. Transp. Syst.* **2015**, *9*, 924–935.

13. Wang, Y.; Peng, Z.; Wang, K.; Song, X.; Yao, B.; Feng, T. Research on Urban Road Congestion Pricing Strategy Considering Carbon Dioxide Emissions. *Sustainability* **2015**, *7*, 10534–10553.

14. Alrawi, F. The importance of intelligent transport systems in the preservation of the environment and reduction of harmful gases. *Transp. Res. Procedia* **2017**, *24*, 197–203. 3rd Conference on Sustainable Urban Mobility, 3rd CSUM 2016, Volos, Greece, 26–27 May 2016.

15. Wang, R.; Xiao, F. *Advances in Wireless Sensor Networks: 6th China Conference, CWSN 2012, Huangshan, China, October 25–27, 2012*; Revised Selected Papers; Communications in Computer and Information Science; Springer: Berlin/Heidelberg, Germany, 2013.

16. Bui, K.H.N.; Pham, X.H.; Jung, J.J.; Lee, O.J.; Hong, M.S. Context-Based Traffic Recommendation System. In *Context-Aware Systems and Applications: Proceedings of the 4th International Conference, ICCASA 2015, Vung Tau, Vietnam, 26–27 November 2015*; Vinh, P.C., Alagar, V., Eds.; Springer International Publishing: Cham, Switzerland, 2016; pp. 122–131.

17. Ugnenko, E.; Uzhvieva, E.; Voronova, Y. Simulation of Traffic Flows on the Road Network of Urban Area. *Procedia Engineering* **2016**, *134*, 153–156. Transbaltica 2015: Proceedings of the 9th International Scientific Conference, Vilnius Gediminas Technical University, Vilnius, Lithuania, 7–8 May 2015.

18. Lv, Y.; Duan, Y.; Kang, W.; Li, Z.; Wang, F.Y. Traffic Flow Prediction With Big Data: A Deep Learning Approach. *IEEE Trans. Intell. Transp. Syst.* **2015**, *16*, 865–873.

19. Hoogendoorn, S.P.; Bovy, P.H.L. State-of-the-art of vehicular traffic flow modelling. *Proc. I MECH E Part I J. Syst. Control Eng.* **2001**, *215*, 283–303.

20. Arem, V.; Arem, B.V.; Hoogendoorn, S.P. Gas kinetic traffic flow modelling including continuous driver behaviour models. *Transp. Res. Rec. J. Transp. Res. Board* **2003**, *1852*, 1–19.

21. Savrasovs, M. Traffic Flow Simulation on Discrete Rate Approach Base. *Transp. Telecommun. J.* **2012**, *13*, 167–173.

22. Treiber, M.; Kesting, A. *Traffic Flow Dynamics*; Springer: Berlin/Heidelberg, Germany, 2013.

23. Huang, B. GIS coupled with traffic simulation and optimization for incident response. *Comput. Environ. Urban Syst.* **2007**, *31*, 116–132.

24. Riouali, Y.; Benhlima, L.; Bah, S. Petri net extension for traffic road modelling. In Proceedings of the 2016 IEEE/ACS 13th International Conference of Computer Systems and Applications (AICCSA), Agadir, Morocco, 29 November–2 December 2016; Volume 7, pp. 7–12.

25. Demongodin, I.; Audry, N.; Prunet, F. Batches Petri nets. In Proceedings of the IEEE Systems Man and Cybernetics Conference (SMC), Le Touquet, France, 17–20 October 1993; Volume 1, pp. 607–617.

26. Demongodin, I. Generalised Batches Petri Net: Hybrid Model For High Speed Systems With Variable Delays. *Discret. Event Dyn. Syst.* **2001**, *11*, 137–162.

27. Riouali, Y.; Benhlima, L.; Bah, S. Toward a Global WSN-Based System to Manage Road Traffic. In Proceedings of the International Conference on Future Networks and Distributed Systems, Cambridge, UK, 19–20 July 2017; pp. 28:1–28:6.

28. Xiao, L.; Peng, X.; Wang, Z.; Xu, B.; Hong, P. Research on Traffic Monitoring Network and Its Traffic Flow Forecast and Congestion Control Model Based on Wireless Sensor Networks. In Proceedings of the 2009 International Conference on Measuring Technology and Mechatronics Automation, Zhangjiajie, Hunan, China, 11–12 April 2009; Volume 1, pp. 142–147.

29. Rahman, M.; Ahmed, N.U.; Mouftah, H.T. City traffic management model using Wireless Sensor Networks. In Proceedings of the 2014 IEEE 27th Canadian Conference on Electrical and Computer Engineering (CCECE), Toronto, ON, Canada, 4–7 May 2014; pp. 1–6.

30. Nafi, N.S.; Khan, R.H.; Khan, J.Y.; Gregory, M. A predictive road traffic management system based on vehicular ad-hoc network. In Proceedings of the 2014 Australasian Telecommunication Networks and Applications Conference (ATNAC), Southbank, Australia, 26–28 November 2014; pp. 135–140.

31. Cárdenas-Benítez, N.; Aquino-Santos, R.; Magaña-Espinoza, P.; Aguilar-Velazco, J.; Edwards-Block, A.; Medina Cass, A. Traffic Congestion Detection System through Connected Vehicles and Big Data. *Sensors* **2016**, *16*, 599.

32. Iwasaki, Y.; Misumi, M.; Nakamiya, T. Robust Vehicle Detection under Various Environmental Conditions Using an Infrared Thermal Camera and Its Application to Road Traffic Flow Monitoring. *Sensors* **2013**, *13*, 7756–7773.

33. Viola, P.; Jones, M. Rapid object detection using a boosted cascade of simple features. In Proceedings of the 2001 IEEE Computer Society Conference on Computer Vision and Pattern Recognition, (CVPR), Kauai, HI, USA, 8–14 December 2001; Volume 1, pp. I–511–I–518.

34. Lienhart, R.; Maydt, J. An extended set of Haar-like features for rapid object detection. In Proceedings of the International Conference on Image Processing, Rochester, NY, USA, 22–25 September 2002; Volume 1, pp. I–900–I–903.

35. Du, R.; Chen, C.; Yang, B.; Lu, N.; Guan, X.; Shen, X. Effective Urban Traffic Monitoring by Vehicular Sensor Networks. *IEEE Trans. Veh. Technol.* **2015**, *64*, 273–286.

36. Singh, V.; Srivastava, H.; Venturino, E.; Resch, M.; Gupta, V. *Modern Mathematical Methods and High Performance Computing in Science and Technology: M3HPCST, Ghaziabad, India, December 2015*; Springer: Singapore, 2016.

37. Mikolajczak, B.; Singh, A. TransCPN—Software Tool for Transformation of Colored Petri Nets. In Proceedings of the 2009 Sixth International Conference on Information Technology: New Generations, Las Vegas, NV, USA, 27–29 April 2009; pp. 211–216.

38. Martínez, D.; González, A.; Blanes, F.; Aquino, R.; Simo, J.; Crespo, A. Formal Specification and Design Techniques for Wireless Sensor and Actuator Networks. *Sensors* **2011**, *11*, 1059–1077.

39. Ehrig, H.; Juhas, G.; Padberg, J.; Rozenberg, G. *Unifying Petri Nets: Advances in Petri Nets*; Lecture Notes in Computer Science; Springer: Berlin/Heidelberg, Germany, 2003.

Article

A Social Environmental Sensor Network Integrated within a Web GIS Platform

Yorghos Voutos [1,*], Phivos Mylonas [1], Evaggelos Spyrou [2] and Eleni Charou [2]

[1] Department of Informatics, Ionian University, 7 Tsirigoti Square, 49100 Corfu, Greece;
fmylonas@ionio.gr

[2] Institute of Informatics and Telecommunications, NCSR Demokritos, Neapoleos 10,
15310 Ag. Paraskevi, Greece; vaggelis.spyrou@gmail.com (E.S.); exarou@iit.demokritos.gr (E.C.)

* Correspondence: george.voutos@gmail.com; Tel.: +30-697-043-7960

Received: 1 October 2017 ; Accepted: 15 November 2017 ; Published: 21 November 2017

Abstract: We live in an era where typical measures towards the mitigation of environmental degradation follow the identification and recording of natural parameters closely associated with it. In addition, current scientific knowledge on the one hand may be applied to minimize the environmental impact of anthropogenic activities, whereas informatics on the other, playing a key role in this ecosystem, do offer new ways of implementing complex scientific processes regarding the collection, aggregation and analysis of data concerning environmental parameters. Furthermore, another related aspect to consider is the fact that almost all relevant data recordings are influenced by their given spatial characteristics. Taking all aforementioned inputs into account, managing such a great amount of complex and remote data requires specific digital structures; these structures are typically deployed over the Web on an attempt to capitalize existing open software platforms and modern developments of hardware technology. In this paper we present an effort to provide a technical solution based on sensing devices that are based on the well-known Arduino platform and operate continuously for gathering and transmitting of environmental state information. Controls, user interface and extensions of the proposed project rely on the Android mobile device platform (both from the software and hardware side). Finally, a crucial novel aspect of our work is the fact that all herein gathered data carry spatial information, which is rather fundamental for the successful correlation between pollutants and their place of origin. The latter is implemented by an interactive Web GIS platform operating oversight in situ and on a timeline basis.

Keywords: IoT; GIS; Wireless Sensor Network; environmental monitoring; participatory

---

1. Introduction

The methodology of identifying and recording natural parameters is straightly connected to environmental degradation, while modern technological achievements have created new prospects of interaction between human and their living environment [1]. Technological solutions derive from complex scientific processes, which offer integrity, scientific relevance and applied continuously could also serve as a stepping stone to minimize environmental impact [2]. The increased accessibility to cutting edge technologies and the variety of skill-set held by the average citizen, generate prospects of novel methodology for protecting and preserving the environment. This study focuses on the development of a prototype platform that records the environmental state of any given place. Open-source technologies (software and hardware) are playing a pivotal role on the implementation of the platform. More specifically, the proposed platform is supported by recording devices based on the Arduino family of boards. Code development take place at all stages of the project and have been implemented exclusively through open-source applications. The monitoring device is calibrated prior deployment, taking into consideration the parameters of each component (software and hardware).

The scarcity and degradation of renewable or non-renewable natural resources are signaling disturbances in the planet's geochemical cycles as well as the reduction of biological diversity and genetic stock [3]. Human activities are characterized as the main source of climate change [4]. It is commonly accepted that the ecosystems of major cities have played an important role on the environmental crisis due to the unceasing accumulation of population within them. Moreover, cities present particular vulnerabilities to climate change and its effects [4]. The multidimensional concept of a human's Quality of Life (QoL) [5] is shaped, among others, by the perceived environmental nuisance, under subjective criteria. QoL deals with the study and documentation of the concept of quality of everyday life, through the synergy of both subjective and objective criteria.

Enriching human activities with technological solutions may act as a springboard to minimize environmental impacts on everyday life. Towards this goal, one of the most promising, yet affordable solutions is the concept of the "Internet-of-Things" (IoT) [6]. IoT denotes the computerization and the utilization of everyday digital objects for the further enrichment of Internet data. It presents new means of interaction between man, machines and computers, indicating natural and essential modus operandi for humans and their environment. Moreover, recent advances in the fields of electronics have allowed consumer mobile Internet-enabled devices (e.g., smart-phones, tablets, smart-watches, etc.) to be equipped or even expandable with numerous features, that allow or facilitate interdisciplinary applications related to human and natural activities. The embodiment of GPS receivers within the aforementioned devices, the usage of novel methods of analytics, as well as means of presentation of geographical data have keenly contributed on broadening environmental science applications in conjunction with the advanced computing.

Finally, the notion of "participatory sensing" [7] has allowed the contribution and access of individuals and or groups to a single core knowledge, allowing users to become active members within digital communities. The rapid growth of computing power on mobile devices has realized large scale environmental sensing, mainly through broad access and visualization provided by web GIS applications.

The herein presented research methodology includes both design and implementation steps. Principles of environmental monitoring [1] guide the deterministic modeling that encloses certain research variables of the case study [8]. In addition to the theoretical approach, software structures are designed according to the system's demand. Accurate environmental sensing depends on the appropriate design and function of hardware elements. Furthermore, communication infrastructure is essential for seamlessly feeding the system from end to end. Subsequently, the recording device is manufactured according to the type of studied physical quantities and networking restrictions. The device needs to be developed and calibrated accordingly in order to follow the system's standardized procedures. Further visualization and analysis is essential to this work because in order to locate and possibly recognize sources of environmental degradation. This purpose serves a Geographic Information System (GIS) platform which is integrated to a web interface developed specifically for this study.

The rest of this paper is organized as follows: In Section 2, we present related research work concerning various applications of remote sensor networks. Then, in Section 3, we present the details regarding hardware components that have been used. Section 4 presents in detail the implementation framework of the of the proposed platform. Results that occurred upon the deployment of the platform into real-life use cases are presented in Section 5 and the proof-of-concept is laid out in Section 6. Finally, the discussion regarding the conclusions and future prospects of the proposed framework is presented in Section 7.

2. Related Work

Recent technology advancements have driven Wireless Sensor Network (WSN) systems to become a feasible solution for many innovative applications [9,10]. Several systems that rely on low-power embedded micro-controller platforms have been proposed [9,11]. Such systems make use of the digital and analog I/O ports of platforms for sensor extensions alongside with custom or open source software components. For instance, Ferdoush and Li [10] proposed a system based upon several hardware and software elements. They focused on the development and integration processes. The overall architecture of their system included a base station and a number of distributed wireless sensor nodes. On the hardware side, both nodes and the base station are developed in an assemblage of micro-controllers (uC), a radio transceiver and an environmental sensor measuring humidity and temperature. Specifically, base stations are implemented using a Raspberry Pi Model B [11], taking advantage of its advanced processing capabilities compared to the Arduino Uno [12], which has been used to incorporate the sensors. Connectivity is established with the help of XBee Pro S2B module [13] Data manipulation is performed by applications that have been installed in both sensors and base station. A gateway application that has been installed in the micro-controllers assists the on-board functionality and acts as an intermediate for the sensor network and the MySQL database. Furthermore, the whole system is monitored by a web application which is controlled by the end user and offers data visualization capabilities. Overall, the system proposed by Ferdoush and Li is low cost, compact and could be easily managed with reduced complexity. On the other hand it has only been deployed for indoor monitoring of temperature and relative humidity and the end user is provided with low data visualization capabilities. Although it shares several fundamental characteristics with our proposed system, we believe that it is strongly differentiated on many aspects. Within our approach, communication is based on Bluetooth protocol and GPRS/WiFi connectivity. Moreover, our approach is structured around cloud computing services and its main aspect is the transmission of produced environmental information; i.e., it has been designed for outdoor use producing seven environmental variables. Finally, our approach strongly focuses on spatial characteristics of natural phenomena and we integrate this on every aspect of our deployment.

Similarly, Kumar and Kumaraswamy [14] developed a WSN using open-source hardware platforms for small-scale ecological monitoring and knowledge collection. Both Raspberry pi and a microcontroller were used as a sensor node and base station setup. Each node has embedded software capable to handle recordings to the base station, which is supported by a user friendly web application. Communication is executed by ZigBee protocol (IEEE 802.15.4 standard), which complies to three types of network topology (star, cluster-tree and mesh). Their proposal is adaptive to many ecological monitoring applications due to its compatibility with several open source hardware and software platforms.

Indoor Environmental Quality (IEQ) is a concept which concerns the work of Salamone et al. [15]. Therein, a WSN has been developed on the purpose of aggregating a set of different categories of comfort, well-being and satisfaction of users of buildings. Sensor nodes were based on an Arduino Uno and monitored air speed, radiant temperature, luminosity and CO_2. Their system, namely nEmOs project, is implemented for recurrence monitoring and improvement of conditions and energy efficiency of buildings. The network's communication is based on WiFi and sensor readings are sent to the Xively [16] cloud service. The notion of base stations is not adopted; instead, an Android App has been developed for the purposes of data distribution and node management. Comparison of the proposed sensor nodes with existing commercial tools indicated a difference of more than 5% in accuracy. Overall, nEmOs may be characterized as a useful monitoring model for confined spaces. The main differences with the proposed system is that contains further sensing complexity which is also applied outdoors. However both approaches aim at the estimation of environmental quality through a series of low cost and open source tools.

The direction of sensing the natural outdoor environment has been adopted by [9]. Their work refers to small distance dense deployment strategy of automated early fire detection through cluster distributed sensor nodes operating with low energy demands. The sensors are deployed to fixed positions in forest areas, feeding base stations (cluster-heads) with specific metrics, which, on their turn, forward the gathered information to a data sink. Network topology includes "adaptive mechanisms" related to fire detection and uses both flat and hierarchical structure. An important technical aspect of the project is the correlation between energy consumption and network performance due to the remote exposure of sensors in adverse conditions. This is achieved by sensing temperature and humidity fluctuations that point out fire threat. An integrated automated monitoring system that relies on network design and implementation has been implemented. It showcases the depth of functional capabilities in automated sensing methodology. The data used are spatial aware and obtain specific fixed positions in the research area. From our perspective, geographical location offers correlated information regarding location and time depending on the environmental aspect in question (humidity or temperature). Likewise, user related capabilities of event aware sensors offer reactive mechanisms. In the proposed system, nodes adjust their sensing parameters according to spatial transitions and warn the end user for abnormal or dangerous fluctuations of the environmental quality.

Sensor related applications and services in automotive vehicles is a direction followed by corporate industries [17]. A moving vehicle can be a source of sensory data that are difficulty acquired by a single system or network. Produced variables benefit drivers and third parties gathering information for environment monitoring, passenger awareness and vehicle operation. Sensory data derive from embedded hardware and network functions supported by vehicles ECU (Electronic Control Unit) and are supported by Global Positioning System's (GPS) operation. The dissemination of data support further implementation on urban and public sensing provide benefits to global information sharing and access with the aid of mobile phones and handled devices, opening novel application domains. Automated environmental data generation through vehicles may considerably widen the source of sensing data while enabling further development of supporting infrastructures (e.g., networking). Built in sensing in vehicles fails to support hardware customization due to restricted production. Nevertheless, social aware passengers convey the potential expansion of environmental sensing inter-connectivity by integrating portable sensor technology into vehicle capabilities [18].

Precision agriculture is a wealthy field of application for automated monitoring as it has been highlighted by both Srbinova et al. [19] and Keshtgary and Delijoo [20] which have both developed WSN systems for improved quality in farming. They both followed the common WSN schema of nodes and base stations while showcasing efficient processes of gathering and distributing environmental parameters. Both studies engaged into the structure of network topologies, attempting to optimize quality in arable areas. More specifically, Srbinova et al. used communication protocols with low connection rates based on energy efficient time frames. Also, Keshtgary and Delijoo concentrated on the creation of performance metric typeset for a bivariate topological model. The initial iteration locates nodes at edge of each field and the latter distributes them randomly. Precision agriculture through WSN distinguishes external factors of monitoring to provide profundity on this field of study. Sensor networks require input from complementary components to complete monitoring and operational routines such as an irrigation system to control water level and humidity.

Hur and Eisenstadt [21] proposed a "low power wireless monitoring system" for mosquito and pathogen related research. The system's purpose is to transmit information regarding humidity, temperature, wind speed and direction and location data for better control of mosquito populations and to prevent the spread related diseases. They've deployed a set of fixed, power autonomous and weather proof wireless climate monitoring devices based on a microcontroller that communicates to a Web based service through a low power Adaptive Network Technology (ANT) module. Moreover, the device security is enhanced through a radio-frequency identification unit (RFID) for secure control and manual user login of the module. The series of data is presented to a web browser application equipped with extensive graphical capabilities, and therein location related information is presented to a Google Maps based platform. Although our project embodies similar concepts, this work is specialized in population control and disease prevention. Additionally, sensors are geostationary and do not feature open source software and hardware properties.

The three year design and deployment of WSN by Naumowicz et al. [22] aimed at seabird monitoring on Skomer Island (a UK National Reserve, located off the west coast of Pembrokeshire, Wales). The research team developed a real-world deployable sensor network to investigate the habitat of Manx Shearwater (Puffinus puffinus) seabird. The project is based on battery powered sensor nodes communicating bi-directionally via Micro-Mesh-Protocol. The sealed devices were based on generic extension boards (MSB430MS) and installed near the entrance of the bird's habitat (burrow) monitoring air temperature and humidity, movement on the entrance (passive infrared PIR), identity of individual bird (were marked previously with RFID tags) and weight of individual gird (with custom made scales). Recordings were initially saved in a SD card and selectively parsed to the repository through Micro-Mesh. Data and nodes were controlled by a custom built firmware with low level API based on ScatterWeb of Freie Universitat Berlin. Remote deployed and custom developed WSNs offer dependable recordings on specific implementations, but lack repeatability and broad applicability.

More et al. [23] proposed a "test-bed for real-world Habitat Monitoring System (HMS)" by acquiring remote physical environmental data. Their project can be implemented in any remote location using the Arduino Uno board, WI-FI connectivity and a Graphical User Interface (GUI). The nodes are consisted by a sensing, a power and a communication unit, which are monitoring temperature, humidity and light, while transmitting them towards a base station. The platform supports live data visualization on a hourly basis and the GUI manages the recorded data through a database built for this purpose. The project of More et al. is an adaptable platform focused in easy deployment at specific remote areas. Our project is concentrated in the spatial aspect of monitoring, proffers portable operation and is compatible with modern mobile devices.

Simbeye et al. [24] dealt with the development of special nodes in order to monitor environmental parameters in aquaculture. Their method concerned the evaluation of monitoring an aquaculture system by deploying for the duration of six months two sensor network nodes in fish ponds. The overall framework consists three monitoring components: "smart sensor nodes", gateway/coordinator nodes—both based on the ZigBee platform—and a PC as monitoring center. The environmental conditions were analyzed through specific software operating on every system component and presented real-time and total recordings in a GUI. The methodology of water monitoring allows to avoid fish mortality and could be applied in various fields of environmental sensing.

The adherence of proper hygiene practices in public health institutions is a subject studied by Bal and Abrishambaf [25] through the implementation of IoT and WSN technologies. Their prototype system aims at monitoring hand hygiene compliance rates through cloud-connected monitoring stations to monitor hand hygiene events in real-time and in large scale. The proposed platform is consisted by a network of "smart hand washing" nodes, which are embedded in a wireless domain through Zigbee communication protocol and UHF-RFID modules. The nodes are divided into Soap Dispenser and Faucet categories that both integrate embedded microprocessors, various sensors and actuators. The automatic soap dispenser, based on Arduino PRO-mini, initiates the hygiene sequence once it is actuated by the user and it is followed by the faucet, based on Raspberry Pi 3, which finalizes the hygiene activity. Networking is based on wireless local area network that establishes communication among nodes and cloud services (Database and Clients) where lower and higher level programming languages have employed on the purpose to measure compliance while counting hand-hygiene occurrences and their total duration. Bal and Abrishambaf proposed a novel approach on public health related human actuated events, outwit the scope of environmental sensing and outdoor monitoring.

The survey of Noel et al. [26] dealt with applications of WSN to Structural Health Monitoring (SHM) which is referred to the monitoring of critical infrastructures in order to expand their lifespan through "early damage detection". This application requires the deployment of numerous sensors throughout a structure for damage localization. Applied WSN for SHM are based on the selection of sensor and sensed parameters—mainly focused on structure's acceleration and velocity through piezoelectric accelerometers. SHM requires the management of a large amount of data with dense population of sensor nodes. Delay in sampling rate depends on the prospect of the monitoring procedure, e.g., long-term allows long delays. Network scalability is highlighted as an important factor in meeting each SHM application quality due to the required "sheer quantity of data collection and transmission" and is related to the maximum network node time-synchronization step. Network architecture is improved through hierarchical relationship between a base station and several sensor nodes. Synchronization among the nodes and the base station is implemented by specialized algorithms that are dependent to Time Synchronization Error (TSE) factor. Furthermore, optimal placing of sensor nodes originate from civil engineering perspective and determines the effectiveness of structural information collection. Relatively to scalability, placement is related to network's lifespan, overall connectivity, robustness and decision regarding the implemented routing protocol. Energy efficiency determines network lifespan and affects system operation. Clustering is highlighted as a common technique to improve scalability, simplify routing, extend network lifespan and conserve bandwidth. In addition to the aforementioned, an SHM is capable of carrying several features such as Mobile Phone Sensing (MPS) that extends the system to the capabilities of smartphones (e.g., GPS, accelerometers, cameras etc). WSN consist an effective tool with SHM applications that requires extensive research prior deployment. The common ground between environmental monitoring and SHM is found on sensor locality, network architecture and communication protocols.

System intelligence in supply chain is provided by the integration among RFID and WSN. Mirsahi et al. [27] suggested an identification and detection system with intercommunicated devices that fulfil several requirements of the user. Based on the analytical Petri Net toolbox the authors proposed a system of "smart nodes" capable of environmental monitoring, location identification and organizing products. Their system is performance oriented by impromptu providing different functions related to the operation of automated guided vehicles (AGV).

Recent research work on the subject of environmental sensing and WSN indicates the popular applicability of IoT projects in several fields of application. In contrast to most of the aforementioned works we consider the significance of spatial and temporal elements in environmental monitoring. Non-linearity of natural phenomena is optimally monitored through the recognition of environmental processes over time and space [28]. Therefore embedded location tracking arise as the distinctive factor of our integrated system along with the potential of widespread implementation by public and private bodies. We propose an adaptable monitoring system based on integrated IoT, web services and popular development platforms that utilizes off the shelf hardware components and portable devices. The system functionality is based on the deployment of sensor nodes in conjunction with an ever available android compatible device. Furthermore, it is adaptable in terms of power supply and communication protocols. The monitoring procedure can be implemented by non-expert users and mainly focuses on qualitative assessment of the perceived environment. Environmental physical quantities are visualized and simplified onto geographical overlay on the prospect of rapid decision making. In conclusion, the proposed platform could be adapted to various environmental sensing applications and is capable for further customization.

3. Implementation

As expected, the proposed integrated system is based on the application of Information and Communication Technologies (ICT). As a result the technical aspect of this work is divided into two distinct parts: hardware development and networking. These allow the system to obtain, carry and disseminate physical variables through a tree type network topology comprised by sensor nodes, base stations and a server (as message broker). Additionally, the conjunction between sensor nodes and base stations operates through merging measurements and location tracking in order to detect spatial trends in reference to environmental deterioration factors. Also, the network supports on the fly visualization capabilities through numerical and cartographic representation. The latter is implemented by heat maps that provide an optimal apprehension of environmental quality on any given location through variable clustering. In this study the heat map is considered to be an environmental assessment system, visualizing the synchronization of physical quantities and spatial position.

Individual values of each variable are aggregated into a geographical matrix on which data are graphically represented through a color scheme. Warmer color variations commonly correspond to dense data concentration and therefore density is related to higher values. The proposed platform is based on distributed recording that assist the aggregation of data, hence the indication of spatial fluctuations in concentration of pollution factors. Each variable refers to its corresponding range (Noise Pollution: 30 to 80 dbA) and is categorized accordingly on the map. Beside individual metrics, integrated environmental quality can be detected through a Global variable. Global Environmental Quality is an assessment methodology attempting to integrate the total of measured variables into a heat map visualization on which non-dense data are considered as noise.

3.1. Hardware

The system developed within this study may be seen as an extension of a wireless sensor network and consists of several hardware parts. The system aims at monitoring the immediate conditions related to the perceived environment. Its hardware components consisted by a control unit and several sensors able to record and disseminate the ambient conditions of a given area. The components need to comply with the conditions of replace-ability, availability and programmability in order to facilitate ease of operation and reproduction. Electronic prototyping offer several off the shelf solutions that follow the aforementioned criteria.

The sensing device is developed using an Arduino developing board. More specifically, we opted for the Arduino YUN [29] which may be easily deployed for both portable and fixed operation due to its networking capabilities and expand-ability. Arduino platform offers low power consumption among popular open source development boards. Additionally, Arduino offers distinctive Digital and Analogue pins, enabling connectivity with several sensors, actuators and modules. The YUN model offers extensive wired and wireless connectivity capabilities along with Arduino's Integrated Development Environment (IDE). The latter is based on C and C++ languages, which loads cyclic programming loops directly through the device's firmware. Physical quantities of specific environmental variables are produced by 5 sensor modules that have been connected on the YUN (Table 1). In addition to monitoring tasks the YUN operates as a communication node that transmits the measurements through WiFi (while being fixed) and Bluetooth (while being mobile). The selected sensor modules have been selected based on low cost and their range of calibration, taking into consideration as many variables as possible. The schematic of the sensor node, built using an Arduino YUN is illustrated in (Figure 1). The selected components are depicted in Table 1 and they have been selected based on their low price and adequate accuracy for the proposed application, i.e., accuracy was sufficient for the goal of qualitative assessment of environmental parameters. We should note that the necessary source code for the sensor node and the mobile phone has been made publicly available (Mobile Sensor: https://goo.gl/oKqw5a, Fixed Sensor: https://goo.gl/9RJvRU, Android App: https://goo.gl/BuPUoh.

Table 1. Expansions, Functions and Units used on the recording devices.

Expansion Type	Model	Function	Measurement Unit
Temperature, Humidity	DHT 22	Temperature, Rel. Humidity, Heat Index	°C, % Humidity, % °C
Photometer	TEMT 2000	Luminosity	Lux (lx)
Microphone	MAX 4466	Noise Pollution/ Noise Intensity	dBm
Gasses microparticles	MQ-7	Carbon Monoxide (CO)	ppm
Gasses microparticles	MQ-4	Methane (CH4)	ppm

When being fixed, the system is directly connected to WiFi, while being portable, An Android device (i.e., a typical smart-phone) complements the system's hardware in order to provide connection to the Internet. More specifically, the smart-phone acts as a base station that receives and transmits flow of data from the sensors to the server. Furthermore it may also offer extensive control and real-time visualization features for the purpose of complete monitoring operation.

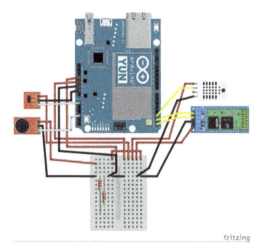

Figure 1. Sensor Circuit schema.

The selection of the aforementioned hardware components attempts to tackle the common problem of insufficient energy resources, especially in mobile operation (Figure 2). The Arduino platform is known to offer several solutions for connecting to power sources, while having a relatively small energy footprint. In our case, the YUN is connected to a typical power bank via USB. This way, the system is able to provide portability, elongated operating times as long as effortless connectivity.

Figure 2. Sensor node in bulk form.

In normal conditions each node's energy requirements averaging 10 mA/h. Using a portable power supply with a nominal power of 2000 mAh it is estimated that each node can reach optimal operation of 200 h. Unfortunately, an external battery cannot be used in full capacity thus mobile operating life of the sensor module is estimated between 12 to 17 h.

3.2. Network Architecture

Data management and storage are the main activities of the proposed sensor network and are supported by exploiting both preexisting hardware capabilities and also extensions of the YUN. It is worth noting that several distribution methodologies exist for both portable and fixed monitoring devices. Portable sensors are dependable to the Android device in order to assert its networking capabilities (Figure 3). Consequently the YUN transmits the data via Bluetooth connection to the mobile device, which then is responsible to forward these readings to the server for further manipulation. On the other hand, fixed nodes set aside Android connectivity and directly forward the readings through WiFi. Both module types are time synchronous through a Unix Timestamp [30] function that is embedded on deployment. Additionally, during mobile monitoring the system validates time-stamp with satellite timing provided by GPS Atomic Clock [31]. This technique expands the recording accuracy of the system's recognition of time related patterns.

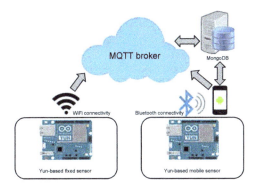

Figure 3. Communication architecture.

A Client-Server schema has been developed for the purpose of the study, utilizing open source software and Cloud Computing technologies. Supportively an MQTT [32] broker has been set up in order to insure the continuity of operation between base station and the server. Heroku [33] is a cloud platform-as-a-service (PaaS) on which a server has been deployed through Node.js [34] to host the operation of the database. Both database design and implementation have been developed through the non-relational Database Management System MongoDB [35]. Therein, every recording is handled as a GeoJSON [36] element by the database to be used subsequently by the Android app. A fragment of the transmitted data in GeoJSON format is depicted below:

```
{  "_id": {
        "$oid": "5819b45914b70931ff6db1"
   },
   "deviceId": "mob03",
   "sensorType": "mobile",
   "timestamp": {
        "$date": "2016-11-01T14:33:03.800Z"
   },
   "geo": {
        "type": "Point",
        "coordinates": [
            23.77108281,
            37.94333254
            ]
     },
     "humidity": 38.2,
     "temperature": 24.8,
     "heatIndex": 24.33,
     "luminosity": 56,
     "methane": 4.73,
     "co": 38.66,
     "noise": 39
}
```

4. Application Framework

The Android platform has been designed to offer numerous hardware and software capabilities to assist development and functioning of heterogeneous types of applications. Upon investigation, the aforementioned capabilities have been proven to fulfill the requirements of the proposed system and its dependencies on complex tasks that require hardware components and are related to the flow of collected data. The implemented app has been designed to exploit the Bluetooth, GPRS, WiFi and GPS capabilities of the mobile phone, which are the prerequisites in terms of the phone's specifications so as to enable data acquisition and collection from the YUN, location tracking and data transmission. Data may then be forwarded to services for database provisioning and cartographic representation.

To avoid message flooding, the app's operating sequence is initiated by the pairing between the sensor and the Android device via Bluetooth and consists of several intervals of predefined duration. Each recording consisting of a set of measurements from all sensors is instantly transmitted as a string message to the phone. This message is enhanced with the exact geographic location of the device and a time stamp (Figure 4). The message is then transformed to the GeoJSON format and transmitted to the MQTT broker, which then forwards it to the server. This flow of data to the dynamic repository enables the interactive mapping operations that allow cartographic representation of the recorded data. The latter is implemented in the server that stores all recordings to the MongoDB database and additionally manages and analyzes the content through logical queries.

The two-way communication among fixed sensor nodes and the server is implemented using the MQTT protocol, which enables message interchange through topics using a publishing subscribing procedure. Moreover, since MQTT is an extremely lightweight protocol, designed to require small code footprint and network bandwidth, guarantees a significantly small message size. Moreover, it is available for many heterogeneous devices and programming languages and fully compatible with all platforms that have been used within our system. Data sharing infrastructure is based on a network server acting as a web service. It consists of a Node.js server and an MQTT broker, both deployed on the Heroku cloud development platform. Ultimately, a non relational database model has been selected for data management and storage of the recordings. MonogDB manages data as individual text documents (JSON) with distinct structure (field and values). In addition to the server, database is based on mLab [37] cloud storage service. Finally, the Android App is developed with Ionic framework [38] that offers simplicity whereas supporting Angular.Js front-end development standard. Ionic utilizes ngCordova [39] framework which functions on top of npm Javascript package [40]. The app is equipped with functional and visualization capabilities, allowing the user to control, monitor and assess environmental quality (Figure 5).

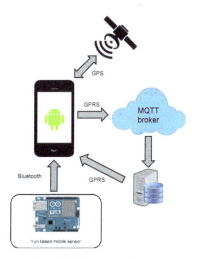

Figure 4. Android App schema.

Figure 5. Data Acquisition on the Android application; Presented values within each line are: Relative Humidity, Temperature, Heat Index, Luminosity, CH4 ppm, CO ppm, dB, longitude, latitude.

Base station's role on this application is to collect and transmit data to a repository. In addition to this, our project exploits the plethora of android platform capabilities. It offers the user live reading and control alongside with geographical overlay of the recordings. The embedded Web Map is developed through the Mapbox platform that represents current and past recordings along with their spatial representation (Figure 6). It provides user an extended apprehension of environmental quality in any given place and time the sensors are deployed.

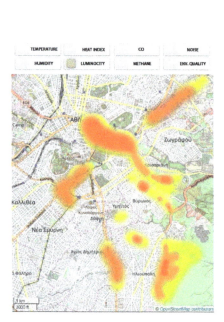

Figure 6. Luminosity map, Athens.

5. Use Case Scenarios

The system has at its disposal multiversal capabilities which allows repeatability among various cases. Assessing environmental quality is a complex multi-parameter procedure and a deployment schema has been created for the purpose of the specific research work. At the operational level, the recording device may be used for both portable and fixed operation while on both occasions requires Internet access for data transmission. Portable sensors depend on Android for spatial recordings and network connection. While being fixed, they have predefined location and autonomous connectivity.

The latter is fastened in specific building infrastructures with the aim of providing the system with continuous baseline data. This operates as a filtering mechanism that minimizes the possibility of spatial errors. On the other hand mobile measurements supply the monitoring system with risk indicators on a given route the sensor has "passed through". Repeated traverses on the same route or on specific spatial points could possibly indicate spatial propagation of nuisance derivatives. The main idea is situated at the operation of the sensor on systematic itineraries by frequent commuters based on un-complicated reproduction of methodology.

Human is an indispensable factor on implementing the aforementioned complex monitoring procedure. The evaluation of the receptive environment is based on criteria originating from qualitative measurements [5]. Small scale implementation and minimum resources restrict wider operation with several nodes dispatched into different locations. The application requires continuous operation of at least two sensing devices (portable and fixed) in order to replete the database with spatial and numerical records and subsequently produce optimal representation and highlight probable system errors or weaknesses. Therefore three realizable user oriented scenarios are determined, depending on spatial dispersion of the sensor nodes.

5.1. Individual

Based on the aforementioned every individual may implement the proposed monitoring methodology on his everyday commute. Sensing could be applied by vehicle users, cyclists, walkers or hikers who follow specific itineraries thus to enrich the repository with spatial oriented data. The screen of the Android device projects an immediate visualization of environmental quality of the crossed area.

5.2. Social

Project's low cost and ease reproduction into multiple iterations facilitate further propagation on a larger scale. Their data inputs will be gathered in clusters, improve collection and enhance interpretation. Beyond hobbyists and enthusiasts the proposed WSN possibly attracts citizen and community groups. Widely employed Android devices urge large scale monitoring processes in residential areas. The proposed WSN could be implemented by local community and school groups, NGOs, tour operators and in general groups with interest into environmental sensing methodology.

5.3. Smart City Infrastructure

The increase of world's population and the shortage of natural resources incline towards the widespread use of information and communication technology (ICT) [41] in everyday life. Efficient changes in urban environments are powered by the trends of Smart Cities under the condition of meeting the needs of the city and its citizens while assisting the management of infrastructure and services [41].

Promoting involvement of state supported facilities in educational and environmental awareness activities. Public buildings and infrastructures operate constantly and are network connected. These edifices consist the ideal point of research interest, thus accommodate a vast number of activities and services. On the other hand private organizations will meliorate their image on environmental corporate social responsibility and assist on further environmental awareness activities.

The adoption by state owned vehicles (e.g., refuse trucks) and public transportation (e.g., bus, tram) services generate surplus value in relation to public service. Most of public vehicles follow the same routes on a daily basis creation a dynamic field of operation that potentially produces baseline data.

6. Validation

The proposed WSN was carried out in a broad area of Athens, Greece employing a deployed pair of fixed and portable sensors. The area of study was mostly set at central Athens region for both node types. Data emanated from recordings deployed on recurrent itineraries by car, bicycle or pedestrian use. Likewise a fixed node was set on different positions for varied time periods. This indicates that the comprehensive implementation of the system requires continuous operation of two or more devices (portable and stationary) in order to replete the Database of records (spatial and numerical). The minimum number of deployed devices used on this research as a detection mechanism for outlying erroneous factors. Subsequently, the expected number of recordings function positively for the further development of the platform, in order to egress errors and reveal system weaknesses for future implementation.

On strictly technical terms, there were few initial inconsistencies between modules and Arduino YUN, which impaired the sensing functionality. Eventually, debugging help solve some of these issues, nevertheless the complex configuration caused erroneous recordings. MQ sensors (Gasses micro-particles) use an internal heater in order to operate in temperatures higher than 50 °C [42], therefore are particularly affected by extreme temperature fluctuations and often produce inaccurate readings. Joint operation with a temperature sensor scale down potential inconsistencies. Additionally, noise pollution is a complex variable that needs specialized equipment [43]. A thirty-second stride per measure was applied so to increase accuracy of noise nuisance responsiveness by the microphone module. The effectiveness of each time step was validated with controlled measurements of a calibrated decibel meter. In addition to sensory there were few connectivity issues between YUN and the Android device. This came as a result of firmware incompatibilities, which resolved by further debugging and the use of different Android devices, with no measurable documentation on this matter.

The most considerable barrier the research came up against is incomplete data, which lead to challenging endeavors regarding automated environmental assessment. Ultimately manual data normalization allowed the production of a final assessment map (Figure 7), carried out by data aggregation (Global Environmental Quality) according to heat map methodology.

Figure 7. Global Environmental Quality Assessment map, Athens.

7. Conclusions and Future Work

The proposed system offers an automated methodology of monitoring the environmental quality. The system's potential is emphasized through the continuous network supply from several devices (nodes) simultaneously, the low resources and energy requirements and both its quantitative and qualitative assessment capabilities. Furthermore it supports various hardware extensions with the derived variables to offer dynamic representation capabilities on a Web GIS environment. Data generalizations caused measurement inaccuracies and hardware–software compatibility issues, which are assessed specifically on every occasion. We should emphasize herein that towards a cost-efficient and open source solution, with minimal implementation time, the way to go is a bottom up approach, such as the one we have followed, i.e., to select off-the-shelf tested solutions in order to compose the full system. We also feel that such an approach may be easily adopted by everyone, e.g., hobbyists, enthusiasts, students, researchers etc., who may easily and at a low cost create their own nodes and connect them to the platform, towards a fully social environmental network. Of course, we should emphasize that any single-board open platform such as the Raspberry Pi [44] or any other platfrom that supports digital and analog sensors and the MQTT protocol may be used for the construction of the sensor node.

The results prospect for further continuation of the research work. Map visualization of geographical variables in web GIS may be further optimized. Additionally, the system allows greater specialization capabilities on recording and development of both hardware and software structures. The implementation scenarios are capable to broaden in many other applications. The importance of channeling the research methodology to the public through crowd-sourcing is appearing while embedding big data methodology. The construction of an integrated Spatial Sensor Web Network requires the adoption of SensorML [45] standard and Sensor Web Enablement SWE [46] action to further support and enrich existing repositories. Implementing manual normalization generated the need for further research on machine learning methodology outward of the server in favor of big data aggregation techniques. Finally, the proposed system could be integrated with small effort on an IoT-ready platform that supports the MQTT protocol, such as the SYNAISTHISI platform [47], which is an integrated platform that allows humans, systems, machines, and devices for the creation and management of services. Initial experiments indicated that the proposed sensors may be seamlessly integrated within the SYNAISTHISI ecosystem. Also, transformation of all processing units into services is straightforward within SYNAISTHISI. This way, the desirable scalability should be guaranteed.

Author Contributions: Yorghos Voutos conceptualized and implemented the research work. Phivos Mylonas contributed to the implementation of application development and programming. Evaggelos Spyrou designed and assisted the implementation of the monitoring devices. Eleni Charou assisted the analysis of the data. All contributors facilitated to the writing of the paper.

Conflicts of Interest: The authors declare no conflict of interest.

References

1. Lein, J.K. Environmental Sensing. In *Environmental Sensing: Analytical Techniques for Earth Observation*; Springer: New York, NY, USA; Dordrecht, The Netherlands; Heidelberg, Germany; London, UK, 2012; Chapter 2, pp. 23–50, ISBN 978-1-46-140142-1.

2. Gomarasca, M.A. *Basics of Geomatics*; Springer: New York, NY, USA, 2009; ISBN 978-1-40-209014-1.

3. Reed, D.H. Impact of Climate Change on Biodiversity. In *Handbook of Climate Change Mitigation and Adaptation*, 2nd ed.; Chen, W.-Y., Seiner, J., Suzuki, T., Lackner, M., Eds.; Springer: New York, NY, USA, 2012; pp. 505–530.

4. Intergovernmental Panel on Climate Change (IPCC). *Climate Change 2014: Synthesis Report. Contribution of Working Groups I, II and III to the Fifth Assessment Report of the Intergovernmental Panel on Climate Change*; Core Writing Team, Pachauri, R.K., Meyer, L.A., Eds.; IPCC: Geneva, Switzerland, 2014; 151p.

5. Mohit, M.A. Quality of Life in Natural and Built Environment An Introductory Analysis. *Procedia-Soc. Behav. Sci.* **2013**, *101*, 33–43.

6. Atzori, L.; Iera, A.; Morabito, G. The Internet of things: A survey. *Comput. Netw.* **2010**, *54*, 2787–2805.

7. Burke et al 2006 Participatory Sensing. Available online: http://remap.ucla.edu/jburke/publications/Burke-et-al-2006_Participatory-sensing.pdf (accessed on 12 September 2017).

8. Uusitalo, L.; Lehikoinen, A.; Helle, I.; Myrberg, K. An overview of methods to evaluate uncertainty of deterministic models in decision support. *Environ. Model. Softw.* **2015**, *63*, 24–31.

9. Emre Aslan, Y.; Korpeoglou, I.; Ulusoy, O. A framework for use of wireless sensor networks in forest fire detection and monitoring. *Comput. Environ. Urban Syst.* **2012**, *36*, 614–625.

10. Ferdoush, S.; Li, X. Wireless Sensor Network System Design using Raspberry Pi and Arduino for Environmental Monitoring Applications. *Procedia Comput. Sci.* **2014**, *34*, 103–110.

11. Raspberry Pi Model B+—Raspberry Pi. Available online: https://www.raspberrypi.org/products/raspberry-pi-1-model-b/ (accessed on 20 October 2017).

12. Arduino Uno Rev3. Available online: https://store.arduino.cc/arduino-uno-rev3 (accessed on 20 October 2017).

13. Digi XBee/XBee-PRO ZigBee Modules (S2B)—Formerly ZB Product Detail—Digi International. Available online: https://www.digi.com/support/productdetail?pid=4549 (accessed on 20 October 2017).

14. Kumar, V.V.; Kumaraswamy, G. Wireless Sensor Network for Environmental Monitoring using Rasberri Pi. *Int. J. Adv. Technol. Innov. Res.* **2016**, *8*, 2084–2086, ISSN 2348-2370.

15. Salamone, F.; Belussi, L.; Danza, L.; Ghellere, M.; Meroni, I. Design and Development of nEMoS, an All-in-One, Low-Cost, Web-Connected and 3D-Printed Device for Environmental Analysis. *Sensors* **2015**, *15*, 13012–13027.

16. IoT Platform for Connected Devices | Xively by LogMeIn. Available online: https://www.xively.com/ (accessed on 20 October 2017).

17. Abdelhamid, S.; Hassanein, H.S.; Takahara, G. Vehicle as a Mobile Sensor. *Procedia Comput. Sci.* **2014**, *34*, 286–295.

18. Rawat, P.; Singh, K.D.; Chaouchi, H.; Bonnin, J.M. Wireless sensor networks: A survey on recent developments and potential synergies. *Supercomput* **2014**, *68*, 1–48.

19. Srbinovska, M.; Gavrovski, C.; Dimcev, V.; Krkoleva, A.; Borozan, V. Environmental parameters monitoring in precision agriculture using wireless sensor networks. *J. Clean. Prod.* **2014**, *88*, 297–307.

20. Keshtgary, M.; Deljoo, A. An Efficient Wireless Sensor Network for Precision Agriculture. *Can. J. Multimed. Wirel. Netw.* **2012**, *3*, 1–5.

21. Hur, B.; Eisenstadt, W.R. Low power Wireless Climate Monitoring System with RDIF Security Access Feature for Mosquitto and Pathogen Research. In Proceedings of the 1st Conference on Mobile and Secure Services, (MOBISECSER), Gainesville, FL, USA, 20–21 February 2015.

22. Naumowicz, T.; Freeman, R.; Kirk, H.; Dean, B.; Calsyn, M.; Liers, A.; Braendle, A.; Guilford, T.; Schiller, J. Wireless Sensor Network for habitat monitoring on Skomer Island. In Proceedings of the 35th Annual IEEE Conference on Local Computer Networks, LCN 2010, Denver, CO, USA, 10–14 October 2010; pp. 882–889.

23. More, A.; Wagh, S.; Joshi, K. A test-bed for habitat monitoring system using Wi-Fi in Wireless Sensor Networks. In Proceedings of the IEEE International Conference on Computational Intelligence and Computing Research (ICCIC), Madurai, India, 10–12 December 2015; pp. 1–6.

24. Simbeye, D.S.; Zhao, J.; Yang, S. Design and deployment of wireless sensor networks for aquaculture monitoring and control based on virtual instruments. *Comput. Electron. Agric.* **2014**, *102*, 31–42.

25. Bal, M.; Abrishambaf, R. A System for Monitoring Hand Hygiene Compliance based-on Internet-of-Things. In Proceedings of the IEEE International Conference on Industrial Technology (ICIT 2017), Toronto, ON, Canada, 22–25 March 2017; p. 18

26. Noel, A.; Abdaoui, A.; Badawy, A.; El-Fouly, T.; Ahmed, M.; Shehata, M. Structural Health Monitoring using Wireless Sensor Networks: A Comprehensive Survey. *IEEE Commun. Surv. Tutor.* **2017**, *19*, 1403–1423.

27. Mirshahi, S.; Uysal, S.; Akbari, A. Integration of RFID and WSN for supply chain intelligence system. In Proceedings of the Electronics, Computers and Artificial Intelligence (ECAI), Pitesti, Romania, 27–29 June 2013; pp. 1–6.

28. Lein, J.K. Sensors and Systems. In *Environmental Sensing: Analytical Techniques for Earth Observation*; Springer: New York, NY, USA; Dordrecht, The Netherlands; Heidelberg, Germany; London, UK, 2012; Chapter 3, pp. 51–82, ISBN 978-1-46-140142-1.

29. ARDUINO YÚN. Available online: https://store.arduino.cc/arduino-yun (accessed on 12 September 2017).

30. Epoch Converter—Unix Timestamp Converter. Available online: https://www.epochconverter.com (accessed on 20 October 2017).

31. GPS.gov: Timing Applications. Available online: https://www.gps.gov/applications/timing (accessed on 20 October 2017).

32. MQTT. Available online: http://mqtt.org/ (accessed on 12 September 2017).

33. Cloud Application Platform I Heroku. Available online: https://www.heroku.com/ (accessed on 12 September 2017).

34. Node.js. Available online: https://nodejs.org/en/ (accessed on 12 September 2017).

35. MongoDB for GIANT Ideas I MongoDB. Available online: https://www.mongodb.com (accessed on 12 September 2017).

36. GeoJSON. Available online: http://geojson.org (accessed on 12 September 2017).

37. MongoDB Hosting: Database-as-Service by mLab. Available online: https://mlab.com/ (accessed on 12 September 2017).

38. Build Amazing Native Apps and Progressive Web Apps with Ionic Framework and Angular. Available online: https://ionicframework.com/ (accessed on 12 September 2017).

39. GitHub—Ionic Team/ng-Cordova. Available online: https://www.npmjs.com (accessed on 12 September 2017).

40. npm. Available online: https://www.npmjs.com (accessed on 12 September 2017).

41. Pellicer, S.; Santa, G.; Bleda, A.L.; Maestre, R.; Jara, A.J.; Skarmeta, A.G. A Global Perspective of Smart Cities: A Survey. In Proceedings of the Seventh International Conference on Innovative Mobile and Internet Services in Ubiquitous Computing, Taichung, Taiwan, 3–5 July 2013.

42. Arduino Playground—MQGasSensors. Available online: http://playground.arduino.cc/Main/MQGasSensors/#heater (accessed on 20 October 2017).

43. Cho, D.S.; Kim, J.H.; Manvell, D. Noise mapping using measured noise and GPS data. *Appl. Acoust.* **2007**, *68*, 1054–1061.
44. Raspberry Pi—Teach, Learn, and Make with Raspberry Pi. Available online: https://www.raspberrypi.org/ (accessed on 20 October 2017).
45. Sensor Model Language (SensorML) | OGC. Available online: http://www.opengeospatial.org/standards/sensorml (accessed on 12 September 2017).
46. Sensor Web Enablement (SWE) | OGC. Available online: http://www.opengeospatial.org/ogc/markets-technologies/swe (accessed on 12 September 2017).
47. Pierris, G.; Kothris, D.; Spyrou, E.; Spyropoulos, C. SYNAISTHISI: An Enabling Platform for the Current Internet of Things Ecosystem. In Proceedings of the Panhellenic Conference on Informatics (PCI), Athens, Greece, 1–3 October 2015.

Journal of
Sensor and
Actuator Networks

Article

User-Generated Services Composition in Smart Multi-User Environments

Vincenzo Catania, Giuseppe La Torre, Salvatore Monteleone, Daniela Panno and Davide Patti *

Department of Electrical, Electronic, and Computer Engineering, University of Catania, V.le A. Doria, 6, 95125 Catania, Italy; vincenzo.catania@dieei.unict.it (V.C.); giuseppe.latorre@dieei.unict.it (G.L.T.); salvatore.monteleone@dieei.unict.it (S.M.); daniela.panno@dieei.unict.it (D.P.)
* Correspondence: davide.patti@dieei.unict.it; Tel.: +39-095-738-2385

Received: 6 July 2017; Accepted: 30 August 2017; Published: 1 September 2017

Abstract: The increasing complexity shown in Smart Environments, together with the spread of social networks, is increasingly moving the role of users from simple information and services consumers to actual producers. In this work, we focus on security issues raised by a particular kind of services: those generated by users. User-Generated Services (UGSs) are characterized by a set of features that distinguish them from conventional services. To cope with UGS security problems, we introduce three different policy management models, analyzing benefits and drawbacks of each approach. Finally, we propose a cloud-based solution that enables the composition of multiple UGSs and policy models, allowing users' devices to share features and services in Internet of Things (IoT) based scenarios.

Keywords: user generated services; smart environments; IoT

---

1. Introduction

The possibility for everyone to create custom content and services, in a simple and reliable way, has been introduced in recent years and is currently supported by a plethora of web based platforms, such as IFTTT [1], OpenMashup [2], and APIANT [3] (formerly known as We-Wired Web). These solutions carry out the composition of services with two different approaches: (i) by aggregating data, existing services, and user's defined tasks; and (ii) by simply creating new views of existing content. The results of these compositions can be referred to as User-Generated Services (UGSs) and User-Generated Content (UGC), respectively [4,5].

The Internet of Things (IoT) vision [6], which emerged in recent years due to a convergence of different communication/computing technologies, is leading to the diffusion of everyday-life Internet-capable objects, such as smartphones, Smart TVs, and health monitoring devices. Thus, IoT represents the ideal ecosystem for composite UGSs and UGC, making users able to generate new content and services not only from scratch, but also gathering data from objects and the environment [7–9]. This process, however, may give rise to several security issues due to the composition of the service-related Access Control Policies (ACP). For example, when an application developer assembles existing services that have their own security policies, he must ensure that the resultant policies do not conflict with the existing ones [10].

This scenario highlights the increasing importance that User-Generated Content and Services are going to assume in the short term. In particular, it is important to outline that there are substantial differences between traditional Web Services based on the Service-Oriented Architecture (SOA) paradigm and User-Generated Services, even more when the latter are integrated in an IoT scenario [11]. In fact, while the first ones are "always on" and regulated by access control policies that usually do not need to be updated frequently, the second ones may be subjected to more frequent changes due to users' actions and context. Let us consider, for example, social networks: when users perform common tasks such as adding/removing content (photos, videos, etc.) or updating the list of friends, the related policies change accordingly. Therefore, we can affirm that, unlike what happens for classical services, policies associated with UGC or UGSs may change very frequently. In addition, the access to a UGS may be regulated by pieces of contextual information connected to the service owner.

Let us consider the following example of context-dependent access control policy: a user belonging to the group "colleagues" can automatically access my gallery via bluetooth when all the following rules are satisfied: (i) My battery charge level is at least 35%; (ii) I'm at my workplace; and (iii) I'm not driving. It is easy to imagine that the user's context may change very rapidly and in a way that implies the continuous change of the current active policy for a device. This is just another example showing how UGSs represent a new class of services that substantially differ from traditional ones.

In this paper, which extends our prior work [12], we first analyze how the composition of services whose access control depends on context-aware policies further complicates the policy enforcement on the resulting composite service. Then, we define three models of policy management that capture the different possibilities available for UGSs. Finally, we demonstrate how a cloud-based approach can be exploited to support such policy models using commonly available open-source components and standard web technologies. The implementation of this approach has been built on top of *webinos* [13] platform, to which the authors contributed.

2. Reference Scenario

As the number of devices such as smartphones, tablets, in-car-devices and so on, increases, the whole electronic industry ecosystem is switching from "multi-user per device" to "multi-device per user" environments. Adopting the terminology and concepts we introduced in the *webinos* project [7], the set of devices associated with a given user can be considered as virtually contained (registered) inside the user's *Personal Zone* (PZ) and might also be shared with others, that is, registered in multiple PZs.

Figure 1 shows two PZs belonging, respectively, to the users Alice and Bob. Alice's PZ contains a smartphone and a camcorder while Bob's contains only a Smart TV. Despite a single device that could be "shared" among several PZs, it is owned by a unique user that is responsible for its policies and whose management may also be delegated to other users/entities. An example policy for Alice's PZ could be the following:

Alice's relatives are allowed to see her smartphone's gallery pictures on their Smart TV when she is connected through Wi-Fi.

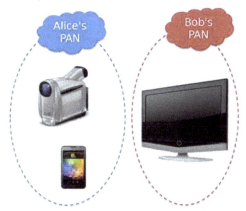

Figure 1. A simple representation of Personal Area Networks.

Each user can set policies for devices registered in his/her PZ. In the case that a device is shared among multiple users (i.e., PZs) and its behavior is regulated by multiple policies (e.g., one for each user), the one written by the owner takes priority over the others. For the sake of simplicity, in the following, we will use the name of the PZ owner to refer to a generic device registered in his/her PZ. For example, a request from Carol is to be intended as a request coming from one of the devices registered in her PZ.

Many different issues could arise when services regulated by context-aware policies are composed. These issues may be experienced for instance considering the scenario depicted in Figure 2, in which services *Videostream* and *Screenshot* are provided by Alice to Bob and by Bob to Carol. In general:

- *Videostream* allows users to receive a video stream from Alice's camcorder/smartphone;
- *Screenshot* allows users to take snapshots of contents reproduced on Bob's Smart TV.

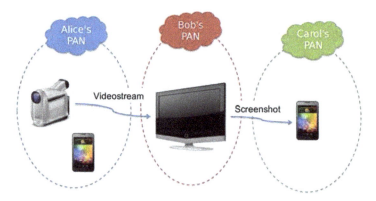

Figure 2. An example of User-Generated Services composition: the *Screenshot* service can make use of the *Videostream* service to provide content.

Let us consider the following:

Example 2.1. Alice's policies for *Videostream* service are:

1. Alice's parents are always allowed to use *Videostream* service;
2. Alice's relatives are allowed to use *Videostream* service only when Alice is in Catania;
3. Every other subject is not allowed to use *Videostream* service.

Moreover, Bob's policies for *Screenshot* service are:

1. Only Bob's house guests are allowed to use *Screenshot* service;
2. Every other subject is not allowed to use *Screenshot* service.

Both Alice's and Bob's policies specify contextual constraints: Alice is willing to offer her service toward her relatives only if she is in Catania (so this policy depends on Alice's context), and Bob's policy instead allows only people who are inside Bob's house (so this policy depends on subject's context). Let us imagine that Bob invites Carol (Alice's aunt) to his home to watch a video and suppose that Carol takes some screenshots of this video with her smartphone using the Smart TV provided service. When Bob's Smart TV receives a screenshot request from Carol, it checks its policies and allows Carol's smartphone to access the service, according to Bob's policy. This scenario might raise some problems if Carol tries to take screenshots of content owned by Alice. In this case, even supposing that Bob (his Smart TV) is aware of Alice's policies at the time that a request from Carol is received, it is not possible to enforce the request if Alice's context information (i.e., location) is not available. In fact, Alice may consider her location as a "private" information or it could not be accessible at that specific moment.

If Bob decides to allow a Carol's request only enforcing his policy (regardless of Alice's decision), the situations listed in Table 1 may occur:

Table 1. Potential situation of conflict between Alice's policy and actual data sharing.

#	Alice's Context	Alice's Policy	Conflict?
1	A is in Catania	C is A's relative	NO
2	A is in Catania	C isn't A's relative	YES
3	A isn't in Catania	C is A's relative	YES
4	A isn't in Catania	C isn't A's relative	YES

According to Alice's and Bob's policies, case 1 is the only that does not cause any conflict between Alice's and Bob's authorization decisions. On the contrary, the conditions considered in cases 2, 3, and 4 lead to conflicting situations that Bob does not take into account Alice's policies and related context information at the enforcement time.

This is just one example of the issues that may arise when multiple UGSs are composed. In the rest of the paper, we will analyze these issues and propose different solutions to cope with them.

3. Security Policy Issues in UGS Composition

The behavior of IoT Services (either traditional or user-generated) is regulated by security access control policies that restrict the access to services to external subjects, represented by applications or other services. In the UGSs scenario, when a user assembles existing services, he/she has to guarantee that the policy of the composite service is coherent with policies of all the other involved services (the component services). For example, suppose that Bob wants to create a new service making use of another one provided by Alice. When Carol requires access to this new service, Bob cannot decide whether to allow or deny Carol's request only evaluating his policy: he also should know Alice's decision toward Carol's request.

In order to avoid ambiguity, it is necessary to define the notation we adopted to describe our case studies.

Let D be the set of service providers d_i, for example, in the considered scenario, the devices of an IoT ecosystem. Let S_i be the set services $s_{i,j}$, where $s_{i,j}$ is the j-th service provided by d_i. Furthermore, let P_i be the set of policies $p_{i,k}$, where $p_{i,k}$ denotes the set of policies for all the services provided by the device d_i. Finally, let $C_{i,j}$ be the set of the *component services* used to produce the *composite service* $s_{i,j}$.

For example, Figure 3 shows a graph representation for a user-generated service composition where:

- Each node is a service provider, e.g., a device owned by a user providing/consuming services;
- Each edge from d_x to d_y indicates a service provided by d_x that is requested by d_y.

Note that $s_{2,1}$ is a composite service having $s_{1,1}$ as component service, that is, $C_{2,1} = \{s_{1,1}\}$. In particular, three main aspects must be considered in the UGSs composition with regard to the access control policy. These aspects are:

- *Dynamicity*: service related policies may change frequently;
- *Context Awareness*: policies may depend on contextual information (e.g., user's context);
- *Degree of Privacy*: users could want to set restrictions on the disclosure degree of their policies towards other subjects (users/services).

These features that characterize UGSs composition may cause new issues to arise as compared with the traditional service composition.

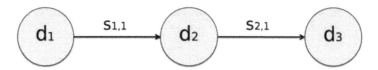

Figure 3. Graph formal representation of User-Generated Services (UGSs) composition.

3.1. Dynamicity

In fast changing environments, to promptly react to policies' changes, a security policy infrastructure with the following features is required:

- It should be able to update/synchronize composite services' policies when component services' policies change. For example, referring again to Figure 3, if the policies related to service $s_{1,1}$ change, it is necessary to synchronize the policies of all composite services that have $s_{1,1}$ as a component service (in this case only $s_{2,1}$);
- It should define efficient strategies to ensure that any change in component services' policies does not lead to conflicting authorization decisions taken by the security policy of the composite service.

In this perspective, already discussed techniques based on static composition of policies such [10,14] may not be suitable for highly dynamic environments.

3.2. Context Awareness

The use of policies referring to contextual information further complicates the authorization decision process to grant access to composite services. In the policy example related to Figure 2, Bob can take a conflict-free decision against a Carol's request only if he knows Alice's context. However it is not available to Bob since only Alice knows her context and it may be changed at the time of Carol's request. Contextual policies, therefore, add additional difficulties in user-generated service composition. In particular, the policy manager of the composite service provider needs to know remote contextual information from which the component services' policies depend on. We call this "context synchronization problem".

3.3. Degree of Privacy

UGSs composition can lead to policy disclosure. To avoid this, the service provider that assembles a composite service, referred in the following as *intermediate provider*, has to ensure that its policy is compliant with all the component services' policies. This is possible only if he knows all the policies that represent the behavior of each component service toward all the possible subjects. In many cases, especially in the UGS scenario, this could be a serious privacy problem since policies contain sensitive information that the owner of the component service might want to disclose partially (partial privacy) or not at all (full privacy) to other users. If all the component services adopted full privacy on their policies, the intermediate service provider would be unable to ensure any compliant authorization decision against a composite service's access request. Similar problems might arise also in the case of partial privacy. In addition, contextual user information could be in turn under partial or fully privacy restrictions, as it often refers to sensitive user's data.

4. Proposed Policy Models

By definition, UGSs are intended as composed services provided by different users. This implies that one of the main issues to address is to ensure the desired privacy criteria to each user involved in the composition process. Ensuring privacy does not only mean specifying a policy to decide who can see content (or use a service), but it also means to protect that policy. For example, in the case of UGC (e.g., in Facebook), the policy "I do not want John to see one of my photos", apart from preventing John to see that content, should imply that John will not be able to to know that he is not allowed to see one of my photos. This problem is even more significant in the case of context-aware policies, where the result of the enforcing may depend on sensitive information whose privacy must be protected. In the following, we introduce three approaches that, taking into account different degrees of privacy, can be used to cope with issues related to dynamicity and context-awareness. Depending on how the policy content is distributed and managed across the devices, we can distinguish the three different models described in the following subsections. These three policy enforcement techniques were primarily designed to preserve privacy (both policy content and user context). They also consider some approaches to cope with the dynamicity of the user context which directly impacts on the enforcement.

4.1. Distributed Policy Enforcement

Distributed Policy Enforcement (DPE) is the solution we propose in the case of full privacy degree for the component services' policies. The DPE approach is based on a distributed algorithm for policy enforcement that involves all the providers (partners) that take part in the service composition process. In this way, each partner is characterized by a "non disclosure" policy strategy that prevents the composite service provider from knowing partner's policies. Using DPE, an authorization decision to deny access to a service is taken only if the individual decisions of all partners have been collected and at least one of them is of the type Deny. The Policy Composition Algorithm (PCA) is therefore of type Deny-Override. When a provider receives an access request to its composite service, it firstly evaluates the request locally and if necessary forwards this request to all the providers involved in the service composition.

We can see in detail how this method works considering Figure 3. Let us suppose d_2 is Bob's Smart TV, which is composing a service $s_{1,1}$ offered by Alice camcorder d_1 to provide the *Screenshot* service $s_{2,1}$. When Carol requires through her smartphone d_3 access to $s_{2,1}$, the Policy Enforcement Point (PEP) of Bob's PZ firstly enforces local policy to decree whether Carol is allowed, and if not, it straight out rejects the request. On the contrary, if Bob's policy allows Carol, Bob's PEP forwards the incoming request to Alice's PEP (on behalf of Carol). At this stage, Alice's policy manager enforces the local policy and evaluates whether Carol can indirectly access $s_{1,1}$. Finally, Alice's PEP sends the decision to Bob's PEP, which issues (or not) the service $s_{2,1}$.

As direct consequence, this method is agnostic to dynamic policy changes of component services. Any change, in fact, is taken into account thanks to the distributed nature of the policy enforcement: each partner takes part in the final decision on the basis of its policy decision. This technique also works well in context based policy systems: the authorization decision of each service's partner will take into account also any other useful contextual information. From a practical point of view, there is a main drawback: this approach may lead to a composite service that could never work due to conflicts among component service's policies. In addition, from a performance point of view, an overhead is introduced by every enforcement. For example, when the intermediate service node forwards an access request to the partners, it has to transfer to them all the requestor's identity information plus the information about the required resources. On the other hand, there are no performance degradation issues due to policy or context synchronization.

4.2. Local Policy Enforcement

When providers' policies do not contain sensitive information, they could be stored and evaluated by intermediate providers. Local Policy Enforcement (LPE), unlike DPE, requires policy evaluation only for those service providers that supply a composite service. This means, for instance, that the intermediate provider d_2, in addition to its set of policies P_2, could store the set P_1 of the component service $s_{1,1}$ and evaluate it whenever a request is received (such as from d_3).

In general, an intermediate provider who stores all component's sets of policies could compose them and then, for each access request, evaluate the composite policy. As already mentioned, deriving from several component policies a composite policy in which there are neither conflicts nor redundancies is quite complex. For this reason, in a UGS scenario, where policies are dynamic and may change frequently, we can affirm that evaluating each single policy is preferable to extracting a composite policy. In this kind of evaluation, an authorization decision that denies service access to a subject is taken if at least one of the component policy returns a "deny" response. The PCA algorithm is therefore of type Deny-Override.

As shown in Section 2 (policy example of Figure 2), given that Bob knows that when Alice is in Catania she is willing to provide *Videostream* service to Carol, he cannot know at the enforcement time where Alice is and thus he cannot allow or deny Carol. Therefore, to evaluate the policy of a component service, an intermediate provider must know the remote context. Two different approaches enable policy enforcement by intermediate providers when context-dependent policies can be adopted. The first approach assumes that Bob stores Alice's policy set that contains n context-dependent policies. However, only a subset of these policies is currently active: those related to the current Alice's context. Thus, Alice sends Bob only information about her context and Bob uses this information to understand which of the policies contained in the policy set are active (applicable). This exchange could happen according to two strategies: (a) Alice tells Bob her context information whenever her context changes; (b) Bob asks Alice her context information whenever he receives a request (e.g., from Carol). If Alice's context changes frequently, it could be better to adopt approach (b). On the contrary, if Alice's context rarely changes, the proposed variant (a) may be preferable. The second approach considers that Bob knows only the current active subset of Alice's policies. In this case, Alice sends to Bob those policies enabled by her context.

Since LPE expects that composite service providers keep component services policies, it is necessary to update these every time they change. As shown in Figure 4, if n users (providers) require the $s_{1,1}$ service in their composition process, Alice's policy manager has to synchronize the policy in all the involved providers each time the policy for $s_{1,1}$ is changed.

Synchronization could be a burdensome task as a provider (e.g., Alice) should maintain information about all the "follower" providers, and it is even more problematic if the provider that supplies the service is a resource-constrained device.

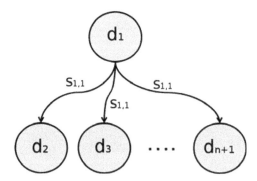

Figure 4. Service provisioning to multiple devices.

In those cases when not only the policy but also the context relative to a service provider may change, knowing these policies might be not enough to be able to evaluate them. As aforementioned, in both of the two approaches, Alice needs to realize when her context changes so that she can advise Bob about sending him her actual policy/context information. Therefore, there is the need to automatically spot every context change. For this purpose, we propose an extension of XACML (eXtensible Access Control Markup Language) architecture (Figure 5) that introduces the Context Listener component. The choice of using XACML as a basis for this work is mainly due to the flexibility and fine grained levels of customizability given by this standard. In detail, the Context Listener reads the policy obtained through the PAP (Policy Administration Point) module and stores both context-dependent parameters and relative boundaries. For example, if a policy rule was

"Permit if battery level is greater than 35%",

the Context Listener will store *"battery_level"* as a parameter and *"greater than 35%"* as related boundary. Using this information, the Context Listener can reorganize a user's policy on the basis of his/her context. In particular, the current values of context-dependent parameters affect the policy selection. For example, the pseudo code reported below may represent the logic followed by the Context Listener to choose the current policy:

```
if (context_params1 < boundary1)
    current_policy = P1
if (context_params2 > boundary2)
    current_policy = P2
```

Thus, the Context Listener periodically polls the PIP (Policy Information Point) module to obtain actual values for the contextual parameters (such as current battery level) and checks whether these values remain within the boundaries defined by the policy. When at least one of the parameters, included in the rule, exceeds its boundary, the Context Listener communicates to interested intermediate providers the current user's context or policy.

In summary, LPE can be adopted if there are no privacy concerns, but the synchronization process requires an overhead that, as we will show in Section 5, may be not acceptable in the case of devices with reduced performance as, for example, mobile phones.

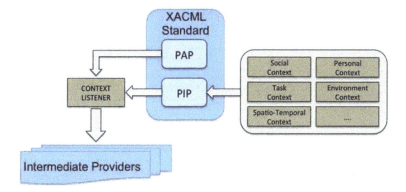

Figure 5. XACML (eXtensible Access Control Markup Language) extension with Context Listener.

4.3. Policy's Context Obfuscation

Local Policy Enforcement requires distribution of policies or parts of them. The process to exchange this kind of data requires some mechanisms to assure content authenticity and avoid tampering. Privacy is the other main aspect to cope with in situations such as this one, where personal information (i.e., contextual data) are exchanged. In fact, the policies themselves are privacy sensitive information because they can contain users' preferences (i.e., rules that are applied to specific subjects) and may depend on context parameters (e.g., users' location details). Policy Information Points are allowed to elicit, from remote providers (i.e., users' devices), personal contextual data in order to allow policy enforcement. This means that, knowing user's policy and the relative decision toward a request, it could be possible to retrieve information about user's context. This obviously leads to privacy issues.

In literature, the problem of policy's content protection is faced in different works as, for example, in [15] where the authors propose techniques based on encryption. Our proposal relies on obfuscation methods in order to mask sensitive information sending the policy structure in plain text.

Suppose that Alice chooses the following policy for the *Videostream* service:

```
1 <policy-set id="Alice's policyset">
2    <policy algorithm="permit-overrides">
3      <target>
4        <subject param="cert" match="Carol.cert"/>
5        <resource param="service" match="videostream"/>
6      </target>
7      <rule id="5ABE" effect="permit">
8        <condition>
9          <context param="location" match="home"/>
10       </condition>
11     </rule>
12     <rule effect="deny"/>
13   </policy>
14   <policy>
15     <target>
16       <subject id="F3MK"/>
17     </target>
18     <rule effect="deny"/>
19   </policy>
20 </policy-set>
```

Since this policy depends on Alice's context (specifically on Alice's location), giving it in plain-text to Bob could give rise to privacy issues: Bob, in fact, knowing the policy, could realize that Alice is at home at the instant when Carol is allowed to get *Videostream* service. This information does not concern Bob: he only should know that Carol will be able to get *Videostream* service (indirectly through *Screenshot* service) when a certain Alice's context will be active, but he should not know which one it is. The policy stored by Bob's devices would be the following:

```
1 <policy-set id="Obfuscated Alice's policyset">
2    <policy algorithm="permit-overrides">
3      <target>
4        <subject param="cert" match="Carol.cert"/>
5        <resource param="service" match="videostream"/>
6      </target>
7      <rule id="5ABE" effect="permit" obfuscated>
8        <condition>
9          <context param="E67QF1" match="AR7MG6"/>
10       </condition>
11     </rule>
12     <rule effect="deny"/>
13   </policy>
14   <policy algorithm="deny-overrides">
15     <target>
16       <subject id="F3MK" obfuscated/>
17     </target>
18     <rule effect="deny"/>
19   </policy>
20 </policy-set>
```

In this way, using LPE, Alice will transfer to Bob the pair $< E67QF1, AR7MG6 >$ representing her context, instead of the sensitive information $< location, home >$.

4.4. Partial Disclosure Policy Enforcement

Describing DPE and LPE, we pointed out some benefits and drawbacks of both solutions. DPE solves problems related to dynamic policy/context changes and privacy issues related to policy disclosure, but it could be very difficult to generate a new service without any knowledge about policies related to component services. This, in fact, may lead to having composite services that do not work properly. For instance, if Bob decides to provide $s_{2,1}$ only after *5:00 p.m.* without knowing that Alice is willing to provide $s_{1,1}$ only before *3:00 p.m.*, his service will never work. On the other hand, with LPE approach, intermediate providers know component policies: this could involve privacy problems (as discussed in previous sections), but it represents the best way, for an intermediate provider, to supply a working service. For these reasons, we want to introduce a new approach that can be considered as somewhere in between DPE and LPE: we call it Partial Disclosure Policy Enforcement (PDPE).

According to the idea behind PDPE, when an intermediate provider wants to supply a composite service to a set of known subjects, he can obtain from the component service provider not the whole policy but only the information regarding these subjects. PDPE thus consists of two phases:

1. the *initialization* phase, in which an intermediate provider (Bob) can "negotiate" the policy disclosure with the component provider (Alice) requiring only the policy's information toward a pre-determined set of subjects;
2. the *incremental update* phase, in which the intermediate provider requires additional information every time a new subject (which is not included in the original set of the considered subjects) requires access to the service.

The first phase can be optional as an intermediate provider could not negotiate the policy disclosure for a first set of subjects building this initial set when a subject requires the service the first time.

For example, suppose Bob does not know Alice's policy for $s_{1,1}$. When Carol requires $s_{2,1}$ Bob informs Alice who sends back to Bob the piece of her policy regarding Carol. From that moment onwards, Bob stores this partial policy, enforcing it every time Carol requires $s_{2,1}$ service. Whenever a new subject (e.g., David) requires $s_{2,1}$, Bob repeats the procedure, and so on. Since even partial policies may depend on user's contextual information, PDPE employs the same approaches shown in Figure 5 to overcome problems related to policy/context changes. In addition, it might apply the obfuscation technique already discussed previously.

4.5. Considerations

The proposed approaches mainly differ in the amount of policy's information revealed by component service providers to intermediate providers. However, all of the discussed approaches can be combined to meet different users' security requirements. Consider the scenario in which Bob wants to provide a service that shows a Google Map decorated with his and his friends' preferred restaurants. This scenario is represented in Figure 6. Alice and David provide two services that give information about their preferred restaurants. We can note that all the considered approaches are employed: Google, using PDPE, gives Alice only a piece of its policy (only the parts related to those subjects that Bob wants to consider), Alice, indeed, does not bother about privacy issues and gives Bob her whole policy (LPE). Finally, David does not want Bob to know his policy, so he adopts DPE.

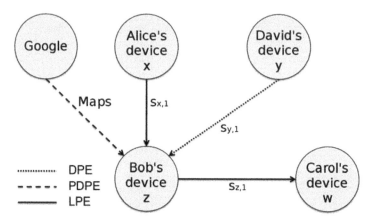

Figure 6. An example of hybrid service composition scenario in which $s_{z,1}$ composes all the other provided services, i.e., $C_{z,1} = \{Maps, s_{x,1}, s_{y,1}\}$.

5. A Cloud Approach

5.1. Mobile Constraints

As aforementioned, the broad diffusion of IoT devices, combined with the presence of platforms able to simplify interactions among them, represent the starting point for the spread of User-Generated Services. In some cases, these services could strictly depend on devices' features and local context. If we consider, for example, the scenario depicted in Section 2 we can find out that the service created by Alice is provided thanks to the presence and the features of her smart device. This scenario is just one example that points out that the next step is represented by those services that are not only generated but also provided by users through their devices (User Provided Services or UPSs). Limitations may be due to the utilization of kind of devices that are not supposed to work as providers. This is the case of smartphones and handsets in general. In fact, it is possible to recognize problems of at least three categories, which are performance, scalability and presence. For what concerns performance, it is clear that providing a service that is resource consuming (e.g., in terms of CPU time, memory and bandwidth) may reduce the usability of devices' main functionalities. Scalability issues are related to the number of users that can concurrently access our self-provided service.

The last point regards presence: some devices could be not reachable in any moment due to a temporary lack of connectivity (for example, a car or a smartphone inside a tunnel or in a place without coverage) or just because they are running out of battery. As is known, devices might provide services or contents and can regulate access to them via context-based policies. In the first case, the device presence is obviously needed to guarantee the service availability, and, in the second case, it is needed to gather the context information without which the policy to access or handle the remote content cannot be enforced. It is also important to notice that the problems described in previous sections still remain. In fact, it is difficult to properly handle policy disclosure and cope with the synchronization process of context and policy, especially in the case of many actors.

5.2. Architecture

In order to cope with the issues described in previous sections, we propose another structure that differs from the one depicted in Figure 3, introducing a new component, namely *service mediator*. The structure of this architecture is shown in Figure 7.

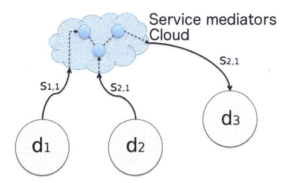

Figure 7. Cloud-based architecture for UGSs composition management.

This architecture still allows using the already described policy models and their combinations: however, it is important to point out that, in this case, the policy is enforced by components in the cloud and not by intermediate providers.

The role of the *service mediator*, which is intended to be a cloud component, is manifold; in fact, it is possible to recognize at least the following functionalities: (a) synchronizing user's preferences, context information and policies; (b) resolving problems related to "device presence"; (c) reducing the disclosure of sensitive data, context information and policies; (d) providing unified service discovery; (e) integrating logic to switch among different policy and context exchange approaches; and (f) enhancing scalability and performance.

One of the main advantages of a cloud approach regards synchronization (a). In fact, compared to the peer-to-peer model presented in the first part of this paper, a cloud based architecture simplifies the process of exchanging and keeping up to date the information needed. This might be done, for example, through a publish/subscribe notification system. Furthermore, such a publish/subscribe mechanism could be useful to resolve presence related issues (b), enabling users and devices to leave online records of taken decisions, context information and other data, also when they are disconnected. This problem, as mentioned before, is very relevant in the case of constrained devices. If we consider, for example, the scenario presented in Section 2 adding the clause that Alice allows Bob to record her videostream and reuse it with the aforementioned restrictions, the knowledge of Alice's location becomes very important. For obvious reasons, it is not possible to know Alice's location at any moment (e.g., all her devices ran out of battery), but, with the cloud approach here presented, it is possible to communicate and preserve context information, e.g., the last location available, for a more accurate evaluation.

The cloud approach also limits disclosure of personal data (c). In fact, the service mediator component could be the only point where sensitive information is stored. In addition, it enforces remote access requests on behalf of the remote service provider with the advantage of limiting exchange of policies, contextual information and sensitive data.

Devices can expose services registering them in the cloud. There the *service mediator* can: make them discoverable (d), manage their status and, as already mentioned, regulate remote access to them through policies. The *service mediator* could also contain some logic in order to switch between the different policy management models described. This smart switching system can allow users to change the desired degree of privacy at run time.

The gain in terms of scalability and performance (f) is due to the fact that the *service provider* will not be directly contacted by clients because exposed services will be accessed by the *service mediator*. It will be able to multiplex a service or serialize access to it in the case he cannot directly provide that service. Considering again the *Videostream* service, it is easy to imagine that a solution like the one proposed—with a server that acquires the videostream (*service provider*) and multiplexes it to other consumers—can reduce the provider's workload.

As a demonstrator prototype of the proposed approach, a policy management component has been implemented through the *webinos* foundation platform in order to expose devices' features to other devices registered in the virtual area called Personal Zone (PZ). The PZ has the main role of providing, in a simple manner, access to local and remote services, thus creating also an abstraction from underlying communication technologies. In particular, the approach proposed in *webinos'* makes use of the architecture depicted in Figure 8. In this architecture, the component called Personal Zone Hub (PZH) implements the behavior of the *service mediator*.

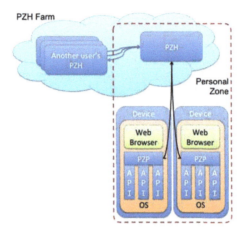

Figure 8. *Webinos* general architecture.

The PZH is the element in which the devices belonging to a PZ are registered. It enables the communication between devices of the same or a different PZ, allows the discovery of other PZHs and manages the synchronization process (e.g., of user's preferences, policy and context data). A PZH also controls security aspects. In fact, it is the certificate authority that issues certificates for each PZP registered in a PZ. These certificates allow mutually authentication and also encryption of the messages exchanged among devices in the zone.

The other main component of *webinos* architecture is the PZP that runs on each *webinos enabled device* and manages the communication between the device and the main hub (PZH). The PZP also stores the information that should be synchronized with the hub in the case it is not reachable in order to start the synchronization process when the PZH again becomes available. The PZP is responsible for the local discovery of features/services, accessible through a set of APIs (Application Programming Interfaces) that expose some capabilities of the underlying Operating System.

From this description, it is possible to notice that the structure proposed by *webinos* well suits the cloud approach where the *service mediator* is an extension of the PZH able to manage not only security and synchronization aspects but also service multiplexing. Choosing *webinos* as a basis for our work made it possible to move the focus on privacy/security issues, removing the necessity of implementing a new system from scratch to synchronize policies, context information and user's preferences. Furthermore, *webinos* provides full specifications for over 30 APIs to manage, for example, authentication, discovery of devices and services, context, contacts, filesystem, media content and streams, sensors and actuators, simplifying the creation of multi-user/multi-device/multi-domain applications in several Operating Systems, such as Android, Windows, MacOs, GNU/Linux, Chrome OS and Firefox OS [16].

The *webinos* platform provides privacy protection and access control features to meet the privacy and security requirements of web applications and users. This means protecting against malware and other users who may attempt to access more data than they should or simply avoid the unnecessary disclosure of personal data. To satisfy these requirements, *webinos* relies on the strong identification of web applications, users and devices, combined with a least-privilege access control, based on XACML. It is an OASIS standard that describes: (i) an XML (eXtensible Markup Language) representation for both a policy language and an access control decision request/response language, and (ii) a data-flow model for policy enforcement and relative involved actors. In *webinos*, the XACML architecture has been adapted using PrimeLife extensions [17], allowing for making access control decisions based on both the request context and user preferences.

The root element defined by XACML is a PolicySet that is made up by both a set of policies (containing at least one policy) and Policy Combination Algorithms (PCA) that take the authorization decision from each policy as input and apply some standard logic to come up with a final decision. Each XACML policy is in turn made up of a Target and a set of Rules.

A Target is basically a set of simplified conditions for the Subject, Resource and Action that must be met for a PolicySet, Policy or Rule to apply to a given request. Each Rule represents the core logic for a policy, and it is made up of a Condition (which is a boolean function and may contain nested sub-conditions) and an Effect (a value of Permit or Deny that is associated with successful evaluation of the Rule).

The Data-flow model introduced by XACML is shown in Figure 9. In short, a Policy Enforcement Point (PEP) is responsible for intercepting a native request for a resource and to forward this to the Context Handler (CH). The CH will form an XML request based on the requester's attributes, the resource in question, the action, and other information pertaining to the request. The CH will then send this request to a Policy Decision Point (PDP), which will look at the request and some policy that applies to the request, and come up with an answer about whether access should be granted. That answer (in XML format) is returned to the Context Handler, which translates this response to the native response format of the PEP. Finally, the PEP, based on the response, allows or denies access to the requester. A more detailed description about XACML is provided by [18] while a description of *webinos* is presented in [19].

The object model depicted in Figure 9 shows the main components of the *webinos* policy framework. Both the PZP and PZH enforce policies using standard XACML components, supplemented by:

- The *Decision Wrapper* creates the initial policy enforcement query based on incoming requests;
- The *Access Manager* makes the final decision by combining pieces of information from XACML access control and Data Handling Decision Function (DHDF);
- The *DHDF Engine* provides privacy and data handling functionalities;
- The *Request Context* manages all contextual information; it stores all the data and credentials released by a user in a given session;
- The *PDP Cache* (PDPC) stores PDP decisions that could be shared among personal devices.

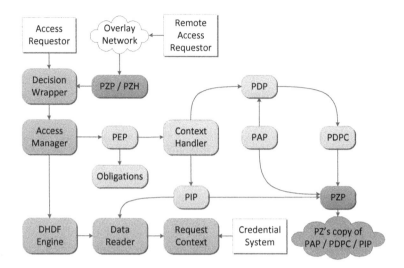

Figure 9. XACML-based Data-flow model of *webinos*.

5.3. Considerations on Design Choices

This work brings together two innovative aspects related to the world of next-generation services. The first is to imagine an extension of the concept of User Generated Content to services, thereby defining User Generated Services as services that are both directly generated and provided by users, for example through their devices (e.g., smartphone, TV, and car). The possibility of composing services to create new ones is certainly one of the key aspects of the SOA paradigm. In the case of UGSs, the composition of multiple services provided by different users introduces a number of privacy issues that have been the main focus of this work. In particular, the management of access control and privacy of a service is managed through policies that, in the case of composite services, are in turn composed, with the risk of creating inconsistencies or conflicts that may invalidate user preferences. The methods presented in previous sections are thought to mitigate the impact that fast changing user-centered environments, characterized by the presence of UGSs and the manipulation of sensitive data, may suffer from not as fast or approximate policies' updates. In facts, when existing services are put together, it is necessary to guarantee that the policy of the resulting composite service is coherent with policies of all the component services to avoid conflicting authorization decisions taken by the security policy of the composite service.

The second innovative aspect concerns the possibility to have service access governed by policies that depend on the user's context. It is important to consider that changes in user-centered environments are usually reflected in a physical (e.g., position and speed) and a logical (e.g., preferences and contacts in social networks) context, each of which contributes to increasing the dynamics to take into account while composing services. This introduces a further complexity in policy enforcement, as it is necessary to know the context of all the users involved in the composition of a service in order to decide whether or not to grant access to that service. In addition, due to the fact that the context of a user is characterized by a strong variability, applying caching strategies is not easy since policy constraints may change along with the context itself. For these reasons, we have considered implementing strategies for composing UGS that consider variations in the context of the users involved in the composition.

Then, it was important to consider the spread of constrained devices that are part of everyday life. To expose UGSs within these devices, it was necessary to take into account different factors, and in particular, the fact that resources needed to expose/exploit UGSs, as far as possible, should not compromise the normal functioning of the device. The cloud-based solution, proposed in this section, has been designed to overcome these limitations regarding performance, scalability, and presence (the latter, in terms of power consumption and network coverage) and to exploit the other policy models introduced in this work. Finally, although the proposed methods introduce an overhead due to the transfer of policy or context information, they provide greater security and privacy protection in scenarios likely to become common over the next few years.

6. Related Work

The scientific interest in UGSs and UGC is growing in these last years. In [5], the authors presented a comprehensive survey of the state-of-the-art UGSs and defined UGSs by comparison with the concept of UGC, describing advantages and limitations of each approach. Ref. [4] introduces some guidelines to support users in the services' creation and management. In [20], the requirements to let the vision of the "super prosumer" become true are investigated. In particular, they review the current technologies that enable an easy creation and discovery of mobile services and list the identified requirements for UGSs. The interest in this topic is further motivated by the result of diverse studies that evaluate, for example, the impact of UGSs and especially UGC on society [21,22], tourism [8], and advertising [23]. With regard to aspects explicitly focused on service composition, some works were proposed to prevent conflicting behaviors when policies are composed. In [14], authors propose a security policy composition mechanism which semi-automatically derives the policy consistency rules. In addition, Ref. [10] presents an approach that merges existing policies and restrictions into a new policy to remove redundancy and inconsistencies. It is important to point out how the process of policy composition might be very expensive from a computational perspective; as a consequence, these solutions can only be applied if we assume static policies (i.e., not changing over the time), so that the composition process can be performed only once off-line, when the composite service is made up. Another approach, proposed in [24], adopts a filtering phase and a differential evolutionary based algorithm to compose services taking into account service providers' mobility.

The composition and deployment of UGSs has also been investigated from the IoT perspective. In [11], the authors proposed an infrastructure to enable developers and designers to dynamically query, select, and use running instances of real-world services. More specifically, Ref. [25] analyzed the notion of ubiquitous services of IoT in connection with their usage in the context of social networks. Other works focused on particular domains of IoT services, such as [26], introducing an interconnection framework for mobile Health (mHealth), or [27,28] where the composition service is enabled by means of a semantic ontology. Some important contributions in this field have been directed through the definition of policy models suitable for context-aware scenarios, as in [28–30]. Access control systems should be able to support and understand existing and new context information types in order to address access control requirements. To make this possible, the authors of [31] presented an extensible access control solution based on XACML (eXtensible Access Control Markup Language) making it able to understand new attributes' data types and the functions that are used in the policy to evaluate the users' requests. Another interesting work is [32], which proposed an access control policy model based on context and the role that can be appropriate for web services. The model takes into account contextual information to define and perform access control policies. It works with contextual information from users, environments and resources to execute dynamic role assignment and constrain the authorization decision. Another approach to address conflicts in context-aware policies is presented in [33], where authors propose a framework in which the policy is chosen at run time based on context information. Recently, the authors of [34] presented a generic framework, OntCAAC (Ontology-based Context-Aware Access Control), modelling dynamic contexts and corresponding access control policies exploiting semantic technologies.

In conclusion, several works have addressed typical problems related to UGSs such as dynamic policy change and context-aware policies; however, to the best of our knowledge, none of these works has yet taken into account the kind of issues assuming the perspective of UGSs composition as the

J. Sens. Actuator Netw. **2017**, *6*, 20

main challenge. The main contribution of this work is to introduce different models that are explicitly focused on a composite service scenario and present a concrete architecture that could address most of the critical issues described here.

7. Conclusions

The composition of User-Generated Services in an IoT environment introduces several security related challenges. In this work, three different approaches have been analyzed showing the available trade-off in policy management. Finally, a cloud based architecture that is flexible enough to embrace the different policy enforcement models has been introduced, together with a prototype based on the *webinos* foundation platform. Future work will focus on the support of those constrained devices, such as very simple sensors, that can be identified but cannot hold policies to regulate access to their features and data.

Acknowledgments: The research described in this paper was initially funded by the EU FP7 *webinos* project (FP7-ICT-2009-05 Objective 1.2). The extension of this work has been partially supported by the Italian Ministry of Education, University and Research on the "PAC" call funding the "SERVIFY (SERVIce FirstlY)" project, Ref. PON03PE_00132_1, CUP B72F14000300005.

Author Contributions: All authors contributed extensively to the work presented in this paper. Giuseppe La Torre, Salvatore Monteleone and Davide Patti wrote the code and performed experiments; Vincenzo Catania and Daniela Panno refined the initial study. All authors discussed enhancements, results and implications, wrote the manuscript and commented on it at all stages.

Conflicts of Interest: The authors declare no conflict of interest. The founding sponsors had no role in the design of the study; in the collection, analyses, or interpretation of data; in the writing of the manuscript, and in the decision to publish the results.

References

1. IFTTT. IF This Then That. 2011. Available online: http://www.ifttt.com (accessed on 5 July 2017).
2. OMA. Open Mashup Alliance. 2009. Available online: https://en.wikipedia.org/wiki/Open_Mashup_Alliance (accessed on 5 July 2017).
3. APIANT. The Cloud Integration and Automation Platform | APIANT. 2016. Available online: https://apiant.com (accessed on 5 July 2017).
4. Jensen, C.S.; Vicente, C.R.; Wind, R. User-Generated Content: The Case for Mobile Services. *Computer* **2008**, *41*, 116–118.
5. Zhao, Z.; Laga, N.; Crespi, N. A survey of user generated service. In Proceedings of the 2009 IC-NIDC IEEE International Conference on Network Infrastructure and Digital Content, Beijing, China, 6–8 November 2009; pp. 241–246.
6. Xia, F.; Yang, L.T.; Wang, L.; Vinel, A. Internet of Things. *Int. J. Commun. Syst.* **2012**, *25*, 1101–1102.
7. Fuhrhop, C.; Lyle, J.; Faily, S. The webinos Project. In Proceedings of the 21st International Conference Companion on World Wide Web, WWW '12 Companion, New York, NY, USA, 16–20 April 2012; pp. 259–262.
8. Marine-Roig, E.; Clavé, S.A. Tourism analytics with massive user-generated content: A case study of Barcelona. *J. Destin. Mark. Manag.* **2015**, *4*, 162–172.
9. Ventura, D.; Monteleone, S.; La Torre, G.; La Delfa, G.C.; Catania, V. Smart EDIFICE—Smart EveryDay interoperating future devICEs. In Proceedings of the 2015 International Conference on Collaboration Technologies and Systems (CTS), Atlanta, GA, USA, 1–5 June 2015; pp. 19–26.
10. Speiser, S. Policy of Composition ≠ Composition of Policies. In Proceedings of the 2011 IEEE International Symposium on Proceedings of the Policies for Distributed Systems and Networks (POLICY), Pisa, Italy, 6–8 June 2011; pp. 121–124.
11. Guinard, D.; Trifa, V.; Karnouskos, S.; Spiess, P.; Savio, D. Interacting with the SOA-Based Internet of Things: Discovery, Query, Selection, and On-Demand Provisioning of Web Services. *IEEE Trans. Serv. Comput.* **2010**, *3*, 223–235.

12. Catania, V.; La Torre, G.; Monteleone, S.; Panno, D.; Patti, D. User-Generated services: Policy Management and access control in a cross-domain environment. In Proceedings of the 2015 International Wireless Communications and Mobile Computing Conference (IWCMC), Dubrovnik, Croatia, 24–28 August 2015; pp. 668–673.

13. Catania, V.; La Torre, G.; Monteleone, S.; Patti, D.; Vercelli, S.; Ricciato, F. A novel approach to Web of Things: M2M and enhanced javascript technologies. In Proceedings of the 2012 IEEE International Conference on Green Computing and Communications (GreenCom), Besancon, France, 20–23 November 2012; pp. 726–730.

14. Satoh, F.; Tokuda, T. Security Policy Composition for Composite Web Services. *IEEE Trans. Serv. Comput.* **2011**, *4*, 314–327.

15. Dong, C.; Russello, G.; Dulay, N. Shared and Searchable Encrypted Data for Untrusted Servers. In *Data and Applications Security XXII*; Lecture Notes in Computer Science; Atluri, V., Ed.; Springer: Berlin/Heidelberg, Germany, 2008; Volume 5094, pp. 127–143.

16. Webinos. Webinos Developer Portal. Available online: https://developer.webinos.org (accessed on 5 July 2017).

17. Ardagna, C.A.; De Capitani di Vimercati, S.; Paraboschi, S.; Pedrini, E.; Samarati, P. An XACML-based privacy-centered access control system. In Proceedings of the first ACM Workshop on Information Security Governance, Chicago, IL, USA, 13 November 2009; pp. 49–58.

18. Moses, T. Extensible Access Control Markup Language 2.0 Specification Set. Available online: http://www.oasis-open.org (accessed on 5 July 2017).

19. Lyle, J.; Monteleone, S.; Faily, S.; Patti, D.; Ricciato, F. Cross-platform access control for mobile web applications. In Proceedings of the 2012 IEEE International Symposium on Policies for Distributed Systems and Networks (POLICY), Chapel Hill, NC, USA, 16–18 July 2012; pp. 37–44.

20. Tacken, J.; Flake, S.; Golatowski, F.; Prüter, S.; Rust, C.; Chapko, A.; Emrich, A. Towards a Platform for User-Generated Mobile Services. In Proceedings of the 2010 IEEE 24th International Conference on Advanced Information Networking and Applications Workshops (WAINA), Perth, Australia, 20–23 April 2010; pp. 532–538.

21. Shelton, T.; Poorthuis, A.; Zook, M. Social media and the city: Rethinking urban socio-spatial inequality using user-generated geographic information. *Landsc. Urban Plan.* **2015**, *142*, 198–211.

22. Venerandi, A.; Quattrone, G.; Capra, L.; Quercia, D.; Saez-Trumper, D. Measuring Urban Deprivation from User Generated Content. In Proceedings of the 18th ACM Conference on Computer Supported Cooperative Work & Social Computing (CSCW), Vancouver, BC, Canada, 14–18 March 2015; pp. 254–264.

23. Stavrianea, A.; Kavoura, A. Social media's and online user-generated content's role in services advertising. *AIP Conf. Proc.* **2015**, *1644*, 318–324.

24. Deng, S.; Huang, L.; Wu, H.; Wu, Z. Constraints-Driven Service Composition in Mobile Cloud Computing. In Proceedings of the 2016 IEEE International Conference on Web Services (ICWS), San Francisco, CA, USA, 27 June–2 July 2016; pp. 228–235.

25. Ortiz, A.; Hussein, D.; Park, S.; Han, S.; Crespi, N. The Cluster Between Internet of Things and Social Networks: Review and Research Challenges. *IEEE Int. Things J.* **2014**, *1*, 206–215.

26. Jara, A.J.; Zamora-Izquierdo, M.A.; Skarmeta, A.F. Interconnection Framework for mHealth and Remote Monitoring Based on the Internet of Things. *IEEE J. Sel. Areas Commun.* **2013**, *31*, 47–65.

27. Lee, S.; Chong, I. User-centric intelligence provisioning in web-of-objects based IoT service. In Proceedings of the 2013 International Conference on ICT Convergence (ICTC), Jeju, Korea, 14–16 October 2013; pp. 44–49.

28. Toninelli, A.; Montanari, R.; Kagal, L.; Lassila, O. A Semantic Context-aware Access Control Framework for Secure Collaborations in Pervasive Computing Environments. In *Proceedings of the 5th International Conference on The Semantic Web*; Springer-Verlag: Berlin, Germany, 2006; pp. 473–486.

29. Yahyaoui, H.; Almulla, M. Context-based specification of Web service policies using WSPL. In Proceedings of the 2010 Fifth International Conference on Digital Information Management (ICDIM), Thunder Bay, ON, Canada, 5–8 July 2010; pp. 496–501.

30. Kapsalis, V.; Hadellis, L.; Karelis, D.; Koubias, S. A Dynamic Context-aware Access Control Architecture for e-Services. *Comput. Secur.* **2006**, *25*, 507–521.

31. Cheaito, M.; Laborde, R.; Barrere, F.; Benzekri, A. An extensible XACML authorization decision engine for context aware applications. In Proceedings of the 2009 Joint Conferences on the Pervasive Computing (JCPC), Tamsui, Taipei, Taiwan, 3–5 December 2009; pp. 377–382.

32. Li, H.; Yang, Y.; He, Z.; Hu, G. Context-aware Access Control Policy Research for Web Service. In Proceedings of the 2011 First International Conference on Instrumentation, Measurement, Computer, Communication and Control (IMCCC), Beijing, China, 21–23 October 2011; pp. 529–532.
33. Mohan, A.; Blough, D.M. An attribute-based authorization policy framework with dynamic conflict resolution. In Proceedings of the 9th Symposium on Identity and Trust on the Internet, Gaithersburg, MD, USA, 13–15 April 2010; ACM: New York, NY, USA, 2010; pp. 37–50.
34. Kayes, A.; Han, J.; Colman, A. An ontology-based approach to context-aware access control for software services. In *International Conference on Web Information Systems Engineering*; Springer: Berlin/Heidelberg, Germany, 2013; pp. 410–420.

Journal of
*Sensor and
Actuator Networks*

Review

Big Sensed Data Meets Deep Learning for Smarter Health Care in Smart Cities

Alex Adim Obinikpo [†] and Burak Kantarci [*,†]

School of Electrical Engineering and Computer Science, University Ottawa, Ottawa, ON K1N 6N5, Canada;
aobin064@uottawa.ca
* Correspondence: burak.kantarci@uottawa.ca; Tel.: +1-613-562-5800 (ext. 6955)
† These authors contributed equally to this work.

Received: 20 October 2017; Accepted: 17 November 2017; Published: 20 November 2017

Abstract: With the advent of the Internet of Things (IoT) concept and its integration with the smart city sensing, smart connected health systems have appeared as integral components of the smart city services. Hard sensing-based data acquisition through wearables or invasive probes, coupled with soft sensing-based acquisition such as crowd-sensing results in hidden patterns in the aggregated sensor data. Recent research aims to address this challenge through many hidden perceptron layers in the conventional artificial neural networks, namely by deep learning. In this article, we review deep learning techniques that can be applied to sensed data to improve prediction and decision making in smart health services. Furthermore, we present a comparison and taxonomy of these methodologies based on types of sensors and sensed data. We further provide thorough discussions on the open issues and research challenges in each category.

Keywords: wearable sensors; biosensors; smart health; deep learning; machine learning; analytics

1. Introduction

Smart cities are built on the foundation of information and communication technologies with the sole purpose of connecting citizens and technology for the overall improvement of the quality of lives. While quality of life includes ease of mobility and access to quality healthcare, amongst others, effective management and sustainability of resources, economic development and growth complement the fundamental requirements of smart cities. These goals are achieved by proper management and processing of the data acquired from dedicated or non-dedicated sensor networks. In most cases, the information gathered is refined continuously to produce other information for efficiency and effectiveness within the smart city.

In the Internet of Things (IoT) era, the interplay between mobile networks, wireless communications and artificial intelligence is transforming the way that humans live and survive via various forms of improvements in technological advancements, more specifically improved computing power, high performance processing and huge memory capacities. With the advent of cyber-physical systems, which comprise the seamless integration of physical systems with computing and communication resources, a paradigm shift from the conventional city concept towards a smart city design has been coined as the term smart city. Basically, a smart city is envisioned to be ICT driven and capable of offering various services such as smart driving, smart homes, smart living, smart governance and smart health, just to mention a few [1]. ICT-driven management and control, as well as the overwhelming use of sensors in smart devices for the good and well-being of citizens yields the desired level of intelligence to these services. Besides continuously informing the citizens, being liveable and ensuring the well-being of the citizens are reported among the requirements of smart cities [2]. Therefore, the smart city concept needs transformation of health services through sensor and IoT-enablement of medical devices, communications and decision support. This ensures availability, ubiquity and personal customization of services, as well as ease of access to these services. As stated in [3], the criteria for smartness of an environment are various. As a corollary to this statement, the authors investigate a smart city in the following dimensions: (1) the technology angle (i.e., digital, intelligent, virtual, ubiquitous and information city), (2) the people angle (creative city, humane city, learning city and knowledge city) and (3) the community angle (smart community).

Furthermore, in the same vein, Anthopoulus (see [4]) divides the smart city into the following eight components: (1) smart infrastructures where facilities utilize sensors and chips; (2) smart transportation where vehicular networks along with the communication infrastructure are deployed for monitoring purposes; (3) smart environments where ICTs are used in the monitoring of the environment to acquire useful information regarding environmental sustainability; (4) smart services where ICTs are used for the the provision of community health, tourism, education and safety; (5) smart governance, which aims at proper delivery of government services; (6) smart people that use ICTs to access and increase humans' creativity; (7) smart living where technology is used for the improvement of the quality of life; and (8) smart economy, where businesses and organizations develop and grow through the use of technology. Given these components, a smart health system within a smart city appears to be one of the leading gateways to a more productive and liveable structure that ensures the well-being of the community.

Assurance of quality healthcare is a social sustainability concept in a smart city. Social sustainability denotes the liveability and wellbeing of communities in an urban setting [5]. The large population in cities is actually a basis for improved healthcare services because one negligence or improper health service might lead to an outbreak of diseases and infections, which might become epidemic, thereby costing much more in curtailing them; however, for these health services to be somewhat beneficial, the methods and channels of delivery need to be top-notch. There have been various research studies into the adequate method required for effective delivery of healthcare. One of these methods is smart health. Smart health basically is the provision of health services using the sensing capabilities and infrastructures of smart cities. In recent years, smart health has gained wide recognition due to the increase of technological devices and the ability to process the data gathered from these devices with minimum error.

As recent research states, proper management and development of smart health is the key to success of the smart city ecosystem [6]. Smart health involves the use of sensors in smart devices and specifically manufactured/prototyped wearable sensors/bio-patches for proper monitoring of the health status of individuals living within a smart city, as shown in Figure 1. This example depicts a scenario for air quality monitoring to ensure healthier communities. Smart city infrastructure builds upon networked sensors that can be either dedicated or non-dedicated. As an integral component of the smart city, smart health systems utilize devices with embedded sensors (as non-dedicated sensing components) for environmental and ambient data collection such as temperature, air quality index (AQI) and humidity. Besides, wearables and carry-on sensors (as the dedicated sensing components) are also utilized to acquire medical data from individuals. Both dedicated and non-dedicated sensory data are transmitted to the data centres as the inputs of processing and further decision making processes. To achieve this goal, the already existing smart city framework coupled with IoT networking needs to be leveraged.

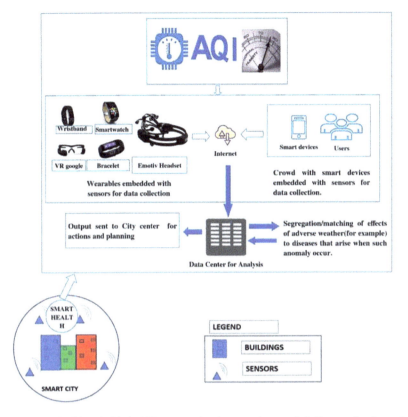

Figure 1. Smart health embedded within a smart city. An example scenario is illustrated to detect the air quality indicator to ensure healthier communities (figure produced by Creately Online Diagram, Cinergix Pvt. Ltd., Mentone, Australia).

In other words, a smart city needs to provide the required framework for smart health to grow rapidly and achieve its aim. Ensuring the quality of big sensed data acquisition is one key aspect of smart health challenges, and the ability to leverage these data is an important aspect of smart health development, as well as building a sustainable smart city structure [7–9]. Applications of smart health within smart cities are various. For example, Zulfiqar et al. [10] proposed an intelligent system for detecting and monitoring patients that might have voice complication issues. This is necessary since a number of services within the smart cities are voice enabled. As such, any disorder with the voice might translate into everyday service problems within the smart city. The same problem has been studied by the researchers in [11], where voice data and ECG signals were used as the inputs to the voice pathology detection system. Furthermore, with the aim of ensuring air quality within a smart city, the researchers in [12] developed a cloud-based monitoring system for air quality to ensure environmental health monitoring. The motivation for environmental health is ensuring the wellness of communities in a smart city for sustainability. The body area network within a smart city can be used for ECG monitoring with the aim of warning an individual of any heart-related problem, especially cardiac arrest [13], and also helps in determining the nature of human kinematic actions with the aim of ensuring improved quality of healthcare whenever needed [14]. Data management of patients is also one of the applications of smart health in smart cities that is of paramount importance. As discussed in [15], proper management of patient records both at the data entry and application levels ensures that patients get the required treatment when due, and this also helps in the development of personalized medicine applications [16]. Furthermore, the scope of smart health in smart cities is not limited to the physiologic phenomena in human bodies; it also extends to the environment and physical building blocks of the smart infrastructure. Indeed, the consequences of mismanaged environment and/or physical structures are potentially unhealthy users and communities, which is not a sustainable case for a smart city. To address this problem, the researchers in [17] created a system to monitor the structural health within a city using wireless sensor networks (WSN). It is worth mentioning that structural health monitoring also leads to inferential decision making services.

With these in mind, calls for new techniques that will ensure proper health service delivery have emerged. As an evolving concept, machine intelligence has attracted the healthcare sector by introducing effective decision support mechanisms applied to sensory data acquired through various media such as wearables or body area networks [18]. Machine learning techniques have undergone substantial improvements during the evolution of artificial intelligence and its integration with sensor and actuator networks. Despite many incremental improvements, deep learning has arisen as the most powerful tool thanks to its high level abstraction of complex big data, particularly big multimedia data [19].

Deep learning (DL) derives from conventional artificial neural networks (ANNs) with many hidden perceptron layers that can help in identifying hidden patterns [20]. Although having many hidden perceptron layers in a deep neural network is promising, when the concept of deep learning was initially coined, it was limited mostly by computational power of the available computing systems. However, with the advent of the improved computational capability of computing systems, as well as the rise of cloudified distributed models, deep learning has become a strong tool for analysing sensory data (particularly multimedia sensory data) and assisting in long-term decisions. The basic idea of deep learning is trying to replicate what the human brain does in most cases. Thus, in a sensor and actuator network setting, the deep learning network receives sensory input and iteratively passes it to subsequent layers until a desirable output is met. With the iterative process, the weights of the network links are adapted so as to match the input with the desirable output during the training process. With the widespread use of heterogeneous sensors such as wearables, medical imaging sensors, invasive sensors or embedded sensors in smart devices to acquire medical data, the emergence and applicability of deep learning is quite visible in modern day healthcare, from diagnosis to prognosis to health management.

While shallow learning algorithms enforce shallow methods on sensor data for feature representation, deep learning seeks to extract hierarchical representations [21,22] from large-scale data. Thus, the idea is using deep architectural models with multiple layers of non-linear transformations [23]. For instance, the authors in [24] use a shallow network with a covariance representation on the 3D sensor data in order to recognize human action from skeletal data. On the other hand, in the study in [25], the AlexNet model and the histogram of oriented gradients features are used to obtain deep features from the data acquired through 3D depth sensors.

In this article, we provide a thorough review of the deep learning approaches that can be applied to sensor data in smart health applications in smart cities. The motivation behind this study is that deep learning techniques are among the key enablers of the digital health technology within a smart city framework. This is due to the performance and accuracy issues experienced by conventional machine learning techniques under high dimensional data. Thus, it is worth noting that deep learning is not a total replacement of machine learning, but an effective tool to cope with dimensionality issues in several applications such as smart health [26]. To this end, this article aims to highlight the emergence of deep learning techniques in smart health within a smart city ecosystem and at the same time to give future directions by discussing the challenges and open issues that are still pertinent. In accordance with these, we provide a taxonomy of sensor data acquisition and processing techniques in smart health applications. Our taxonomy and review of deep learning approaches pave the way for providing insights for deep learning algorithms in particular smart health applications.

This work is organized as follows. In Section 2, we briefly discuss the transition from conventional machine learning methodologies to the deep learning methods. Section 3 gives a brief overview of the use of deep learning techniques on sensor network applications and major deep learning techniques that are applied on sensory data, while Section 4 provides insights for the smart health applications where deep learning can be used to process and interpret sensed data. Section 5 presents outstanding challenges and opportunities for the researchers to address in big sensed health data by deep learning. Finally, Section 6 concludes the article by summarizing the reviewed methodologies and future directions.

2. Analysis of Sensory Data in E-Health

2.1. Conventional Machine Learning on Sensed Health Data

With the advent of the WSN concept, machine learning has been identified as a viable solution to reduce the capital and operational expenditures on the design of the network, as well as to improve the lifetime of the network [27]. Presently, the majority of the machine learning techniques use a combination of feature extraction and modality-specific algorithms that are used to identify/recognize handwriting and/or speech [28]. This normally requires a dataset that is big in volume and powerful computing resources to support tremendous amount of background tasks. Furthermore, despite tedious efforts, there are always bound to be certain issues, and these perform poorly in the presence of inconsistencies and diversity in the dataset. One of the major advantages of machine learning in most cases is feature learning where a machine is trained on some datasets and the output provides valuable representation of the initial feature.

Applications of machine learning algorithms on sensory data are various such as telemedicine [18,29,30], air quality monitoring [31], indoor localization [32] and smart transportation [33]. However, conventional machine learning still has certain limitations such as inability to optimize non-differentiable discontinuous loss functions or not being able to obtain results following a feasible training duration at all times. These and many other issues encountered by machine learning techniques paved the way for deep learning as a more robust learning tool.

2.2. Deep Learning on Sensed Health Data

In [34], deep learning is defined as a collection of algorithmic procedures that 'mimic the brain'. More specifically, deep learning involves learning of layers via algorithmic steps. These layers enable the definition of hierarchical knowledge that derives from simpler knowledge [35]. There have been several attempts to build and design computers that are equipped with the ability to think. Until recently, this effort has been translated into rule-based learning, which is a 'top down' approach that involves creating rules for all possible circumstances [36]. However, this approach suffers from scalability since the number of rules is limited while its rule base is finite.

These issues can be remedied by adopting learning from experience instead of rule-based learning via a bottom-up approach. Labelled data form the experience. Labelled data are used as training input to the system where the training procedure is built upon past experiences. The learning from experience approach is well suited for applications such as spam filtering. On the other hand, the majority of the data collected by multimedia sensors (e.g., pictures, video feeds, sounds, etc.) are not properly labelled [37].

Real-world problems that involve processing of multimedia sensor data such as speech or face recognition are challenging to represent digitally due to the possibly infinite the problem domain. Thus, describing the problem adequately suffers especially in the presence of multi-dimensional features, which in turn leads to an increase in the volume of the space in such a way that the available data become sparse, and training on sparse data would not lead to meaningful results. Nevertheless, such 'infinite choice' problems are common in the processing of sensory data that are mostly acquired from multimedia sensors [38]. These issues pave the way for deep learning as deep learning algorithms have to work with hard and/or intuitive problems, which are defined with no or very few rules on high dimensional features. The absence of a rule set enforces the system to learn to cope with unforeseen circumstances [34].

Another characteristic of deep learning is the discovery of intricate structure in large datasets. To achieve this, deep learning utilizes a back propagation algorithm to adjust the internal parameters in each layer based on the representation of the parameters in the previous layer [34]. As such, it can be stated that representation learning is possible on partially labelled or unlabelled sensory data.

Acharya et al. [39] used deep learning techniques (specifically CNN) in the diagnosis and detection of coronary artery disease from the signals acquired from the electrocardiogram (ECG) and achieved an accuracy of 94.95%. The authors in [38] proposed the use of deep neural networks (DNN) for the active and automatic classification of ECG signals. Furthermore, in order to detect epileptic conditions early enough, deep learning with edge computing for the localization of epileptogenicity using electroencephalography (EEG) data has been proposed in [40]. Emotional well-being is a key state in the life of humans. With this in mind, the authors in [41] classified positive and negative emotions using deep belief networks (DBN) and data from EEG. The aim is to accurately capture the moment an emotional swing occurs. Their work yielded an 87.62% classification accuracy. The authors in [42] designed a BGMonitor for detecting blood glucose concentration and used a multi-task deep learning approach to analyse and process the data, and to make further inferences. The research yielded an accuracy of 82.14% when compared to the conventional methods.

3. Deep Learning Methods and Big Sensed Data

3.1. Deep Learning on Sensor Network Applications

Sensors are key enablers of the objects (things) of the emerging IoT networks [43]. The aggregation of sensors forms a network whose purpose amongst others is to generate and aggregate data for inferential purposes. The data generated from sensors need to be fine-tuned prior to undergoing any analytics procedure. This has led to various methods to formulate proper and adequate processing of sensed data from sensor and actuator networks. These methods are dependent on the type and applications of the sensed data. Deep learning (one of such methods) can be applied on sensor and actuator network applications to process data generated from sensors effectively and efficiently [44]. The output of a deep learning network can be used for decision making. Costilla-Reyes et al. used a convolutional neural network to learn spatio-temporal features that were derived from tomography sensors, and this yielded an effective and efficient way of performance classification of gait patterns using a limited number of experimental samples [45]. Transportation is another important service in a smart city architecture. The ability to acquire quality (i.e., high value) data from users is key to developing a smart transportation architecture. As an example study, the authors in [46] developed a mechanism using a deep neural network to learn the transportation modes of mobile users. In the same study, the integration of a deep learning-driven decision making system with a smart transportation architecture has been shown to result in 95% classification accuracy. Besides these, deep learning helped in the power usage pattern analysis of vehicles using the sensors embedded in smart phones [47]. The goal of the study in [47] is the timely prediction of the power consumption behaviour of vehicles using smart phones. The use of sensors in healthcare has been leading to significant achievements, and deep learning is being used to leverage the use of sensors and actuators for proper healthcare delivery. For instance, in assessing the level of Parkinson's disease, Eskofier et al. [48] used convolutional neural networks (CNN) for the classification and detection of the key features in Parkinson's disease based on data generated from wearable sensors. The results of the research proved that deep learning techniques work well with sensors when compared to other methods. Moreover, deep learning techniques, particularly CNNs, were used in estimating energy consumption while using wearable sensors for health condition monitoring [49]. Furthermore, by using sensory data generated from an infrared distance sensor, a deep learning classifier was developed for fall detection especially amongst the elderly population [50]. Besides these, with respect to security, combining biometric sensors and CNNs has resulted in a more robust approach for spoofing and security breach detection in digital systems [51]. Yin et al. [52] used a deep convolution network for proper visual object recognition as another application area of deep learning in the analysis of big sensed data, whereas for early detection of deforestation, Barreto et al. [53] proposed using a multilayer perceptron technique. In both studies, the input data are acquired via means of remote sensing.

3.2. Major Deep Learning Methods in Medical Sensory Data

In this subsection, we discuss the major deep learning methods that are used in e-health applications on medical sensory data. The following are the major deep learning methods in e-health, and a table of all notation used is given as Table 1.

Table 1. Basic notations used in the article. Notations are grouped into three categories: stand-alone symbols, vectors between units of different layers and symbols for functions.

Notations	Definition
x	Samples
y	Outputs
v	Visible vector
h	Hidden vector
q	State vector
W	Matrix of weight vectors
M	Total number of units for the hidden layer
w_{ij}	Weights vector between hidden unit h_j and visible unit v_i
S_j	Binary state of a vector
s_i^q	Binary state assigned to unit i by state vector q
Z	Partition factor
d_j	Biased weights for the j-th hidden units
c_i	Biased weights for the i-th visible units
z_i	Total i-th inputs
v_i	Visible unit i
w_{kj}^2	Weight vector from the k-th unit in the hidden Layer 2 to the j-th output unit
w_{ji}^1	Weight vector from the j-th unit in the hidden Layer 1 to the i-th output unit
W_{ji}^1	Matrix of weights from the j-th unit in the hidden Layer 1 to the i-th output unit
$E(q)$	Energy of a state vector q
σ	activation function
$P_r(q)$	Probability of a state vector q
$E(v, h)$	Energy function with respect to visible and hidden units
$pdf(v, h)$	Probability distribution with respect to visible and hidden units

3.2.1. Deep Feedforward Networks

Deep feed-forward networks can be counted among the first generation deep learning models and are based on multilayer perceptrons [34,54]. Basically, a feed-forward network aims at approximating a function f^*. A mapping $y = f(x; \Theta)$ is defined by a feed-forward network to learn the value of the Θ parameters by approximating with respect to the best function. Information flow in these networks is usually from the variables x being evaluated with respect to the outputs y.

During training, the aim is to ensure matching of $f(x)$ to $f^*(x)$, where each example of x is accompanied by a label $y \approx f^*(x)$. In most cases, the learning algorithm decides how to use these layers in order to get the best approximation of f^*. Since these layers do not obtain the desired output from the training data, they are referred to as hidden layers such as Layer 2 in the illustration in Figure 2 below.

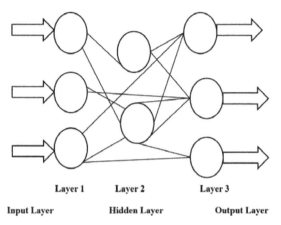

Layer 1   **Layer 2**   **Layer 3**

Input Layer   **Hidden Layer**   **Output Layer**

Figure 2. A basic deep feed-forward network.

A typical model for the deep forward network is described as follows. Given K outputs $y_1, ..., y_k$ for a given input x and the hidden layer, which consists of M units, then the output is formulated as shown in Equation (1) where σ is the activation function, $W_{ji}^{(1)}$ denotes the matrix of weights from unit j of hidden Layer 1 to the output unit i. In the equation, $w_{ji}^{(1)}$ and $w_{ki}^{(2)}$ stand for the weight vector from unit j of hidden Layer 1 to output unit i, and the weight vector from unit k of hidden Layer 2 to output unit i, respectively.

$$y_k(x, w) = \sigma\left(\sum_{j=1}^{M} w_{kj}^{(2)} h\left(\sum_{j=1}^{M} w_{ji}^{(1)} x_i + W_{ji}^{(1)}\right) + w_{ki}^{(2)}\right) \tag{1}$$

3.2.2. Autoencoder

An autoencoder is a neural network that is trained to copy its input to its output [22,55]. In most cases, an autoencoder is implemented as a three-layer neural network (see Figure 3) by directly connecting output units back to input units. In the figure, every output i is linked back to input i. The hidden layer h in the autoencoder represents the input by a code. Thus, a minimalist description of the network can be made by two main components as follows: (1) an encoder function $h = f(x)$; (2) a decoder function that is used to reconstruct the input, $r = g(h)$. Previously, autoencoders were used for dimensionality reduction or feature learning, but currently, the main purpose of autoencoder use is generative modelling because of the connection between autoencoders and latent variables.

Output Layer

Hidden Layer

Input Layer

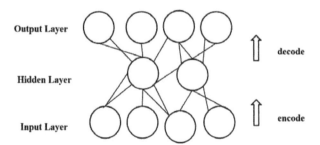

decode

encode

Figure 3. Autoencoder network.

Below are the various types of autoencoders.

- Undercomplete autoencoders [54] are suitable for the situation where the dimension of the code is less than the dimension of the input. This phenomenon usually leads to the inclusion of important features during training and learning.
- Regularized autoencoders [56] enable training any architecture of autoencoder successfully by choosing the code dimension and the capacity of the encoder/decoder based on the complexity of the distribution to be modelled.
- Sparse autoencoders [54] have a training criterion with a sparsity penalty, which usually occurs in the code layer with the purpose of copying the input to the output. Sparse autoencoders are used to learn features for another task such as classification.
- Denoising autoencoders [22] change the reconstruction error term of the cost function instead of adding a penalty to the cost function. Thus, a denoising autoencoder minimizes $L(x, g(f(\tilde{x})))$, where $\tilde{x}$ is a copy of x that has been distorted by noise.
- Contractive autoencoders [57] introduce an explicit regularizer on $h = f(x)$ making the derivatives of f as small as possible. The contractive autoencoders are trained to resist any perturbation of the input; as such, they map a neighbourhood of input points to a smaller neighbourhood of output points.

3.2.3. Convolutional Neural Networks

Convolutional neural networks (CNNs) replace matrix multiplication with convolutions in at least one of their layers [54,58,59]. CNNs have multiple layers of fields with small sets of neurons where an input image is partially processed [60]. When the outputs of these sets of neurons are tiled, their input regions overlap, leading to a new representation of the original image with higher resolution. This sequence is repeated in each sublayer. It is also worth mentioning that the dimensions of a CNN are mostly dependent on the size of the data.

The CNN architecture consists of three distinct layers: (1) the convolutional layer, (2) pooling layer and (3) fully-connected layer. Although it is not a requirement for the CNNs, as illustrated in Figure 4, fully-connected layers can follow a number of convolutional and subsampling layers.

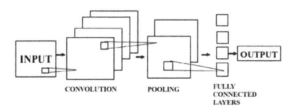

Figure 4. CNN architecture.

- Convolutional layer: The convolutional layer takes an $m \times m \times r$ image as the input, where m and r denote the height/width of the image and the number of channels, respectively. The convolutional layer contains k filters (or kernels) of size $n \times n \times q$, where $n < m$ and q can be less than or equal to the number of channels r (i.e., $q \leq r$). Here, q may vary for each kernel, and the feature map in this case has a size of $m - n + 1$.
- Pooling layers: These are listed as a key aspect of CNNs. The pooling layers are in general applied following the convolutional layers. A pooling layer in a CNN subsamples its input. Applying a max operation to the output of each filter is the most common way of pooling. Pooling over the complete matrix is not necessary. With respect to classification, pooling gives an output matrix with a fixed size thereby reducing the dimensionality of the output while keeping important information.

- Fully-connected layers: The layers here are all connected, i.e., both units of preceding and subsequent layers are connected

3.2.4. Deep Belief Network

The deep belief network (DBN) is a directed acyclic graph that builds on stochastic variables. It is a type of neural network composed of latent variables connected between multiple layers [36,61]. Despite the connections between layers, there are no connections between units within each layer. It can learn to reconstruct its inputs, then is trained to perform classification. In fact, the learning principle of DBNs is "one layer at a time via a greedy learning algorithm".

The properties of DBN are:

- Learning generative weights is through a layer-by-layer process with the purpose of determining the dependability of the variables in layer ℓ on the variables in layer ℓ' where ℓ denotes the index of any upper layer.
- Upon observing data in the bottom layer, inferring the values of the latent variables can be done in a single attempt.

It is worth noting that a DBN with one hidden layer implies a restricted Boltzmann machine (RBM). To train a DBN, first an RBM is trained using constructive divergence or stochastic maximum likelihood. The second RBM is then trained to model the defined distribution by sampling the hidden units in the first RBM. This process can be iterated as many times as possible to add further layers to the DBN.

3.2.5. Boltzmann Machine

As a special type of neural network, the Boltzmann machine (BM) consists of nodes that are connected symmetrically as shown in Figure 5, where neurons help a BM make on/off decisions [62]. In order to identify features that exhibit complex data regularities, a BM utilizes learning algorithms that are well-suited for search and learning problems.

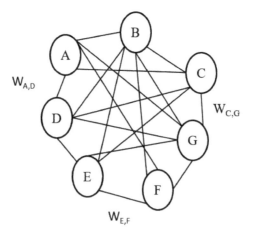

Figure 5. Boltzmann network.

To visualize the operation of a BM better, suppose unit i is able to continuously change its state. First, the node calculates the total input z_i, which is formulated as the sum of b_i (bias) and all the weights on the connections from other units as formulated in Equation (2). In the equation, w_{ij} denotes the weights on connections between i and j, and s_j is defined as in Equation (3). The probability for unit i is formulated as shown in Equation (4).

$$z_i = b_i + \sum_j s_j w_{ij} \tag{2}$$

$$s_j = \begin{cases} 1, & if \quad j \quad is \quad on \\ 0, & if \quad j \quad is \quad off \end{cases} \tag{3}$$

$$P_r(s_i = 1) = \frac{1}{1 + e^{-z_i}} \tag{4}$$

If all neurons are updated sequentially, the network is expected to reach a BM distribution with state vector probability q and energy $E(q)$ as shown in Equations (5) and (6), respectively

$$P_r(q) = \frac{e^{-E(q)}}{\sum_u e^{-E(u)}} \tag{5}$$

$$E(q) = -\sum_i s_i^q b_i - \sum_{i<j} s_i^q s_j^q w_{ij} \tag{6}$$

With a view toward discarding the local optima, the weights on the connections could be chosen in such a way that each energy of the individual vectors represents the cost of these vectors. Learning in BM takes place in two different manners; either with hidden units or without hidden units.

There are various types of BM, and some of them are listed below:

Conditional Boltzmann machines model the data vectors and their distribution in such a way that any extension, no matter how simple it is, leads to conditional distributions.

Mean field Boltzmann machines compute the state of a unit based on the present state of other units in the network by using the real values of mean fields.

Higher-order Boltzmann machines have structures and learning patterns that can accept complex energy functions.

Restricted Boltzmann machines (RBMs): Two types of layers (i.e., visible vs. hidden) are included in the RBMs with no two similar connections [21,55].

In order to obtain unbiased elements from the set $\langle s_i s_j \rangle_{data}$, the hidden units h need to be conditionally independent of the visible unit v. However, heavy computation is required to get unbiased samples from $\langle s_i s_j \rangle_{data}$ [63].

Mathematically, the energy function of an RBM is given as formulated in Equation (7) and has a probability distribution as shown in Equation (8). In the equations, d_j and c_i stand for the biased weights for the hidden and visible units, respectively, whereas Z in the probability distribution function denotes the partition factor.

$$E(v, h) = -\sum_i c_i v_i - \sum_j d_j h_j - \sum_i \sum_j v_i w_{i,j} h_j \tag{7}$$

$$pdf(v, h) = \frac{1}{Z} e^{-E(v,h)} \tag{8}$$

Upon learning one hidden layer, the outcome can be treated as the input data required for training another RBM. This in turn leads to cascaded learning of multiple hidden layers, thus making the entire network be viewed as one model with improvements done on the lower bound [64].

4. Sensory Data Acquisition and Processing Using Deep Learning in Smart Health

Accurate data acquisition and processing is key to effective healthcare delivery. However, ensuring the accuracy of the acquired data has been one of the typical challenges in smart healthcare systems. This is due to the nature of data needed for quality assurance of healthcare delivery and the methods used for data acquisition. This phenomenon in the acquisition of sensory data in healthcare applications has led to the development of innovative techniques for data acquisition with the aim of complementing the "already in use", but upgraded methods. Due to these improvements in data acquisition methods, processing and interpreting sensory data have experienced an upward improvement, as well. These improvements have recently translated into improved quality of healthcare delivery. In this section, we briefly discuss the methods of sensory health data acquisition and processing as they relate to deep learning. Furthermore, we discuss how the generated sensory data types are processed using deep learning techniques. Figure 6a presents a brief taxonomy of data acquisition and processing. Data acquisition is performed mainly via wearables and probes as dedicated sensors and via built-in sensors of mobile devices as non-dedicated sensors.

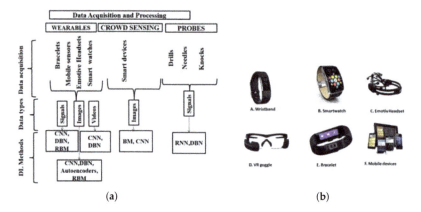

(a)　　　　　　　　　　(b)

Figure 6. Data acquisition methods and processing techniques. (**a**) Taxonomy of sensory data acquisition and processing techniques; (**b**) types of wearables/carry-ons.

4.1. Sensory Data Acquisition and Processing via Wearables and Carry-Ons

Wearables and carry-ons have appeared as crucial components of personalized medicine aiming at performance and quality improvement in healthcare delivery. All wearables are equipped with built-in sensors that are used in data acquisition, and these smart devices with built-in sensors are in various forms as shown in the Figure 6b. The sensors in smart watches acquire data for the heart rate, movement, blood oxygen level and skin temperature. The virtual reality (VR) goggle captures video/image data, whereas the emotive headset senses mostly the brain signals. The wrist band and bracelets sense heart rate, body mass index (BMI), movement data (i.e., accelerometer and gyroscope) and temperature. Mobile devices provide non-dedicated sensing by acquiring sensory data regarding location, movement and BMI. While they all have similar functions, sensing functions mainly depend on the situations or needs for which they are required. The sensors embedded in these devices are the main resources for data acquisition and generation. The data output can be in the form of signals, images or videos; all with various importance and usefulness.

Processing of data generated from wearables and carry-ons is done based on the data types. Deep learning techniques used in this regards are also dependent on the data types and intended applications. This section aims to discuss the various deep learning methods used to process various data types generated from wearables and carry-ons.

- Image processing: Deep learning techniques play a major role in image processing for health advancements. Prominent amongst these methods are CNN, DBN, autoencoders and RBM. The authors in [65] use CNNs to help create a new network architecture with the aim of multi-channel data acquisition and also for supervised feature learning. Extracting features from brain images (e.g., magnetic resonance imaging (MRI), functional Magnetic resonance imaging (fMRI)) can help in early diagnosis and prognosis of severe diseases such as glioma. Moreover, the authors in [66] use DBN for the classification of mammography images in a bid to detect calcifications that may be the indicators of breast cancer. With high accuracy achieved in the detection, proper diagnosis of breast cancer becomes possible in radiology. Kuang and He in [67] modified and used DBN for the classification of attention deficit hyperactivity disorder (ADHD) using images from fMRI data. In a similar fashion, Li et al. [68] used the RBM for training and processing the dataset generated from MRI and positron emission tomography (PET) scans with aim of accurately diagnosing Alzheimer's disease. Using deep CNN and clinical images, Esteva et al. [69] were able to detect and classify melanoma, which is a type of skin cancer. According to their research, this method outperforms the already available skin cancer classification techniques. In the same context, Peyman and Hamid [70] showed that CNN performs better in the preprocessing of clinical and dermoscopy images in the lesion segmentation part of the skin. The study argues that CNN requires less preprocessing procedure when compared to other known methods.

- Signal processing: Signal processing is an area of applied computing that has been evolving since its inception. Signal processing is an utmost important tool in diverse fields including the processing of medical sensory data. As new methods are being improved for accurate signal processing on sensory data, deep learning, as a robust method, appears as a potential technique used in signal processing. For instance, Ha and Choi use improved versions of CNN to process the signals derived from embedded sensors in mobile devices for proper recognition of human activities [71]. Human activity recognition is an important aspect of ubiquitous computing and one of the examples of its application is the diagnosis and provision of support and care for those with limited movement ability and capabilities. The authors in [72] propose applying a CNN-based methodology on sensed data for the prediction of sleep quality. In the corresponding study, the CNN model is used with the objective of classifying the factors that contribute to efficient and poor sleeping habits with wearable sensors [72]. Furthermore, deep CNN and deep feed-forward networks on the data acquired via wearable sensors are used for the classification and processing of human activity recognition by the researchers in this field [73].
- Video processing: Deep learning techniques are also used for processing of videos generated from wearable devices and carry-ons. Prominent amongst these applications is the human activity recognition via CNNs to process video data generated by wearables and/or multimedia sensors [74–76].

4.2. Data Acquisition via Probes

Data acquisition using probes was an early stage data gathering technique. Their development has been made possible using technological enhancements attached to these probing tools. With these enhancements, acquiring sensory readings of medical data has become possible. Probes can be in the form of needles, drills and sometimes knocks, with feedbacks generated via the technological enhancements attached to the probing tools. Probes have seen a revolution since modern science and traditional medicine are being harmonized, with both playing vital roles in healthcare delivery.

Data generated via probes are usually in the form of signals. Processing probe data requires certain deep learning techniques that are augmented in most cases for this purpose. As an example, Cheron et al. [77] used the invasive electrode injection method to acquire signals needed to formulate the kinematic relation between electromyography (EMG) and the trajectory of the arm during movements. To this end, the authors used a dynamic recurrent neural network to process these signals and showed the correlation between EMG and arm trajectory.

4.3. Data Acquisition via Crowd-Sensing

Mobile crowd-sensing is a non-dedicated sensing concept where data are acquired using built-in sensors of smart devices. As the capabilities of smart devices such as smartphones and tablets have tremendously improved during the last decade, any smartphone today is equipped with tens of built-in sensors. Thus, ubiquity, improved sensing, computing and communication capabilities in mobile smart devices have enabled these devices to be used as data acquisition tools in critical applications including smart health and emergency preparedness [78,79]. This type of data acquisition involves users moving towards a particular location and being implicitly recruited to capture required data by the built-in sensors in their smart devices [80]. Crowdsensing envisions a robust data collection approach where users have the leverage and the ability to choose and report more data for experimental purposes in real time [81]. Consequently, this type of data acquisition increases the amount of data required for any purpose especially for the applications under smart health and smart cities [82]. Moreover, it is worth noting that crowd-sensed data are big especially in volume and velocity; hence, application-specific and effective processing methods are required to analyse crowd-sensed datasets. Application-specific data analytics techniques are required for the following reason in mobile crowd-sensing: Besides volume and velocity, the variety and heterogeneity of sensors in mobile crowd-sensing are also phenomenal, which results in producing a gigantic amount of data, which might be partially labelled in some cases.

As an example smart health application where mobile crowd-sensed data are used, Pan et al. [83] have introduced AirTick, which utilizes crowd-sensed image data to obtain air quality information. To this end, AirTick applies Boltzmann machines as the deep learning method on the crowd-sensed image to process the data for eventual results. Furthermore, the authors in [84] have introduced a proposal for cleaner and healthier neighbourhoods and have developed a mobile crowd-sensing application called SpotGarbage, which allows users to capture images of garbage in their locality and send them to the data hub where the data are analysed. In the SpotGarbage application, CNNs are used as the deep learning method to analyse the crowd-sensed images.

Based on the review of different data acquisition techniques and the corresponding deep learning methodologies applied to sensed data under those acquisition techniques, a brief review is presented in Table 2. The table provides a summary of data acquisition techniques, their corresponding data types and some examples of the deep learning techniques used.

Table 2. Summary of data acquisition methods, data types and examples of deep learning technique used. Three types of data acquisition categories are defined, which acquire images, one-dimensional signals and videos. CNN, DBN, restricted Boltzmann machine (RBM) and BM are the deep learning methods that are used to analyse big sensed data.

Data Acquisition Technique	Data Type	Deep Learning Technique
Wearables	Image	CNN [65,69,70], DBN [66,67], RBM [68],
	Signal	CNN [71–73]
	Video	CNN [74–76]
Probes	Signal	RNN [77]
Crowd-sensing	Image	BM [83], CNN [84]

5. Deep Learning Challenges in Big Sensed Data: Opportunities in Smart Health Applications

Deep learning can assist in the processing of sensory data by classification, as well as prediction via learning. Training a dataset by a deep learning algorithm involves prediction, detection of errors and improving prediction quality with time. Based on the review of the state of the art in the previous sections, it can be stated that integration of sensed data in smart health applications with deep learning yields promising outcomes. On the other hand, there are several challenges and open issues that need to be addressed prior to realization of such integration. As those challenges arise from the nature of deep learning, sensor deployment and sensory data acquisition, addressing those challenges paves the way towards robust smart health applications. As a corollary, in this section, we introduce challenges and open issues in the integration of deep learning with smart health sensory data; and pursuant to these, we present opportunities to cope with these challenges in various applications with the integration of deep learning and the sensory data provided.

5.1. Challenges and Open Issues

Deep learning techniques have attracted researchers from many fields recently for sustainable and efficient smart health delivery in smart environments. However, it is worth noting that the application of deep learning techniques on sensory data still experiences challenges. Indeed, in most smart health applications, CNNs have been introduced as revolutionized methodologies to cope with the challenges that deep learning networks suffer. Thanks to the improvements in CNNs, to date, CNN has been identified as the most useful tool in most cases when smart health is involved.

To be able to fully exploit deep learning techniques on medical sensory data, certain challenges need to be addressed by the researchers in this field. The challenges faced by deep learning techniques in smart health are mostly related to the acquisition, quality and dimensionality of data. This is due to the fact that inferences or decisions are made based on the output/outcome of processed data. As seen in the previous section, data acquisition takes place on heterogeneous settings, i.e., various devices with their own sampling frequency, operating system and data formats. The heterogeneity phenomenon generally results in a data plane with huge dimensions. The higher the dimension gets, the more difficult the training of the data, which ultimately leads to a longer time frame for result generation. Moreover, determining the depth of the network architecture in order to get a favourable result is another challenge since the depth of the network impacts the training time, which is an outstanding challenge to be addressed by the researchers in this field.

Value and trustworthiness of the data comprise another challenge that impacts the success of deep learning algorithms in a smart health setting. As any deep learning technique is supposed to be applied to big sensed health data, novel data acquisition techniques that ensure the highest level of trustworthiness for the acquired data are emergent.

Uncertainty in the acquired sensor data remains a grand challenge. A significant amount of the acquired data is partially labelled or unlabelled. Therefore, novel mechanisms to quantify and cope with the uncertainty phenomenon in the sensed data are emergent to improve the accuracy, as well as the efficiency of deep learning techniques in smart health applications.

Furthermore, data acquisition via non-dedicated sensors is also possible in smart cities sensing [85]. In the presence of non-dedicated sensors for data acquisition in smart health, it is a big challenge to know how much data should be acquired prior to processing. Since dedicated and non-dedicated sensors are mostly coupled in smart health applications, determining the amount of data required from different wearables becomes a grand challenge, as well. Recent research proposes the use of compressing sensing methods in participatory or opportunistic sensing via mobile devices [86]; hence, data explosion in non-dedicated acquisition can be prevented. However, in the presence of non-dedicated sensing system, dynamic determination of the number of wearables/sensors that can ensure the desired amount of data is another open issue to be addressed prior to analysing the big sensed data via deep learning networks.

In addition to all this, ensuring trustworthiness of the acquired sensory data prior to deep learning analysis remains an open issue, while auction and game theoretic solutions have been proposed to increase user involvement in the trustworthiness assurance stage of the data that are acquired via non-dedicated sensors [87,88]. In the presence of a collaboration between dedicated and non-dedicated sensors in the data acquisition, coping with the reliability of the non-dedicated end still requires efficient solutions. It is worth noting that deep learning can also be used for behaviour analysis of non-dedicated sensors in such an environment with the aim of eliminating unreliable sensing sources in the data acquisition.

Last but not least, recent research points out the emergence of IoT-driven data acquisition systems [78,89].

5.2. Opportunities in Smart Health Applications for Deep Learning

In this section, we discuss some of the applications of deep learning. To this end, we categorize these applications into three main groups for easy reference. Table 3 shows a summary of these applications together with the deep learning methods used under the three categories, namely medical imaging, bioinformatics and predictive analysis. The table is a useful reference to select the appropriate deep learning technique(s) while aiming to address the challenges and open issues in the previous subsection.

Table 3. Smart health applications with their respective deep learning techniques on medical sensory data. Applications are grouped into three categories: Medical imaging, bioinformatics and predictive analysis. Each application addresses multiple problems on sensed data through various deep learning techniques. DNN, deep neural network.

Application	Problem	Deep Learning Techniques	References
Medical Imaging	Neural Cells Classification	CNN	[65]
	3D brain reconstruction	Deep CNN	[90]
	Brain Tissue Classification	DBN	[67,68]
	Tumour Detection	DNN	[65,66]
	Alzheimer's Diagnosis	DNN	[91]
Bioinformatics	Cancer Diagnosis	Deep Autoencoder	[92]
	Gene Classification	DBN	[93]
	Protein Slicing	DBN	[94,95]
Predictive Analysis	Disease prediction and analysis	Autoencoder	[96]
		RNN	[97]
		CNN	[97,98]

- Medical imaging: Deep learning techniques have actually helped the improvement of healthcare through accurate disease detection and recognition. An example is the detection of melanoma. To do this, deep learning algorithms learn important features related to melanoma from a group of medical images and run their learning-based prediction algorithm to detect the presence or likelihood of the disease.

  Furthermore, using images from MRI, fMRI and other sources, deep learning has been able to help 3D brain construction using autoencoders and deep CNN [90], neural cell classification using CNN [65], brain tissue classifications using DBN [67,68], tumour detection using DNN [65,66] and Alzheimer's diagnosis using DNN [91].

- Bioinformatics: The applications of deep learning in bioinformatics have seen a resurgence in the diagnosis and treatment of most terminal diseases. Examples of these could be seen in cancer diagnosis where deep autoencoders are used using gene expression as the input data [92]; gene selection/classification and gene variants using micro-array data sequencing with the aid of deep belief networks [93]. Moreover, deep belief networks play a key role in protein slicing/sequencing [94,95].

- Predictive analysis: Disease predictions have gained momentum with the advent of learning-based systems. Therefore, with the capability of deep learning to predict the occurrence of diseases accurately, predictive analysis of the future likelihood of diseases has experienced significant progress. Particular techniques that are used for predictive analysis of diseases are autoencoders [96], recurrent neural networks [97] and CNNs [97,98]. On the other hand, it is worth mentioning that in order to improve the accuracy of prediction, sensory data monitoring medical phenomena have to be coupled with sensory data monitoring human behaviour. Coupling of data acquired from medical and behavioural sensors helps in conducting effective analysis of human behaviour in order to find patterns that could help in disease predictions and preventions.

6. Conclusions

With the growing need and widespread use of sensor and actuator networks in smart cities, there is a growing demand for top-notch methods for the acquisition and processing of big sensed data. Among smart city services, smart healthcare applications are becoming a part of daily life to prolong the lifetime of members of society and improve quality of life. With the heterogeneous and various types of data that are being generated on a daily basis, the existence of sensor and actuator networks (i.e., wearables, carry-ons and other medical sensors) calls for effective acquisition of sensed data, as well as accurate and efficient processing to deduce conclusions, predictions and recommendations for the healthiness state of individuals. Deep learning is an effective tool that is used in the processing of big sensed data especially under these settings. Although deep learning has evolved from the traditional artificial neural networks concept, it has become an evolving field with the advent of improved computational power, as well as the convergence of wired/wireless communication systems. In this article, we have briefly discussed the growing concept of smart health within the smart city framework by highlighting its major benefits for the social sustainability of the smart city infrastructure. We have provided a comprehensive survey of the use of deep learning techniques to analyse sensory data in e-health and presented the major deep learning techniques, namely deep feed-forward networks, autoencoders, convolutional neural networks, deep belief networks, Boltzmann machine and restricted Boltzmann machine. Furthermore, we have introduced various data acquisition mechanisms, namely wearables, probes and crowd-sensing. Following these, we have also linked the surveyed deep learning techniques to existing use cases in the analysis of medical sensory data. In order to provide a thorough understanding of these linkages, we have categorized the sensory data acquisition techniques based on the available technology for data generation. In the last part of this review article, we have studied the smart health applications that involve sensors and actuators and visited specific use cases in those applications along with the existing deep learning solutions to effectively analyse sensory data. To facilitate a thorough understanding of these applications and their requirements, we have classified these applications under the following three categories: medical imaging, bioinformatics and predictive analysis. In the last part of this review article, we have studied smart health applications that involve sensors and actuators and visited specific problems in those applications along with the existing deep learning solutions to effectively address those problems. Furthermore, we have provided a thorough discussion of the open issues and challenges in big sensed data in smart health, mainly focusing on the data acquisition and processing aspects from the standpoint of deep learning techniques.

Acknowledgments: This material is based upon work supported by the Natural Sciences and Engineering Research Council of Canada (NSERC) under Grant RGPIN/2017-04032.

Author Contributions: Alex Adim Obinikpo and Burak Kantarci conceived and pursued the literature survey on deep learning techniques on big sensed data for smart health applications, reviewed the state of the art, challenges and opportunities, and made conclusions. They both wrote the paper. Alex Adim Obinikpo created the illustrative images.

Conflicts of Interest: The authors declare no conflict of interest.

References

1. Guelzim, T.; Obaidat, M.; Sadoun, B. Chapter 1—Introduction and overview of key enabling technologies for smart cities and homes. In *Smart Cities and Homes*; Obaidat, M.S., Nicopolitidis, P., Eds.; Morgan Kaufmann: Boston, MA, USA, 2016; pp. 1–16.
2. Liu, D.; Huang, R.; Wosinski, M. Development of Smart Cities: Educational Perspective. In *Smart Learning in Smart Cities*; Springer: Singapore, 2017; pp. 3–14.

3. Nam, T.; Pardo, T.A. Conceptualizing smart city with dimensions of technology, people, and institutions. In Proceedings of the 12th Annual International Digital Government Research Conference: Digital Government Innovation in Challenging Times, College Park, MD, USA, 12–15 June 2011; ACM: New York, NY, USA, 2011; pp. 282–291.

4. Anthopoulos, L.G. The Rise of the Smart City. In *Understanding Smart Cities: A Tool for Smart Government or an Industrial Trick?* Springer: Cham, Switzerland, 2017; pp. 5–45.

5. Munzel, A.; Meyer-Waarden, L.; Galan, J.P. The social side of sustainability: Well-being as a driver and an outcome of social relationships and interactions on social networking sites. *Technol. Forecast. Soc. Change* **2017**, in press.

6. Fan, M.; Sun, J.; Zhou, B.; Chen, M. The smart health initiative in China: The case of Wuhan, Hubei province. *J. Med. Syst.* **2016**, *40*, 62.

7. Ndiaye, M.; Hancke, G.P.; Abu-Mahfouz, A.M. Software Defined Networking for Improved Wireless Sensor Network Management: A Survey. *Sensors* **2017**, *17*, 1031.

8. Pramanik, M.I.; Lau, R.Y.; Demirkan, H.; Azad, M.A.K. Smart health: Big data enabled health paradigm within smart cities. *Expert Syst. Appl.* **2017**, *87*, 370–383.

9. Nef, T.; Urwyler, P.; Büchler, M.; Tarnanas, I.; Stucki, R.; Cazzoli, D.; Müri, R.; Mosimann, U. Evaluation of three state-of-the-art classifiers for recognition of activities of daily living from smart home ambient data. *Sensors* **2015**, *15*, 11725–11740.

10. Ali, Z.; Muhammad, G.; Alhamid, M.F. An Automatic Health Monitoring System for Patients Suffering from Voice Complications in Smart Cities. *IEEE Access* **2017**, *5*, 3900–3908.

11. Hossain, M.S.; Muhammad, G.; Alamri, A. Smart healthcare monitoring: A voice pathology detection paradigm for smart cities. *Multimedia Syst.* **2017**, doi:10.1007/s00530-017-0561-x.

12. Mehta, Y.; Pai, M.M.; Mallissery, S.; Singh, S. Cloud enabled air quality detection, analysis and prediction—A smart city application for smart health. In Proceedings of the 2016 3rd MEC International Conference on Big Data and Smart City (ICBDSC), Muscat, Oman, 15–16 March 2016; pp. 1–7.

13. Sahoo, P.K.; Thakkar, H.K.; Lee, M.Y. A Cardiac Early Warning System with Multi Channel SCG and ECG Monitoring for Mobile Health. *Sensors* **2017**, *17*, 711.

14. Kim, T.; Park, J.; Heo, S.; Sung, K.; Park, J. Characterizing dynamic walking patterns and detecting falls with wearable sensors using Gaussian process methods. *Sensors* **2017**, *17*, 1172.

15. Yeh, Y.T.; Hsu, M.H.; Chen, C.Y.; Lo, Y.S.; Liu, C.T. Detection of potential drug-drug interactions for outpatients across hospitals. *Int. J. Environ. Res. Public Health* **2014**, *11*, 1369–1383.

16. Venkatesh, J.; Aksanli, B.; Chan, C.S.; Akyurek, A.S.; Rosing, T.S. Modular and Personalized Smart Health Application Design in a Smart City Environment. *IEEE Internet Things J.* **2017**, *PP*, 1, doi:10.1109/JIOT.2017.2712558.

17. Rajaram, M.L.; Kougianos, E.; Mohanty, S.P.; Sundaravadivel, P. A wireless sensor network simulation framework for structural health monitoring in smart cities. In Proceedings of the 2016 IEEE 6th International Conference on Consumer Electronics-Berlin (ICCE-Berlin), Berlin, Germany, 5–7 September 2016; pp. 78–82.

18. Hijazi, S.; Page, A.; Kantarci, B.; Soyata, T. Machine Learning in Cardiac Health Monitoring and Decision Support. *IEEE Comput.* **2016**, *49*, 38–48.

19. Ota, K.; Dao, M.S.; Mezaris, V.; Natale, F.G.B.D. Deep Learning for Mobile Multimedia: A Survey. *ACM Trans. Multimedia Comput. Commun. Appl.* **2017**, *13*, 34.

20. Yu, D.; Deng, L. Deep Learning and Its Applications to Signal and Information Processing [Exploratory DSP]. *IEEE Signal Process. Mag.* **2011**, *28*, 145–154.

21. Larochelle, H.; Bengio, Y. Classification using discriminative restricted Boltzmann machines. In Proceedings of the 25th International Conference on Machine Learning, Helsinki, Finland, 5–9 July 2008; pp. 536–543.

22. Vincent, P.; Larochelle, H.; Lajoie, I.; Bengio, Y.; Manzagol, P.A. Stacked denoising autoencoders: Learning useful representations in a deep network with a local denoising criterion. *J. Mach. Learn. Res.* **2010**, *11*, 3371–3408.

23. Wang, L.; Sng, D. Deep Learning Algorithms with Applications to Video Analytics for A Smart City: A Survey. *arXiv* **2015**, arXiv:1512.03131.

24. Cavazza, J.; Morerio, P.; Murino, V. When Kernel Methods Meet Feature Learning: Log-Covariance Network for Action Recognition From Skeletal Data. In Proceedings of the 2017 IEEE Conference on Computer Vision and Pattern Recognition Workshops (CVPRW), Honolulu, HI, USA, 21–26 July 2017; pp. 1251–1258.

25. Keceli, A.S.; Kaya, A.; Can, A.B. Action recognition with skeletal volume and deep learning. In Proceedings of the 2017 25th Signal Processing and Communications Applications Conference (SIU), Antalya, Turkey, 15–18 May 2017; pp. 1–4.

26. LeCun, Y.; Bengio, Y.; Hinton, G. Deep learning. *Nature* **2015**, *521*, 436–444.

27. Alsheikh, M.A.; Lin, S.; Niyato, D.; Tan, H.P. Machine Learning in Wireless Sensor Networks: Algorithms, Strategies, and Applications. *IEEE Commun. Surv. Tutor.* **2014**, *16*, 1996–2018.

28. Mohri, M.; Rostamizadeh, A.; Talwalkar, A. *Foundations of Machine Learning*; MIT Press: Cambridge, MA, USA, 2012.

29. Clifton, L.; Clifton, D.A.; Pimentel, M.A.F.; Watkinson, P.J.; Tarassenko, L. Predictive Monitoring of Mobile Patients by Combining Clinical Observations with Data from Wearable Sensors. *IEEE J. Biomed. Health Inform.* **2014**, *18*, 722–730.

30. Tsiouris, K.M.; Gatsios, D.; Rigas, G.; Miljkovic, D.; Seljak, B.K.; Bohanec, M.; Arredondo, M.T.; Antonini, A.; Konitsiotis, S.; Koutsouris, D.D.; et al. PD_Manager: An mHealth platform for Parkinson's disease patient management. *Healthcare Technol. Lett.* **2017**, *4*, 102–108.

31. Hu, K.; Rahman, A.; Bhrugubanda, H.; Sivaraman, V. HazeEst: Machine Learning Based Metropolitan Air Pollution Estimation from Fixed and Mobile Sensors. *IEEE Sens. J.* **2017**, *17*, 3517–3525.

32. Tariq, O.B.; Lazarescu, M.T.; Iqbal, J.; Lavagno, L. Performance of Machine Learning Classifiers for Indoor Person Localization with Capacitive Sensors. *IEEE Access* **2017**, *5*, 12913–12926.

33. Jahangiri, A.; Rakha, H.A. Applying Machine Learning Techniques to Transportation Mode Recognition Using Mobile Phone Sensor Data. *IEEE Trans. Intell. Transp. Syst.* **2015**, *16*, 2406–2417.

34. Schmidhuber, J. Deep Learning in Neural Networks: An Overview. *Neural Netw.* **2014**, *61*, 85–117.

35. Deng, L.; Yu, D. Deep learning: Methods and applications. *Found. Trends Signal Process.* **2014**, *7*, 197–387.

36. Hinton, G.E.; Osindero, S.; Teh, Y.W. A fast learning algorithm for deep belief nets. *Neural Comput.* **2006**, *18*, 1527–1554.

37. Do, T.M.T.; Gatica-Perez, D. The places of our lives: Visiting patterns and automatic labeling from longitudinal smartphone data. *IEEE Trans. Mob. Comput.* **2014**, *13*, 638–648.

38. Al Rahhal, M.M.; Bazi, Y.; AlHichri, H.; Alajlan, N.; Melgani, F.; Yager, R.R. Deep learning approach for active classification of electrocardiogram signals. *Inform. Sci.* **2016**, *345*, 340–354.

39. Acharya, U.R.; Fujita, H.; Lih, O.S.; Adam, M.; Tan, J.H.; Chua, C.K. Automated Detection of Coronary Artery Disease Using Different Durations of ECG Segments with Convolutional Neural Network. *Knowl.-Based Syst.* **2017**, *132*, 62–71.

40. Hosseini, M.P.; Tran, T.X.; Pompili, D.; Elisevich, K.; Soltanian-Zadeh, H. Deep Learning with Edge Computing for Localization of Epileptogenicity Using Multimodal rs-fMRI and EEG Big Data. In Proceedings of the 2017 IEEE International Conference on Autonomic Computing (ICAC), Columbus, OH, USA, 17–21 July 2017; pp. 83–92.

41. Zheng, W.L.; Zhu, J.Y.; Peng, Y.; Lu, B.L. EEG-based emotion classification using deep belief networks. In Proceedings of the 2014 IEEE International Conference on Multimedia and Expo (ICME), Chengdu, China, 14–18 July 2014; pp. 1–6.

42. Gu, W. Non-intrusive blood glucose monitor by multi-task deep learning: PhD forum abstract. In Proceedings of the 16th ACM/IEEE International Conference on Information Processing in Sensor Networks, Pittsburgh, PA, USA, 18–20 April 2017; ACM: New York, NY, USA, 2017; pp. 249–250.

43. Anagnostopoulos, T.; Zaslavsky, A.; Kolomvatsos, K.; Medvedev, A.; Amirian, P.; Morley, J.; Hadjieftymiades, S. Challenges and Opportunities of Waste Management in IoT-Enabled Smart Cities: A Survey. *IEEE Trans. Sustain. Comput.* **2017**, *2*, 275–289.

44. Taleb, S.; Al Sallab, A.; Hajj, H.; Dawy, Z.; Khanna, R.; Keshavamurthy, A. Deep learning with ensemble classification method for sensor sampling decisions. In Proceedings of the 2016 International Wireless Communications and Mobile Computing Conference (IWCMC), Paphos, Cyprus, 5–9 September 2016; pp. 114–119.

45. Costilla-Reyes, O.; Scully, P.; Ozanyan, K.B. Deep Neural Networks for Learning Spatio-Temporal Features from Tomography Sensors. *IEEE Trans. Ind. Electron.* **2018**, *65*, 645–653, doi:10.1109/TIE.2017.2716907.

46. Fang, S.H.; Fei, Y.X.; Xu, Z.; Tsao, Y. Learning Transportation Modes From Smartphone Sensors Based on Deep Neural Network. *IEEE Sens. J.* **2017**, *17*, 6111–6118.

47. Xu, X.; Yin, S.; Ouyang, P. Fast and low-power behavior analysis on vehicles using smartphones. In Proceedings of the 2017 6th International Symposium on Next Generation Electronics (ISNE), Keelung, Taiwan, 23–25 May 2017; pp. 1–4.

48. Eskofier, B.M.; Lee, S.I.; Daneault, J.F.; Golabchi, F.N.; Ferreira-Carvalho, G.; Vergara-Diaz, G.; Sapienza, S.; Costante, G.; Klucken, J.; Kautz, T.; et al. Recent machine learning advancements in sensor-based mobility analysis: Deep learning for Parkinson's disease assessment. In Proceedings of the 2016 IEEE 38th Annual International Conference of the Engineering in Medicine and Biology Society (EMBC), Orlando, FL, USA, 16–20 August 2016; pp. 655–658.

49. Zhu, J.; Pande, A.; Mohapatra, P.; Han, J.J. Using deep learning for energy expenditure estimation with wearable sensors. In Proceedings of the 2015 17th International Conference on E-health Networking, Application & Services (HealthCom), Boston, MA, USA, 14–17 October 2015; pp. 501–506.

50. Jankowski, S.; Szymański, Z.; Dziomin, U.; Mazurek, P.; Wagner, J. Deep learning classifier for fall detection based on IR distance sensor data. In Proceedings of the 2015 IEEE 8th International Conference on Intelligent Data Acquisition and Advanced Computing Systems: Technology and Applications (IDAACS), Warsaw, Poland, 24–26 September 2015; Volume 2, pp. 723–727.

51. Menotti, D.; Chiachia, G.; Pinto, A.; Schwartz, W.R.; Pedrini, H.; Falcao, A.X.; Rocha, A. Deep representations for iris, face, and fingerprint spoofing detection. *IEEE Trans. Inform. Forensics Secur.* **2015**, *10*, 864–879.

52. Yin, Y.; Liu, Z.; Zimmermann, R. Geographic information use in weakly-supervised deep learning for landmark recognition. In Proceedings of the 2017 IEEE International Conference on Multimedia and Expo (ICME), Hong Kong, China, 10–14 July 2017; pp. 1015–1020.

53. Barreto, T.L.; Rosa, R.A.; Wimmer, C.; Moreira, J.R.; Bins, L.S.; Cappabianco, F.A.M.; Almeida, J. Classification of Detected Changes from Multitemporal High-Res Xband SAR Images: Intensity and Texture Descriptors From SuperPixels. *IEEE J. Sel. Top. Appl. Earth Obs. Remote Sens.* **2016**, *9*, 5436–5448.

54. Goodfellow, I.; Bengio, Y.; Courville, A. *Deep Learning*; MIT Press: Cambridge, MA, USA, 2016.

55. Hinton, G.E.; Salakhutdinov, R.R. Reducing the dimensionality of data with neural networks. *Science* **2006**, *313*, 504–507.

56. Alain, G.; Bengio, Y.; Rifai, S. Regularized auto-encoders estimate local statistics. *Proc. CoRR* **2012**, 1–17.

57. Rifai, S.; Bengio, Y.; Dauphin, Y.; Vincent, P. A generative process for sampling contractive auto-encoders. *arXiv* **2012**, arXiv:1206.6434.

58. Abdulnabi, A.H.; Wang, G.; Lu, J.; Jia, K. Multi-Task CNN Model for Attribute Prediction. *IEEE Trans. Multimedia* **2015**, *17*, 1949–1959.

59. Deng, L.; Abdelhamid, O.; Yu, D. A deep convolutional neural network using heterogeneous pooling for trading acoustic invariance with phonetic confusion. In Proceedings of the 2013 IEEE International Conference on Acoustics, Speech and Signal Processing, Vancouver, BC, Canada, 26–31 May 2013; pp. 6669–6673.

60. Aghdam, H.H.; Heravi, E.J. *Guide to Convolutional Neural Networks: A Practical Application to Traffic-Sign Detection and Classification*; Springer: Cham, Switzerland, 2017.

61. Huang, G.; Lee, H.; Learnedmiller, E. Learning hierarchical representations for face verification with convolutional deep belief networks. In Proceedings of the 2012 IEEE Conference on Computer Vision and Pattern Recognition, Providence, RI, USA, 16–21 June 2012; pp. 2518–2525.

62. Ackley, D.H.; Hinton, G.E.; Sejnowski, T.J. A learning algorithm for boltzmann machines. *Cognit. Sci.* **1985**, *9*, 147–169.

63. Salakhutdinov, R.; Mnih, A.; Hinton, G. Restricted Boltzmann machines for collaborative filtering. In Proceedings of the 24th international conference on Machine learning, Corvalis, OR, USA, 20–24 June 2007; pp. 791–798.

64. Ribeiro, B.; Gonçalves, I.; Santos, S.; Kovacec, A. Deep Learning Networks for Off-Line Handwritten Signature Recognition. In Proceedings of the 2011 CIARP 16th Iberoamerican Congress on Pattern Recognition, Pucón, Chile, 15–18 November 2011; pp. 523–532.

65. Nie, D.; Zhang, H.; Adeli, E.; Liu, L.; Shen, D. *3D Deep Learning for Multi-Modal Imaging-Guided Survival Time Prediction of Brain Tumor Patients*; Springer: Cham, Switzerland, 2016.

66. Rose, D.C.; Arel, I.; Karnowski, T.P.; Paquit, V.C. Applying deep-layered clustering to mammography image analytics. In Proceedings of the 2010 Biomedical Sciences and Engineering Conference, Oak Ridge, TN, USA, 25–26 May 2010; pp. 1–4.

67. Kuang, D.; He, L. Classification on ADHD with Deep Learning. In Proceedings of the 2014 International Conference on Cloud Computing and Big Data, Wuhan, China, 12–14 November 2014; pp. 27–32.

68. Li, F.; Tran, L.; Thung, K.H.; Ji, S.; Shen, D.; Li, J. A Robust Deep Model for Improved Classification of AD/MCI Patients. *IEEE J. Biomed. Health Inform.* **2015**, *19*, 1610–1616.

69. Esteva, A.; Kuprel, B.; Novoa, R.A.; Ko, J.; Swetter, S.M.; Blau, H.M.; Thrun, S. Dermatologist-level classification of skin cancer with deep neural networks. *Nature* **2017**, *542*, 115–118.

70. Sabouri, P.; GholamHosseini, H. Lesion border detection using deep learning. In Proceedings of the 2016 IEEE Congress on Evolutionary Computation (CEC), Vancouver, BC, Canada, 24–29 July 2016; pp. 1416–1421.

71. Ha, S.; Choi, S. Convolutional neural networks for human activity recognition using multiple accelerometer and gyroscope sensors. In Proceedings of the 2016 International Joint Conference on Neural Networks (IJCNN), Vancouver, BC, Canada, 24–29 July 2016; pp. 381–388.

72. Sathyanarayana, A.; Joty, S.; Fernandez-Luque, L.; Ofli, F.; Srivastava, J.; Elmagarmid, A.; Arora, T.; Taheri, S. Sleep quality prediction from wearable data using deep learning. *JMIR mHealth uHealth* **2016**, *4*, e125.

73. Hammerla, N.Y.; Halloran, S.; Ploetz, T. Deep, convolutional, and recurrent models for human activity recognition using wearables. *arXiv* **2016**, arXiv:1604.08880.

74. Baccouche, M.; Mamalet, F.; Wolf, C.; Garcia, C.; Baskurt, A. Sequential deep learning for human action recognition. In *International Workshop on Human Behavior Understanding*; Springer: Berlin/Heidelberg, Germany, 2011; pp. 29–39.

75. Ji, S.; Xu, W.; Yang, M.; Yu, K. 3D convolutional neural networks for human action recognition. *IEEE Trans. Pattern Anal. Mach. Intell.* **2013**, *35*, 221–231.

76. Karpathy, A.; Toderici, G.; Shetty, S.; Leung, T.; Sukthankar, R.; Fei-Fei, L. Large-scale video classification with convolutional neural networks. In Proceedings of the 2014 IEEE Conference on Computer Vision and Pattern Recognition, Columbus, OH, USA, 23–28 June 2014; pp. 1725–1732.

77. Cheron, G.; Draye, J.P.; Bourgeios, M.; Libert, G. A dynamic neural network identification of electromyography and arm trajectory relationship during complex movements. *IEEE Trans. Biomed. Eng.* **1996**, *43*, 552–558.

78. Page, A.; Hijazi, S.; Askan, D.; Kantarci, B.; Soyata, T. Research Directions in Cloud-Based Decision Support Systems for Health Monitoring Using Internet-of-Things Driven Data Acquisition. *Int. J. Serv. Comput.* **2016**, *4*, 18–34.

79. Guo, B.; Han, Q.; Chen, H.; Shangguan, L.; Zhou, Z.; Yu, Z. The Emergence of Visual Crowdsensing: Challenges and Opportunities. *IEEE Commun. Surv. Tutor.* **2017**, *PP*, 1, doi:10.1109/COMST.2017.2726686.

80. Ma, H.; Zhao, D.; Yuan, P. Opportunities in mobile crowd sensing. *IEEE Commun. Mag.* **2014**, *52*, 29–35.

81. Haddawy, P.; Frommberger, L.; Kauppinen, T.; De Felice, G.; Charkratpahu, P.; Saengpao, S.; Kanchanakitsakul, P. Situation awareness in crowdsensing for disease surveillance in crisis situations. In Proceedings of the Seventh International Conference on Information and Communication Technologies and Development, Singapore, 15–18 May 2015; p. 38.

82. Cardone, G.; Foschini, L.; Bellavista, P.; Corradi, A.; Borcea, C.; Talasila, M.; Curtmola, R. Fostering participaction in smart cities: a geo-social crowdsensing platform. *IEEE Commun. Mag.* **2013**, *51*, 112–119.

83. Pan, Z.; Yu, H.; Miao, C.; Leung, C. Crowdsensing Air Quality with Camera-Enabled Mobile Devices. In Proceedings of the Twenty-Ninth IAAI Conference, San Francisco, CA, USA, 6–9 February 2017; pp. 4728–4733.

84. Mittal, G.; Yagnik, K.B.; Garg, M.; Krishnan, N.C. SpotGarbage: Smartphone app to detect garbage using deep learning. In Proceedings of the 2016 ACM International Joint Conference on Pervasive and Ubiquitous Computing, Heidelberg, Germany, 12–16 September 2016; pp. 940–945.

85. Habibzadeh, H.; Qin, Z.; Soyata, T.; Kantarci, B. Large Scale Distributed Dedicated- and Non-Dedicated Smart City Sensing Systems. *IEEE Sens. J.* **2017**, *17*, 7649–7658, doi:10.1109/JSEN.2017.2725638.

86. Xu, L.; Hao, X.; Lane, N.D.; Liu, X.; Moscibroda, T. More with Less: Lowering User Burden in Mobile Crowdsourcing through Compressive Sensing. In Proceedings of the 2015 ACM International Joint Conference on Pervasive and Ubiquitous Computing, Osaka, Japan, 7–11 September 2015; ACM: New York, NY, USA, 2015; pp. 659–670.

87. Pouryazdan, M.; Kantarci, B. The Smart Citizen Factor in Trustworthy Smart City Crowdsensing. *IT Prof.* **2016**, *18*, 26–33.

88. Pouryazdan, M.; Kantarci, B.; Soyata, T.; Song, H. Anchor-Assisted and Vote-Based Trustworthiness Assurance in Smart City Crowdsensing. *IEEE Access* **2016**, *4*, 529–541.

89. Farahani, B.; Firouzi, F.; Chang, V.; Badaroglu, M.; Constant, N.; Mankodiya, K. Towards fog-driven IoT eHealth: Promises and challenges of IoT in medicine and healthcare. *Future Gener. Comput. Syst.* **2018**, *78*, 659–676.

90. Kleesiek, J.; Urban, G.; Hubert, A.; Schwarz, D.; Maier-Hein, K.; Bendszus, M.; Biller, A. Deep MRI brain extraction: A 3D convolutional neural network for skull stripping. *Neuroimage* **2016**, *129*, 460–469.

91. Fritscher, K.; Raudaschl, P.; Zaffino, P.; Spadea, M.F.; Sharp, G.C.; Schubert, R. Deep Neural Networks for Fast Segmentation of 3D Medical Images. In *Medical Image Computing and Computer-Assisted Intervention—MICCAI*; Springer: Cham, Switzerland, 2016.

92. Fakoor, R.; Ladhak, F.; Nazi, A.; Huber, M. Using deep learning to enhance cancer diagnosis and classification. In Proceedings of the 30th International Conference on Machine Learning, Atlanta, GA, USA, 16–21 June 2013.

93. Khademi, M.; Nedialkov, N.S. Probabilistic Graphical Models and Deep Belief Networks for Prognosis of Breast Cancer. In Proceedings of the 2015 IEEE 14th International Conference on Machine Learning and Applications, Miami, FL, USA, 9–11 December 2016; pp. 727–732.

94. Angermueller, C.; Lee, H.J.; Reik, W.; Stegle, O. DeepCpG: Accurate prediction of single-cell DNA methylation states using deep learning. *Genome Biol.* **2017**, *18*, 67.

95. Tian, K.; Shao, M.; Wang, Y.; Guan, J.; Zhou, S. Boosting Compound-Protein Interaction Prediction by Deep Learning. *Methods* **2016**, *110*, 64–72.

96. Che, Z.; Purushotham, S.; Khemani, R.; Liu, Y. Distilling Knowledge from Deep Networks with Applications to Healthcare Domain. *Ann. Chirurgie* **2015**, *40*, 529–532.

97. Lipton, Z.C.; Kale, D.C.; Elkan, C.; Wetzell, R. Learning to Diagnose with LSTM Recurrent Neural Networks. In Proceedings of the International Conference on Learning Representations (ICLR 2016), San Juan, Puerto Rico, 2–4 May 2016.

98. Liang, Z.; Zhang, G.; Huang, J.X.; Hu, Q.V. Deep learning for healthcare decision making with EMRs. In Proceedings of the IEEE International Conference on Bioinformatics and Biomedicine, Belfast, UK, 2–5 November 2014; pp. 556–559.

Journal of
*Sensor and
Actuator Networks*

Article

Enhanced IoT-Based End-To-End Emergency and Disaster Relief System

Dhafer Ben Arbia [1,2,*]**, Muhammad Mahtab Alam** [3]**, Abdullah Kadri** [1]**, Elyes Ben Hamida** [1] **and Rabah Attia** [2]

[1]   Qatar Mobility Innovations Center (QMIC), Qatar University, Doha P.O. Box. 210531, Qatar;
    dhafera@qmic.com (D.B.A); abdullahk@qmic.com (A.K.); elyes.ben-hamida@irt-systemx.fr (E.B.H.)
[2]   SERCOM Lab, Polytechnic School of Tunisia, University of Carthage, P.O. Box 743, La Marsa 2078, Tunisia;
    rabah.attia@enit.rnu.tn
[3]   Thomas Johann Seebeck Department of Electronics, School of Information Technology,
    Tallinn University of Technology, P.O. Box 10120 Tallinn, Estonia; muhammad.alam@ttu.ee
*   Correspondence: dhafera@qmic.com; Tel.: +974-5010-8593

Received: 30 June 2017; Accepted: 9 August 2017; Published: 21 August 2017

Abstract: In this paper, we present a new enhancement for an emergency and disaster relief system called Critical and Rescue Operations using Wearable Wireless sensors networks (CROW^2). We address the reliability challenges in setting up a wireless autonomous communication system in order to offload data from the disaster area (rescuers, trapped victims, civilians, media, etc.) back to a command center. The proposed system connects deployed rescuers to extended networks and the Internet. CROW^2 is an end-to-end system that runs the recently-proposed Optimized Routing Approach for Critical and Emergency Networks (ORACE-Net) routing protocol. The system integrates heterogeneous wireless devices (Raspberry Pi, smart phones, sensors) and various communicating technologies (WiFi IEEE 802.11n, Bluetooth IEEE 802.15.1) to enable end-to-end network connectivity, which is monitored by a cloud Internet-of-Things platform. First, we present the CROW^2 generic system architecture, which is adaptable to various technologies integration at different levels (i.e., on-body, body-to-body, off-body). Second, we implement the ORACE-Net protocol on heterogeneous devices including Android-based smart phones and Linux-based Raspberry Pi devices. These devices act as on-body coordinators to collect information from on-body sensors. The collected data is then pushed to the command center thanks to multi-hop device-to-device communication. Third, the overall CROW^2 system performance is evaluated according to relevant metrics including end-to-end link quality estimation, throughput and end-to-end delay. As a proof-of-concept, we validate the system architecture through deployment and extracted experimental results. Finally, we highlight motion detection and links' unavailability prevention based on the recorded data where the main factors (i.e., interference and noise) that affect the performance are analyzed.

Keywords: tactical multi-hop routing protocol; Internet-of-Things; optimized routing approach for critical and emergency networks; disaster relief system; body-to-body communication

1. Introduction

According to the United Nations Office of Disaster Risk Reduction (UNISDR), the financial impact due to natural and man-made disasters is paramount. It is reported that by 2030, the global average of annual losses due to disasters is forecasted to increase and reach 415 billion USD [1]. These losses surely decrease when a preventive communication strategy is ready to be triggered in a disaster incident.

Indeed, two recent crises showed how important communication alternatives could be during the disaster relief operations. (1) In March 2011, a 9.0 magnitude earthquake caused a tsunami of 30 feet in Japan, the fourth-largest earthquake on record (since 1900), and six nuclear reactors in Fukushima Daiichi plant were affected (two pools of reactors exploded). Japan's Fire and Disaster Management Agency confirmed that 22,000 people are dead or missing. During the Fukushima disaster, emergency teams and the army were using classic High Frequency (HF) military radio communication without data transmission. Local taxi drivers were coordinating rescue operations using their on-board radio communication devices traditionally used for reservations. (2) In January 2010, Haiti earthquake, of a 7.0 magnitude, was another example of the use of Very High Frequency (VHF) radio communication and satellite phones. During the 24 h after the disaster, disaster task forces did not have a clear vision of the whole situation. Such catastrophes' relief operations are impossible to conduct without an alternative data communication system immediately deployable and operational.

To that end, we have recently proposed a new routing protocol called Optimized Routing Approach for Critical and Emergency Networks (ORACE-Net) [2]. ORACE-Net is a multi-hop routing protocol, which rates every end-to-end link with regards to its quality (i.e., end-to-end link quality estimation). This metric varies according to the nodes' mobility, which is the most relevant criteria for reliable emergency systems.

Our previous work [3] was constrained by the following factors: First, there were no real on-body sensors. We generated data for a fictitious network on the mobile nodes as the application layer payload. Second, the initial experimental results indicate that the average disconnections increase significantly when the end-to-end route has more than two hops. Third, as the achieved results were collected in an indoor scenario, several wireless devices were causing interference on the deployed network and consequently reducing the global network performance. Fourth, with reference to one of the most studied problem in network design, the Capacitated Network Design Problem (CNDP) detailed in [4] on the basis of the results in [5], we re-studied the number of deployed nodes with regards to the network traffic uncertainty. Indeed, eight nodes caused an overhead on the routing layer and made the routing process too slow and, consequently, the round trip time was high. Thus, we reduced the number of deployed tactical nodes to four. It is important to note here that this given number of tactical devices must be carefully selected according to the area dimensions. Bertsekas in [6] provides a complete study of the discrete network optimization problems, and Marotta et al. in [7] propose a heuristic that can be used to warm-start the solution process of the solver, accelerating the convergence towards the optimum. The latter proposed solution approach would be perfect for selecting the optimal number of tactical nodes considering traffic uncertainty in discrete network optimization problems. For small and medium-sized networks (up to 25 nodes), an analytical study given in [8] consists of a reference to converge to an optimized network design independently of the traffic uncertainty. Finally, according to the collected results, we were unable to evaluate the throughput accuracy due to the significant number of disconnections and high round trip time delay.

Some of the benefits of this paper are addressing the above limitations and improving the proposed routing approach behavior, in particular the average throughput, the round trip time delay (RTT_{Delay}) and the end-to-end link quality estimation ($E2E_{LQE}$). This work provides the following main contributions:

- The Critical and Rescue Operations using Wearable Wireless sensors networks (CROW^2) system is one of the rare proof-of-concept implementations of emergency ad hoc autonomous systems. Unlike the detailed works in Section 2, as an application layer payload, we use real-time human vital signs (motion data, heartbeat, magnetometer, etc.) collected from the on-body sensors and pushed to the IoT platform. The evaluation of the proposed system is realized on a real indoor test-bed under realistic conditions. Indeed, we experimentally investigate the mobile devices' behavior with regards to key performance metrics, such as throughput, end-to-end delay, end-to-end link quality estimation during sensing and disseminating data onto the IoT platform.

- The implemented scenario is a reference experiment for researchers and professionals to evaluate concretely the trade-off between the $\{E2E_{LQE}, throughput\}$ and $\{RTT_{Delay}, jitter\}$ in the disaster relief context [9]. Additionally, this work emphasizes the difference between UDP and TCP transport mode performances in disaster relief applications and may be considered as a reference for upcoming application implementations with regards to the bandwidth limitations. Moreover, the realized experiment advises also on the optimal hop count to guarantee the required throughput for the critical applications (medical support, military, firefighters, press and media, etc.).
- The proposed system is back-ended by an IoT platform. Indeed, at the IoT platform level, we prove the system's capability for mobility pattern recognition and prediction. Then, we discuss the overall interference affecting the mobile devices behavior for the considered indoor scenario. The proposed system shows also a global connectivity status of all of the deployed devices during the disaster relief operations.

The remainder of this paper is organized as follows: In Section 2, we present research works proposed recently related to the emergency relief operation systems. In Section 3, we introduce the CROW^2 system generic architecture. In Section 4, we focus on the implementation technologies in accordance with the on-body and body-to-body communications. In the last section, we describe the experimentation scenario, and we discuss the obtained results. Finally, we conclude by summarizing the paper's contributions, and we present some promising directions for future research.

2. Related Works

When conducting disaster relief operations, two relevant challenges arise: (i) setting up an immediate emergency wireless network to inter-connect on-the-field rescuers with trapped survivors; and (ii) relaying the emergency network to the Internet and extended networks.

Chen et al. in [10] classify the applications into three main classes: (i) remote health and fitness monitoring, (ii) military and training and (iii) intelligent biosensors for vehicle area networks. Moreover, the authors in [10] discuss a list of research projects and implementations, in particular the Advanced Health and Disaster Aid Network (AID-N) [11], which targets disaster and public safety applications. AID-N uses a wired connection for BAN communication and mesh and ZigBee for the Body-to-Body Network (BBN). Off-body communication in AID-N is fulfilled through WiFi, cellular networks and the Internet. AID-N aims to sense pulse, blood pressure, temperature and ECG. Negra et al. in [12] focus more on the following major medical applications: (i) telemedicine and remote patient monitoring, (ii) rehabilitation and therapy, (iii) biofeedback and (iv) ambient assisted living. The latter work discusses also the QoS requirements for the medical context.

Recently, research trends have aimed at relying on large-scale LTE/4G-enabled networks to inter-connect deployed devices during disaster relief operations. For instance, the authors in [13] introduced the Device-to-Device (D2D) communication scheme to allow user equipment (UE) to communicate within the reachable neighborhood. The proposed scheme sets up an ad hoc wireless network, which relies on the base stations evolved NodeBs (eNBs) at the network startup. Therefore, the solution still depends on the 4G network infrastructure. Definitely, the unavailability of the 4G backbone causes the unavailability of the proposed D2D wireless network.

We cite among, other works, approaches that studied and implemented alert messaging systems, such as the Reliable Routing Technique (RRT) [14] and TeamPhone [15]. Both approaches consist of setting up a smartphone messaging system, which is able to send alert notifications by bridging cellular networks or over ad hoc and opportunistic networks. These proposed systems seem to solve the connectivity issues on-the-field between rescuers and trapped survivors. However, devices in the disaster area may only communicate within one hop. Devices select one next hop only, and no neighborhood discovery is done. Thus, RRT and TeamPhone are not topology-aware and do not consider external network extension with the Internet or other networks.

The authors in [16] propose a localization-based and network congestion adaptive approach called "DistressNet". DistressNet is claimed to be efficient in congestion avoidance during disaster relief operations; however, this approach is not appropriate for indoor rescue operations due to its localization mechanism, which renders multi-hop algorithms inefficient. The authors in [17] adopted the WiFi Direct standard for the "Emergency Direct Mobile App", which is intended to divide the set of smart phones into groups communicating in peer-to-peer mode assured by WiFi Direct. One of the devices is selected as the Group Owner (GO) and acts as the access point for its group and as a gateway elsewhere. The rest of the devices act as Group Relays (GR). The network topology formation in this strategy causes an important delay. Additionally, with regards to the high mobility imposed by the emergency context, the network topology update (i.e., GO negotiation and election, GR selection) increases data transmissions latency.

The earliest proposed schemes aim to enhance the on-body devices' transmission reliability and to improve the energy efficiency. Chen et al. in [18] proposed a novel Cross-Layer Design Optimization (CLDO) scheme. Indeed, the design of CLDO relies on the three lower layers (i.e., PHY, MAC and network layer). Power consumption is firstly optimized by selecting optimal power relays. Then, the remaining energy in leaf nodes is utilized to increase the lifetime and the reliability. An optimal packet size is given for energy efficiency. Chen et al. claim that an inevitably slight overhead accompanies CLDO processing for different factors. First, during network initialization, complex procedures are run. Second, the algorithm uses a certain number of iterations, which influences the overall performance. Third, CLDO lacks the capacity to manage dynamic location situations.

Another approach presented by Tsouri et al. in [19] relies on Dijkstra's algorithm augmented with novel link cost function designed to balance energy consumption across the network. This latter technique avoids relaying through nodes, which spent more accumulated energy than others. Indeed, routing decisions are made based on the energy optimization. The authors claim that the proposed approach increases the network lifetime by 40% with a slight increase of the energy consumed per bit. However, this work does not fulfill the operational application requirements, which rely on the BBN network for connectivity and routing.

D'Andreagiovanni et al. in [4] introduced a new approach able to handle the uncertainty that affects traffic demands in the Multi-Period Capacitated Network Design Problem (MP-CNDP). Additionally, a hybrid primal heuristic based on the combination of a randomized fixing algorithm was proposed by the authors based on ant colony optimization and exact large neighborhood search. This previous strategy has been improved by D'Andreagiovanni et al. in [20]. The authors adopt a best performance solution based on the min-max approach algorithm, which relies on a combination of a probabilistic fixing procedure, guided by linear relaxations, and an exact large variable neighborhood search, which has been proposed in [4]. D'Andreagiovanni et al. extended their preliminary work [20] by the new Integer Linear Programming (ILP) heuristic to solve the design problem. Furthermore, new techniques detailed in [21] fix the variables expressing routing decisions and employ an initial deterministic fixing phase of the variables modeling the activation of relay nodes. Experiments conducted in this work show that the proposed approach outperforms the existing optimization solvers' strategies.

Miranda et al. in [22] implemented and evaluated a complete Common Recognition and Identification Platform (CRIP) for the healthcare IoT. CRIP enables a basic configuration and communication standardization of healthcare 'things'. Security and privacy and health devices' integration are also covered within this approach. Miranda et al. deployed CRIP according to different communication standards, such as NFC, biometrics (fingerprints) and Bluetooth.

The above proposed approaches are limited for various reasons according to two main classes (O: Operational; T: Technical): (O1) the implemented network is not open to be connected to extended networks (i.e., Internet or military communication platforms); (O2) no command center is considered on-the-field for operations conduct, and therefore, nodes only share their status between each other; (O3) limited services (i.e., alert messages, notifications, etc., only); (T1) nodes in the network have no visibility on the neighborhood and the network topology; (T2) routes (which do not exist for some non-multihop approaches) are neither updated according to the quality of the links' variations based on the mobility, nor according to energy efficiency and commanding proximity. To summarize the various protocols and systems, a benchmark comparison is given in Table 1.

Table 1. Recent implemented disaster management systems benchmark. RRT, Reliable Routing Technique.

Protocols and Systems	Wireless Standard	Multi-Hop	Topology Awareness	Infrastructure Dependency	Network Extensibility	Sensing Devices Integration
RRT [14]	N/A	No	No	No	No	N/A
DistressNet [16]	ad hoc WiFi	Yes	Yes	No	No	N/A
Disaster 4 G [13]	LTE/4G	Yes	Yes	Yes	Yes	N/A
Emergency Direct [17]	WiFi Direct	No	Yes	No	No	N/A
TeamPhone [15]	ad hoc WiFi/SMS	No	No	Yes	No	N/A
CROW² (this work)	ad hoc WiFi	Yes	Yes	**No**	Yes	**Yes**

3. The CROW² System

The Critical Rescue Operation using Wearable Wireless sensor networks (CROW²) is a standalone system that enables a wireless ad hoc network in order to connect human beings (rescuers, trapped survivors, civilians, media and press, etc.) to each other, from one side, and to the Internet (or any extended network), from the other side, during disaster relief operations. The overall objectives and challenges to be addressed were initially described in [23].

3.1. History of the CROW² System

The CROW² system is realized under the CROW² project. Among the contributions of the project, notably, we proposed realistic channel models and simulation environment for Body Area Networks (BAN) and Body-to-Body Networks (BBN or B2B) [24]. We evaluated the IEEE 802.15.6 WBAN standard under the realistic channel, radio and mobility models; in particular, the proposed MAC protocols were compared for application-specific design; additionally, new dynamic MAC protocols were proposed in [25,26]. Furthermore, at the MAC layer, the IEEE 802.15.6 standard's proposed coexistence schemes for co-channel were evaluated in order to investigate the impact of interference from co-located BANs [24].

For that, we studied and compared the effectiveness of distributed and cluster-based architectures for Body-to-Body communications (BBNs or B2B). Then, various routing protocols among different classes including proactive, reactive, geographic-based and gradient-based were simulated and evaluated in [2]. Finally, we proposed a new optimized routing protocol specifically designed for the emergency and disaster relief communication networks. The routing protocol was implemented and evaluated on the WSNet [27] simulator within a realistic disaster mobility pattern. Finally, we implement the entire system on real mobile devices (smart phones and Raspberry Pi devices) for performance assessment within this paper.

3.2. CROW² System Architecture

The CROW² system is a set of wireless distributed devices equipped with wireless sensors intended to collect real-time data (i.e., vital signs, stress level, locations, ambient intelligence [28], etc.) from Wireless Body Area Network (WBAN) nodes towards a cloud IoT platform. Figure 1 depicts the general architecture of the next generation WBAN. A node in the proposed system could be either: (i) tactical (deployed by rescuers while moving inside the disaster area) or (ii) mobile (carried on-body by rescuers or trapped survivors). Tactical nodes establish a wireless tactical backbone, which extends the network coverage. Mobile nodes, being in proximity of the tactical backbone, could route packets through it as depicted in Figure 2b. We call these tactical devices ORACE-Net Tactical Devices (OTDs). Mobile devices carried on-body rely on both the OTDs and the other mobile devices to route data. Data collected from deployed nodes (i.e., tactical and mobile) are routed through the network towards the Command Center node (CC node). The CC node is a tactical command center deployed as a gateway allowing the emergency network to be linked to wide infrastructure networks (e.g., Internet, military platforms, other emergency networks, etc.). The CC node is also the node through which the operations' commanders send their instructions to the rescuers and the rescuers send back their feedback to the CC node. It is important to note here that multiple CC nodes could be deployed and activated in the case of single CC failure.

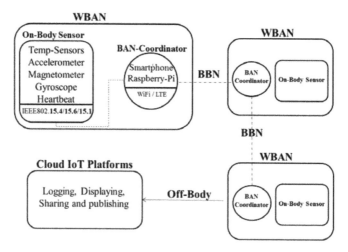

Figure 1. General architecture of the wireless body-area-network system. BAN: Body-Area-Network, BBN: Body-to-Body communication, Off-Body communication: all non-BAN and non-BBN communications.

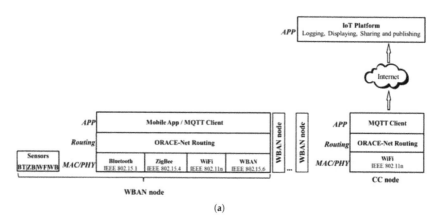

(a)

Figure 2. *Cont.*

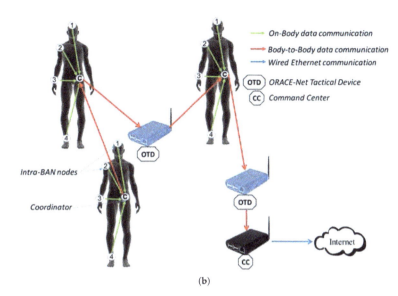

(b)

Figure 2. (**a**) CROW^2 system layer-based architecture. BT: Bluetooth, ZB: ZigBee, WF: WiFi, WB: WBAN. For the CROW^2 system, we considered Bluetooth between sensors and the coordinator and WiFi IEEE802.11n between WBANs and the Command Center node (CC node). (**b**) Multi-hop aspect in CROW^2; Data are routed from/through mobile/tactical nodes towards the Internet. MQTT, Message Queuing Telemetry Transport.

3.3. CROW^2 System Enhancement

As depicted in the layer-based architecture in Figure 2a, CROW^2 consists of two Wireless Body Area Networks (WBANs), or more, connected to a cloud IoT platform through the CC node. Each WBAN node is composed of: (i) a WBAN coordinator, which is a wireless device with advanced energy and communication features, (ii) on-body sensors, which may feature different communications technologies (i.e., Bluetooth IEEE802.15.1, WiFi IEEE802.11a/b/g/n, ZigBee IEEE802.5.4 and WBAN IEEE802.15.6). Sensors are connected among one of the previous technologies to the WBAN coordinator. The BBN routing is assured by the ORACE-Net routing protocol according to the architecture depicted in Figure 1. As the payload at the application layer, we deployed an Message Queuing Telemetry Transport [29] client (on tactical and mobile devices) to push data to the IoT platform.

The CROW^2 system is improved through this work. Compared to our previous work [3], we have installed on-body sensors provided by Shimmer [30]. Therefore, the current system payload consists of real sensed vital sign data from the human body towards the IoT platform. To improve connectivity and mitigate interference, we reduced the tactical devices (OTDs) to four. Additionally, we reduced the number of active indoor wireless access points, since we assume that during the disaster, they will be damaged.

4. CROW^2 System Implementation

In this section, we explain how the CROW^2 system is implemented. We present first the on-body communication; then, we present the body-to-body communication implementation. Finally, we describe the off-body components' implementation, in particular the Labeeb-IoT platform.

4.1. On-Body Communication

WBAN covers the communication between the coordinator (which is the main on-body device responsible for communication with other BANs and off-body devices) and the rest of the on-body or under skin sensors. For the CROW[2] system, on-body communication is established between sensors (i.e., Shimmer [31]) and the Android mobile application (i.e., Labeeb-IoT Shimmer Sensing Android App).

Shimmer sensors [31] are sensing devices capable of measuring physical quantities (e.g., acceleration, gyroscope X, Y, Z and angle, triple axis magnetic field, pressure, etc.) and sharing them via Bluetooth. Shimmer provides a Service Development Kit (SDK) that affords the possibility to read real-time data from the sensor by an Android or IOS mobile application. We place the Shimmer sensor on-body as shown in Figure 3. Once connected via Bluetooth, our mobile application (Labeeb-IoT Shimmer Sensing Android App) starts reading data from the sensor and sharing them with the IoT platform.

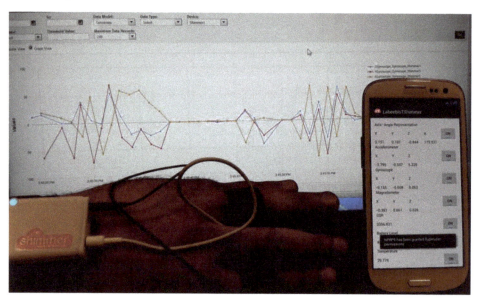

Figure 3. Real-time data collected by the ORACE-Net Mobile Device (OMD), routed through the ORACE-Net network and then displayed on the Labeeb-IoT platform.

The Labeeb-IoT Shimmer Sensing Android App is responsible for collecting data from sensors and transmitting them onto the Labeeb-IoT platform using the Message Queuing Telemetry Transport (MQTT) protocol [29]. Figure 4a depicts a screenshot from the live activity of the mobile app with the different real-time sensed parameters before being pushed to the Labeeb-IoT platform.

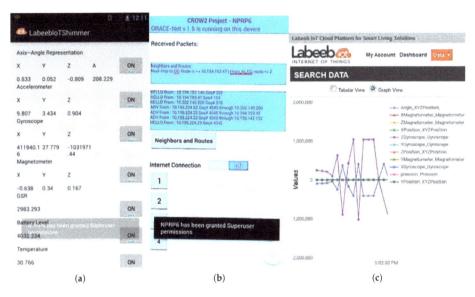

(a)	(b)	(c)

Figure 4. (**a**) A screen-shot from the Labeeb-IoT Shimmer sensing mobile app, which collects data from Shimmer [31] sensors and pushes them to the Internet of Things platform (Labeeb-IoT). (**b**) Testbed: a photo of the ORACE-Net mobile devices displaying the real-time events (received "Hello" and Advertisement ("ADV") packets) and the current route. (**c**) The Labeeb-IoT [32] interface shows the variation of the sensed data from the Shimmer sensor connected to the mobile node.

4.2. Body-To-Body Communication

Body-to-body communications consist of the communications between coordinators (i.e., mobile devices) carried by the rescuers, survivors and also the communications between coordinators and tactical devices, as shown in Figure 2b. The ORACE-Net routing protocol assures routing between CROW^2 devices. With regards to the operational requirements of a disaster relief mission, we assume that the first rescue teams reaching the incident area deploy wireless tactical devices (i.e., OTDs) to enable a wireless ad hoc tactical network on site. We describe these in the two following subsections. The implementation of the ORACE-Net routing protocol is describe for: (i) ORACE-Net Tactical Devices (OTDs) (ii) and ORACE-Net Android Mobile Device (OMD). Both devices are depicted in Figure 5.

4.2.1. Android Mobile Devices

These devices are designed based on the ORACE-Net Android application, which is a mobile app coded in Java and deployed on Android v4.2.2 CyanogenMod 10.0 distribution. This mobile app is dedicated to route data through the emergency network based on the ORACE-Net routing protocol. The ORACE-Net Android application is implemented at the user level as depicted in Figure 6a. It exploits the features of the Linux operating system at the kernel layer through the Dalvik Virtual Machine. Figure 6b depicts the ORACE-Net mobile application components, which are: (1) events listener, (2) broadcast receivers, (3) services, (4) content providers and (5) display activities. The relevant component in the architecture is the events listener, which triggers the rest of the tasks. An events listener is used to catch events (e.g., unicasted, multicasted or broadcasted packets, clicked button, typed text, etc.). In the ORACE-Net Android application, the events listener is implemented as a socket with a multi-cast IP address/Port: 224.0.0.1/10000. A similar socket is implemented with the C-language on Linux for the tactical deployed devices. Received packets through the events listener are handled by the broadcast receivers component to be hulled. Particularly, the content provider allows the application to share the application output with other servers or platforms. Figure 4b is a screenshot of the ORACE-Net mobile app showing the received/transmitted Hello and Advertisement (ADV)packets, the next-hop and the hop count to the CC node.

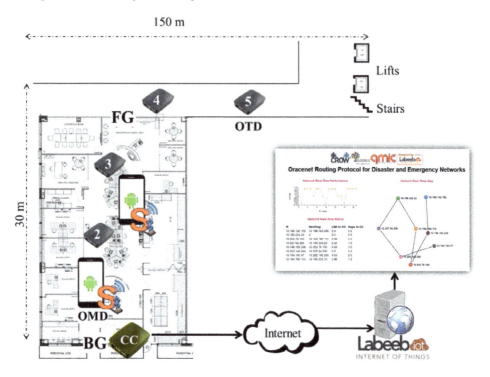

Figure 5. Experimentation scenario and data flow from deployed nodes to the Labeeb-IoT platform. The Command Center (CC node) is placed at the Back Gate (BG); ORACE-Net Mobile Devices (OMD) are mobile devices carried by the rescuers to which Shimmer sensors are connected via Bluetooth. The tactical ORACE-Net network is established through ORACE-Net Linux Tactical Devices (OTD). All collected data go through the CC node to the Labeeb-IoT platform. A real-time dynamic topology website instantly displays the network topology.

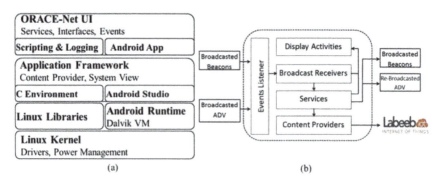

Figure 6. (a) ORACE-Net system-oriented stack over Linux and Android. (b) ORACE-Net Android application architecture.

4.2.2. ORACE-Net Tactical Devices

These tactical devices are implemented based on Linux applications. Indeed, we implemented the ORACE-Net protocol on Raspbian v8.0, a free operating system based on Debian optimized for the Raspberry Pi hardware. Linux libraries are used to operate various protocol events (i.e., socket connections, packets encapsulation, multicasting and broadcasting). We use shell scripts to display the status and statistics and to manage the processes of the protocol. The logging system in the tactical devices is based on the operating system logging service Syslog. Finally, data are pushed to the Labeeb-IoT platform via the MQTT protocol client installed on every OTD.

4.3. Off-Body Communication

Communication between the CC node and the Labeeb-IoT platform covers the off-body communication of the CROW^2 system, as depicted in Figures 1 and 5.

The Internet of Things (IoT) is an emerging technology developed for smart living solutions. IoT solutions are online platforms capable of receiving sensed real-time data from diverse types of devices (including sensors, actuators, coordinators, gateways, etc.) that could be deployed in a vast geographic area. Such platforms are able to collect, store, publish and analyze data according to many parameters. With respect to the MQTT standard [29], the Labeeb-IoT platform uses a publish/subscribe architecture in contrast with the HTTP request/response paradigm architecture. Publish/subscribe is event-driven and enables messages to be pushed by clients using the MQTT protocol. The MQTT client communicates with the broker using predefined methods (e.g., connect, disconnect, subscribe, publish). Labeeb-IoT offers various APIs and RESTful and/or JavaScript Object Notation (JSON) web services.

In our experiments, ORACE-Net devices (mobile and tactical) push continuously and instantly the following data to the Labeeb-IoT platform: (1) device identifier ($Device_{Id}$), (2) device location ($Location$), (3) device neighbors' list ($Neighbors$), (4) next-hop to the CC node (NH_{CC}), (5) $E2E_{LQE}$ and (6) Hop_{count} to the CC node. Data are stored in the platform database and then could be extracted and displayed on Labeeb-IoT as shown in Figure 4c.

5. Experimentation

5.1. Deployment Scenario and Experimental Setup

In our experiments, we consider a disaster scenario in our office, Qatar Mobility Innovations Center (QMIC), in Qatar Science and Technology Park (QSTP). Our test-bed consists of four Raspberry Pi devices (Raspberry Pi Foundation, Cambridge, UK) and two rooted Samsung Galaxy S3-I9300 smart phones (Samsung Electronics Co. Ltd., Suwon, South Korea) with the ORACE-Net routing protocol implemented. The office map is shown in Figure 5. The scenario is as follows: rescue teams access the office from the Back Gate (BG). First, they deploy the CC node in a trusted and safe location (near the entrance gate) where they are connected to the Internet through an Ethernet or WiFi access point (these links could be provided with military microwave or satellite connections). Upon their entrance inside the office, rescuers start deploying tactical devices (OTD) as base stations in order to have the maximum wireless network coverage in the operations area. Two to five OTDs are deployed (as shown in Figure 5). Mobile nodes (smart phones) carried by the rescuers are connected (to the CC node) through the tactical network. Shimmer sensors are connected to ORACE-Net mobile devices via Bluetooth. Since the experimentation area is limited, we reduced the Raspberry Pi's and smart phone's WiFi antenna transmission power to 0 dBm. Experimentation parameters and configuration settings are detailed in Table 2.

Table 2. Experimentation parameters and configuration settings.

General Settings	
Parameter	**Setting**
ORACE-Net Tactical Devices	4 (Raspberry Pi 2) OS: Raspbian v8.0
Mobile nodes	2 (Samsung Galaxy S3-I9300, rooted) OS: Android 4.2.2 CyanogenMod 10.0
Wireless mode	Ad hoc
ESSID	CROW2
Wireless standard	IEEE 802.11n/2.412 GHz (Channel 1)
Transmission power	0 dBm
Experiment area	30 m × 150 m
CC-node connection	Ethernet to Internet Ad hoc WiFi to ORACE-Net network
Experimentation duration	30 min/iteration
Power batteries	- Smart phone: 2100 mAh Li-Ion (3.7 v) - Raspberry-Pi: 10,000-mAh Li-ion (12 v) - CC-node: 12 V power supply
ORACE-Net Protocol Settings	
Application layer	MQTT client used for pushing data to the Labeeb-IoT platform
MQTT msgsize/intervals	30 Kb/1 s
Hello/ADV packet size	20/25 bytes
Hello/ADV intervals	3 s
Multicast address/port	224.0.0.0/10000
Shimmer Sensing Settings [30]	
Wireless standard	Bluetooth IEEE 802.15.1
Sensed data	Pressure, Temperature, Gyroscope (x, y, zaxis-angle), acceleration (x, y, z), magnetometer (x, y, z), battery level
Device/Body	1 (with multiple sensors)
Buffer [31]	1024 bytes
Message interval	1 s

5.2. Results and Discussion

In this subsection, we present the results of the experiment aimed to evaluate the CROW^2 system performance based on the ORACE-Net routing protocol on a real test-bed. To do so, we consider the following metrics: throughput and jitter, End-to-End delay ($E2E_{delay}$) and End-to-End Link Quality Estimation ($E2E_{LQE}$). Throughput is the maximum amount of data processed for sending from the source node (i.e., ORACE-Net mobile device) to the destination node (i.e., Labeeb-IoT platform). "Jitter" is the amount of variation in latency/response time (typically in milliseconds). Reliable connections consistently report back the same latency over and over again. Much variation (or 'jitter') is an indication of connection issues. Jitter is a relevant indicator of the network performance because it defines what kind of applications the network is able to support. The $E2E_{LQE}$ is calculated by the ORACE-Net protocol to estimate end-to-end links. The $E2E_{delay}$ is the round trip time delay recorded from the source node to the destination node. This latter metric informs also about nodes' disconnections. In addition to the above performance metrics, we discuss the collected data from the IoT platform to detect motions and prevent unavailability. Finally, we discuss the overall approximate interference and noise affecting the indoor signal using an academic version of the AirMagnet software.

5.2.1. Throughput and Jitter

The average throughput and jitter recorded on the mobile device over the time during the experiment plotted by UDP/TCP packets is depicted in Figure 7. These results are collected using local Linux logging tools, runnable also on Android (i.e., iptraf and trafshow). It can be seen that the UDP throughput is higher than the TCP throughput. Indeed, the TCP protocol uses connected mode, and it is highly optimized to make reliable use of the link. Therefore, this decreases the throughput and increases the jitter compared to UDP because of the handshake mechanism for the pre-/post-connection process. However, UDP is used for real-time data (e.g., voice and video over IP) and recommended for high-latency links.

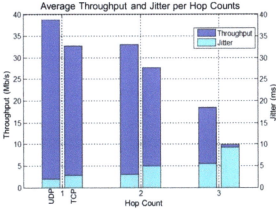

Figure 7. Average TCP and UDP throughput (Mbit/s) and jitter (ms) per hop count.

Now, with regards to the hop counts, UDP and TCP throughput averages within one hop are 38.8 and 32.71 Mb/s, respectively. Throughput decreases when the hop count increases to reach 18.47 and 9.87 Mb/s for UDP and TCP, respectively, within three hops. According to the authors of [33], a minimum data rate of 10 Mb/s is required for audio, medical imaging and video and hundreds of kbps for other WBAN applications. It is perceived that CROW^2 achieved a real throughput higher than the data rate requirements. It is also important to note that the throughput is expected to decrease significantly starting from four hops based on the behavior shown in Figure 7. The average throughput reduction is accompanied by jitter increase. Recorded jitter values increase also following the same pattern as the throughput. It is important to note here that the maximum accepted jitter for the video streaming application must be less than 40 ms according to [34] and under 30 ms according to Cisco for interactive video (video-conferencing) [35]. Indeed, jitter reaches 9.227 ms with TCP mode within three hops, which stays under the limits of the use of video-streaming. According to the results of throughput and jitter, we conclude that the recommended hop count that guarantees throughput for audio/video streaming and files (i.e., photos, reports, etc.) might be less than or equal to three hops, according to the standard definition video (3 Mb/s). The CROW^2 system assures an acceptable throughput and jitter for routes less than or equal to three hops with regards to the required thresholds cited above.

5.2.2. End-To-End Delay and Link Quality Estimation

Figure 8 depicts the average round trip time delay ($E2E_{delay}$) recorded from the OMD to the Labeeb-IoT platform versus $E2E_{LQE}$. It can be seen that the $E2E_{LQE}$ decreases with the rise of $E2E_{delay}$.

Indeed, $E2E_{delay}$ exceeds 1 s when $E2E_{LQE}$ reaches less than 0.7 between 1030 and 1070 s. The same behavior appears between 1155 and 1175 s. $E2E_{LQE}$ and $E2E_{delay}$ are proportional. An $E2E_{LQE}$ equal to zero means that the link is disconnected; the same link shows an infinite $E2E_{delay}$. Figure 8 shows also the effectiveness of the metric used in the ORACE-Net routing protocol (i.e., $E2E_{LQE}$). The route update mechanism based on the optimal $E2E_{LQE}$ then is validated by our experiment. Indeed, ORACE-Net prevents the link quality degradation, then looks for a better route with optimized link quality, delay and disconnection avoidance.

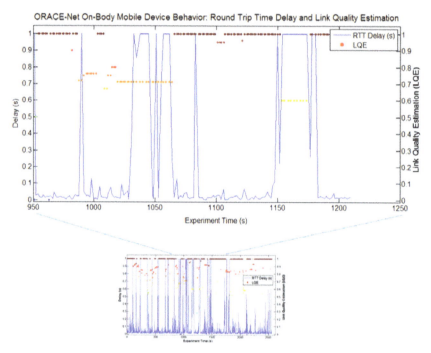

Figure 8. ORACE-Net on-body mobile device behavior: round trip time delay and link quality estimation.

5.2.3. Motion Detection and Link Unavailability Prevention

On-body sensors carried by the rescuers push data regularly to the IoT platform. Based on the type of recorded data, we can extract several human behaviors. For instance, gyroscope data recorded and depicted by the Labeeb-IoT platform in Figure 9 inform about human mobility. Sensors placed on the hand detect and send gyroscope variations tending to zero when the human has stopped and is not moving. Small variations may be distinguished in the first part of the figure when the human is walking and higher variations of the gyroscope when he/she is running. Figure 10 depicts the gyroscope angle variations over more than 2000 s. The gyroscope angle informs about the movement direction. Furthermore, some vital sign information may help the command center to switch rescue teams and send support there; we cite for example magnetometer and heart beat variations reflecting the stress level. All collected data on the IoT platform side could provide also the connectivity status for every deployed node, as can be seen in Figure 10. Disconnected nodes inform about the unavailable intermediate links or network over-saturation.

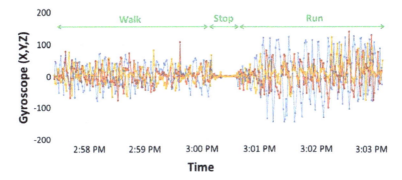

Figure 9. Gyroscope records over 5 min during the experiment. The X-axis is real time.

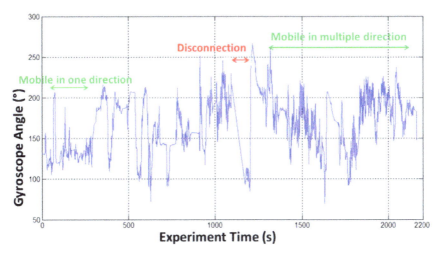

Figure 10. Gyroscope angle variation over 2200 s of the experiment.

5.2.4. Interference Score and Noise

As given by Table 2, the CROW^2 ad hoc network is configured on WiFi Channel 1. Figure 11a shows a sample of the interference score recorded indoors along 25 s. Interference varies from 0–53 dBm (as the maximum peak recorded). We assumed during our previous work [3] that the overall network achievements were affected by the indoor interference caused by WiFi access points, microwaves, etc. Thus, we have recorded the interference score and noise to verify whether these facts affect the overall behavior of the emergency network or not. The recorded interference is important compared to the Received Signal Strength Indicator (RSSI), so the signal is notably affected by the interference. However, the overall interference score is likely to decrease because the wireless infrastructure devices and access points are mostly out-of-order post-disaster. Figure 11b shows a sample of real-time variation for signal and noise strength as a percentage for Channel 1 during 50 s. The noise floor is given by the red curved waves, and the Signal-to-Noise Ratio (SNR) is depicted in yellow color. The figure shows that the signal strength varies between 3 and 50%. To conclude, interference clearly affects the RSSI and, then, the overall performance of the system. Interference is an important factor that must be considered in indoor emergency operations.

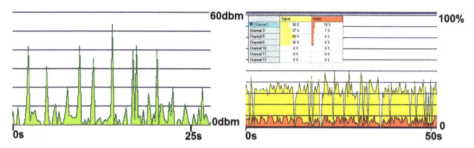

Figure 11. (**a**) Interference score (in dBm) recorded over 25 s on the channel at 2.412 GHz (AirMagnet WiFi Analyzer Limited Edition). (**b**) Screen-shot of signal and noise (as a percentage) recorded over 50 s (AirMagnet WiFi Analyzer Limited Edition).

6. Conclusions

In this article, we presented the CROW^2 system, an IoT end-to-end emergency and disaster relief system. CROW^2 is implemented based on the ORACE-Net routing protocol, especially designed for the disaster context. To evaluate the performance of the proposed system, we deployed the routing protocol and the payload applications on two different platforms (Raspberry Pi and Android smart phone). We equipped a rescuer with on-body sensors connected to a smart phone via Bluetooth. The entire system uses an IoT platform as a back-end to push, record, publish and analyze sensed data. The performance of the system is investigated according to the following relevant metrics: average throughput and jitter, average end-to-end delay and average link quality estimation. We emphasized also motion detection and links' unavailability prevention based on the collected data. Finally, we sampled the indoor interference score and noise to estimate its impact on the system behavior. It can be concluded that the CROW^2 system outperformed the given requirements for wireless body-to-body communications in terms of throughput and jitter. However, being effected by the indoor environment, the behaviors of $E2E_{LQE}$ and $E2E_{delay}$ are moderately fair. This article validates a few research works, especially simulation-based ones, with a real implementation and experiment. Further, it highlights also the limitation of other theoretical proposals, specifically those adopting low power consumption wireless standards for body-to-body communications. This work could be considered as a reference to researchers for real wireless body-to-body implementation using a dedicated routing protocol for the disaster relief context. It is also a reference for routing and technology standards' adoption for similar use cases. As future works, an outdoor experiment could be conducted to provide a complete overview of the system behavior in different situations. Furthermore, a study supported by implementation could be provided to advise on the optimal number of tactical devices for both indoor and outdoor scenarios. An autonomous disaster mode in wireless devices may be proposed based on the ORACE-Net routing approach.

Acknowledgments: This publication was made possible thanks to NPRPGrant #[6-1508-2-616] from the Qatar National Research Fund (a member of the Qatar Foundation). Funding of this paper was through the first author.

Author Contributions: This paper was prepared through the collective efforts of all authors. In particular, Dhafer Ben Arbia prepared the manuscript based on the suggestions and guidance of Muhammad Mahtab Alam, Abdullah Kadri and Elyes Ben Hamida. Dhafer Ben Arbia made substantial contributions towards the overall writing, organization and presentation of the paper. He also conducted the experiment, based on which the results were discussed. In particular, he contributed to the Introduction, Related Works and the CROW^2 system implementation. He detailed also the experiment scenario and discussed the achieved results. Muhammad Mahtab Alam introduced the scope of the paper within the Abstract, then helped to present the CROW^2 system and the WBAN technologies. Elyes Ben Hamida advised on the conducted experiment and coded the C sources on the tactical devices. Muhammad Mahtab Alam, Abdullah Kadri and Rabah Attia did a critical revision of the paper and provided detailed feedback to improve the manuscript content.

J. Sens. Actuator Netw. **2017**, *6*, 19

Abbreviations

The following abbreviations are used in this manuscript:

WBAN	Wireless Body Area Networks
CROW^2	Critical and Rescue Operations for Wearable-WSNs
$E2E_{LQE}$	End-to-End Link Quality Estimation
$E2E_{delay}$	End-to-End Delay
RTT	Round Trip Time
ORACE-Net	Optimized Routing Approach for Critical and Emergency Networks
Labeeb-IoT	an IoT Platform (www.labeeb-iot.com)

References

1. UNISDR. *Unisdr—Annual Report*; Technical Report; United Nations Office of Disaster Risk Reduction: Geneva, Switzerland, 2015.
2. Ben Arbia, D.; Alam, M.M.; Attia, R.; Ben Hamida, E. ORACE-Net: A novel multi-hop body-to-body routing protocol for public safety networks. *Peer-to-Peer Netw. Appl.* **2016**, *10*, 726–749.
3. Ben Arbia, D.; Alam, M.M.; Kadri, A.; Attia, R.; Ben Hamida, E. Implementation and Benchmarking of a Novel Routing Protocol for Tactical Mobile Ad-Hoc Networks. In Proceedings of the 12th IEEE WiMob Conference on Wireless and Mobile Computing, Networking and Communications (WiMob), New York, NY, USA, 17–19 October 2016.
4. D'Andreagiovanni, F.; Krolikowski, J.; Pulaj, J. A fast hybrid primal heuristic for multiband robust capacitated network design with multiple time periods. *Appl. Soft Comput.* **2015**, *26*, 497–507.
5. Büsing, C.; D'Andreagiovanni, F. New results about multi-band uncertainty in robust optimization. In Proceedings of the International Symposium on Experimental Algorithms, Bordeaux, France, 7–9 June 2012; Springer: Berlin, Germany, 2012; pp. 63–74.
6. Bertsekas, D.P. *Network Optimization: Continuous and Discrete Models*; Athena Scientific Belmont: Belmont, MA, USA, 1998.
7. Marotta, A.; D'Andreagiovanni, F.; Kassler, A.; Zola, E. On the energy cost of robustness for green virtual network function placement in 5G virtualized infrastructures. *Comput. Netw.* **2017**, in press.
8. Bauschert, T.; Busing, C.; D'Andreagiovanni, F.; Koster, A.C.; Kutschka, M.; Steglich, U. Network planning under demand uncertainty with robust optimization. *IEEE Commun. Mag.* **2014**, *52*, 178–185.
9. Union, I.T. *Overview of Disaster Relief Systems, Network Resilience and Recovery*; Technical Report; International Telecommunication Union: Geneva, Switzerland, 2014.
10. Chen, M.; Gonzalez, S.; Vasilakos, A.; Cao, H.; Leung, V.C.M. Body Area Networks: A Survey. *Mob. Netw. Appl.* **2011**, *16*, 171–193.
11. Gao, T.; Massey, T.; Selavo, L.; Crawford, D.; Chen, B.R.; Lorincz, K.; Shnayder, V.; Hauenstein, L.; Dabiri, F.; Jeng, J.; et al. The advanced health and disaster aid network: A light-weight wireless medical system for triage. *IEEE Trans. Biomed. Circuits Syst.* **2007**, *1*, 203–216.
12. Negra, R.; Jemili, I.; Belghith, A. Wireless Body Area Networks: Applications and Technologies. *Procedia Comput. Sci.* **2016**, *83*, 1274–1281, doi:10.1016/j.procs.2016.04.266.
13. Gomez, K.; Goratti, L.; Rasheed, T.; Reynaud, L. Enabling disaster-resilient 4G mobile communication networks. *IEEE Commun. Mag.* **2014**, *52*, 66–73.
14. Varun, G.; Menon, J.P.P.; Priya, J. Ensuring Reliable Communication in Disaster Recovery Operations with Reliable Routing Technique. *Mob. Inf. Syst.* **2016**, *2016*, doi:10.1155/2016/9141329.
15. Lu, Z.; Cao, G.; Porta, T.L. Networking Smartphones for Disaster Recovery. *IEEE Trans. Mob. Comput.* **2016**, *PP*, doi:10.1109/TMC.2017.2695452.
16. George, S.M.; Zhou, W.; Chenji, H.; Won, M.; Lee, Y.O.; Pazarloglou, A.; Stoleru, R.; Barooah, P. DistressNet: A wireless ad hoc and sensor network architecture for situation management in disaster response. *IEEE Commun. Mag.* **2010**, *48*, 128–136.

17. Felice, M.D.; Bedogni, L.; Bononi, L. The Emergency Direct Mobile App: Safety Message Dissemination over a Multi-Group Network of Smartphones Using Wi-Fi Direct. In Proceedings of the MobiWac '16, 14th ACM International Symposium on Mobility Management and Wireless Access, Malta, 13–17 November 2016; ACM: New York, NY, USA, 2016; pp. 99–106.

18. Chen, X.; Xu, Y.; Liu, A. Cross Layer Design for Optimizing Transmission Reliability, Energy Efficiency, and Lifetime in Body Sensor Networks. *Sensors* **2017**, *17*, 900.

19. Tsouri, G.R.; Prieto, A.; Argade, N. On increasing network lifetime in body area networks using global routing with energy consumption balancing. *Sensors* **2012**, *12*, 13088–13108.

20. D'Andreagiovanni, F.; Nardin, A. Towards the fast and robust optimal design of Wireless Body Area Networks. *Appl. Soft Comput.* **2015**, *37*, 971–982.

21. D'Andreagiovanni, F.; Nardin, A.; Natalizio, E. A Fast ILP-Based Heuristic for the Robust Design of Body Wireless Sensor Networks. In *European Conference on the Applications of Evolutionary Computation, Proceedings of the EvoApplications 2017, 20th European Conference Applications of Evolutionary Computation, Amsterdam, The Netherlands, 19–21 April 2017*; Squillero, G., Sim, K., Eds.; Lecture Notes in Computer Science; Part I; Springer: Berlin, Germany, 2017; Volume 10199, pp. 234–250.

22. Miranda, J.; Cabral, J.; Wagner, S.R.; Fischer Pedersen, C.; Ravelo, B.; Memon, M.; Mathiesen, M. An Open Platform for Seamless Sensor Support in Healthcare for the Internet of Things. *Sensors* **2016**, *16*, 2089.

23. Ben Hamida, E.; Alam, M.; Maman, M.; Denis, B.; D'Errico, R. Wearable Body-to-Body networks for critical and rescue operations—The CROW2 project. In Proceedings of the 2014 IEEE 25th Annual International Symposium on Personal, Indoor, and Mobile Radio Communication (PIMRC), Washington, DC, USA, 2–5 September 2014; pp. 2145–2149.

24. Alam, M.M.; Ben Hamida, E. Performance Evaluation of IEEE 802.15.6-based WBANs under Co-Channel Interference. *Int. J. Sens. Netw.* **2016**, doi: 10.1504/IJSNET.2016.10001274.

25. Alam, M.M.; Ben Hamida, E.; Ben Arbia, D. Joint Throughput and Channel Aware (TCA) Dynamic Scheduling Algorithm for Emerging Wearable Applications. In Proceedings of the 2016 IEEE Wireless Communications and Networking Conference (WCNC), Doha, Qatar, 3–6 April 2016.

26. Maman, M.; Mani, F.; Denis, B.; D'Errico, R. Evaluation of Multiple Coexisting Body Area Networks Based on Realistic On-Body and Body-to-Body Channel Models. In Proceedings of the 10th International Symposium on Medical Information and Communication Technology (ISMICT'16), Worcester, MA, USA, 20–23 March 2016.

27. WSNET 3.0 Simulator. Available online: http://wsnet.gforge.inria.fr/ (accessed on 30 November 2015).

28. Martínez-Pérez, F.E.; González-Fraga, J.Á.; Cuevas-Tello, J.C.; Rodríguez, M.D. Activity inference for ambient intelligence through handling artifacts in a healthcare environment. *Sensors* **2012**, *12*, 1072–1099.

29. *Information Technology Message Queuing Telemetry Transport (MQTT) v3.1.1*; ISO/IEC 20922; ISO/IEC: Geneva, Switzerland, 2016.

30. Shimmer Sensing. Available online: http://www.shimmersensing.com/products/ecg-development-kit (accessed on 15 January 2017).

31. Burns, A.; Greene, B.R.; McGrath, M.J.; O'Shea, T.J.; Kuris, B.; Ayer, S.M.; Stroiescu, F.; Cionca, V. SHIMMER: A Wireless Sensor Platform for Noninvasive Biomedical Research. *IEEE Sens. J.* **2010**, *10*, 1527–1534.

32. Qatar Mobility Innovations Center. *Labeeb IoT Platform and Solutions*; QMIC: Doha, Qatar, 2016.

33. Chakraborty, C.; Gupta, B.; Ghosh, S.K. A review on telemedicine-based WBAN framework for patient monitoring. *Telemed. e-Health* **2013**, *19*, 619–626.

34. Al-Madani, B.; Al-Roubaiey, A.; Baig, Z.A. Real-Time QoS-Aware Video Streaming: A Comparative and Experimental Study. *Adv. Multimed.* **2014**, *2014*, doi:10.1155/2014/164940.

35. Quality of Service Design Overview. Available online: http://www.ciscopress.com/articles/article.asp?p=357102&seqNum=2 (accessed on 20 February 2017).

MDPI AG

St. Alban-Anlage 66

4052 Basel, Switzerland

Tel. +41 61 683 77 34

Fax +41 61 302 89 18

http://www.mdpi.com

Journal of Sensor and Actuator Networks Editorial Office

E-mail: jsan@mdpi.com

http://www.mdpi.com/journal/jsan

www.ingramcontent.com/pod-product-compliance
Lightning Source LLC
LaVergne TN
LVHW071357070326
832902LV00028B/4636